Picking Presidents

Picking Presidents

HOW TO MAKE THE MOST
CONSEQUENTIAL DECISION IN
THE WORLD

Gautam Mukunda

UNIVERSITY OF CALIFORNIA PRESS

University of California Press
Oakland, California

© 2022 by Gautam Mukunda

Library of Congress Cataloging-in-Publication Data

Names: Mukunda, Gautam, author.
Title: Picking presidents : how to make the most consequential decision
    in the world / Gautam Mukunda.
Description: Oakland, California : University of California Press, [2022] |
    Includes bibliographical references and index.
Identifiers: LCCN 2021060596 (print) | LCCN 2021060597 (ebook) |
    ISBN 9780520379992 (cloth) | ISBN 9780520977037 (ebook)
Subjects: LCSH: Presidents—United States—Election.
Classification: LCC JK524 .M85 2022 (print) | LCC JK524 (ebook) |
    DDC 324.973—dc23/eng/20220308
LC record available at https://lccn.loc.gov/2021060596
LC ebook record available at https://lccn.loc.gov/2021060597

Manufactured in the United States of America

31 30 29 28 27 26 25 24 23 22
10 9 8 7 6 5 4 3 2 1

To Eva Maria—the love of my life. Your support made finishing this book possible. Your love made my life complete.

"Presidents are selected, not elected."

President Franklin Delano Roosevelt

"No real-world human being brings to the U.S. presidency the range of attributes necessary for full success in the job."

James Fallows

"Nothing comes to my desk that is perfectly solvable. Otherwise, someone else would have solved it."

President Barack Obama, to Michael Lewis

Contents

List of Tables and Figure

Preface

I decided to write this book a few days after the 2016 election, prompted by a friend asking if I "had a time machine." My first book, *Indispensable: When Leaders Really Matter,* had come out four years earlier. It proposed an answer to an age-old question—do individuals make history, or are historical outcomes all just the product of larger impersonal forces? I found that most of the time, individual leaders didn't matter. Most leaders are organizational products—they have risen through the ranks and been evaluated by elites. They're basically reflections of their context, and so largely interchangeable with any number of other people who could have been in the same situation. That was the conventional view in social science, and it's usually right.

Sometimes, however, individual leaders can have a huge impact. Some leaders take power from the outside, or over the opposition of elites. Such leaders can be very different from all the other people who could have risen to power and make choices no one else would have. Because they are unique, these choices would tend to be either very successful or disastrous. This wasn't just an academic exercise. This describes historical leaders ranging from Abraham Lincoln to Adolf Hitler. And, of course, it also describes Donald Trump.

Being able to predict that a leader will be extraordinarily good or bad is interesting, but it would be far more practically useful if we could predict which. In *Indispensable* I briefly suggested that leaders with a variety of traits would be very likely to fail and were therefore not worth the risk. The examples of such traits I chose to highlight were personality disorders like narcissism and sociopathy, incompetent or risk-prone managerial styles, out-of-the-mainstream ideologies, and unearned advantages (like inherited wealth). Four years later, the United States of America elected someone who seemed like he had stepped out of the pages of my book.

Perhaps no figure in modern American history has inspired a wider variety of assessments than Trump. I, like many, viewed his candidacy with alarm, and was enormously pessimistic about the likely impact of his administration. Yet, as I noted in articles and interviews during the campaign, my work also kept open the possibility that he would be a brilliantly successful president. I needed a better way to be able to predict the outcome—not just for him, but for anyone who seeks the presidency. I needed to be able to answer the question—can he or she do the job? And I wasn't the only person. Every American does.

This book is my attempt to give everyone who reads it the ability to answer that question—based not on partisan preferences or gut feelings, but on the best research in social science and history. Whatever your politics, if you've ever wondered about what it takes to succeed as president of the United States, this book is for you.

Acknowledgments

First and most importantly, of course, I need to thank my wife, Eva Maria Janerus. We first met when this book's manuscript was in its final stages, and it was her support that got me through the long process from manuscript to publication. Along with Eva Maria, I need to thank Rudy, the World's Greatest Dog, who graciously agreed to allow me to join the family as long as I became his Emotional Support Human. This book's final revisions were made with Rudy in my lap insisting that *both* hands are meant for petting, not typing.

I also need to thank my wonderful editor, Tim Sullivan—this is the second time we've done a book together, and I couldn't ask for a better thought partner. Equally, I must thank my amazing agent, Jim Levine, who fought for this book far more than I could ever have asked him to.

Many others were of great assistance during the process of researching and writing this book. Fareed Zakaria originally suggested that this research question made more sense as a book than as an article (my original intention). Daniel Summers-Minette was critical to doing the Monte Carlo analysis, and J. Chappell Lawson made excellent suggestions about the other statistical analyses. Clayton Christensen provided invaluable mentorship and encouragement for fifteen years—without him, I doubt I would have been able to push this (or many other) projects through to completion.

Thomas LeBien was of great assistance in shaping early drafts of this book. Dylan Rem wrangled footnotes superbly, far exceeding what anyone could expect from someone his age. The entire faculty support team at Schwarzman College helped with some of the initial research. John Dickerson pushed my thinking during a series of interviews—I hope that I helped his book as much as he helped mine.

Julie Battilana, Hannah Riley Bowles, and David Gergen greatly sharpened my analysis and gave me a home at the Kennedy School's Center for Public Leadership—I owe them enormous thanks. Thomas Friedman, Nitin Nohria and Samuel Popkin provided much useful advice at various stages of the process, as did Tsedal Neeley, Rebecca Henderson, Ken Oye, and David Moss. Mike Tushman and Joshua Margolis put long hours into helping me bridge the (enormous) gap between political science and organizational theory, as did Lakshmi Ramarajan, Ryan Raffaelli, and Boris Groysberg.

I would also like to thank the team at University of California Press for all the work they did converting a manuscript into a book in the midst of the COVID-19 pandemic. Francisco Reinking, my production editor, Ben Alexander, my copy editor, and Jen Burton, my indexer, all came through time and time again.

Finally, I need to thank Eva Maria's parents, Ingolf and Eva, for so generously welcoming me into their family, and my parents, Ram and Meera, for a lifetime of support. No one could ask for better in-laws, and no one could imagine better parents. I will be forever grateful.

1 The Fateful Choice

Every four years the American people choose the most powerful person on earth. They do it using a system created by the Founding Fathers in the 1780s based on the theories of Enlightenment philosophers and their knowledge of the Roman Republic.[1] That system has evolved haphazardly ever since, leaving us today with what is at best an imperfect method for choosing the so-called leader of the free world.

The forty-five men—and to date they have all been men—who have held the presidency have varied in party, education, social class, and personality. They present a dizzying array of temperaments, styles, and capabilities. Each, however, triumphed in America's baroque and ever-changing presidential selection process.

It's worth asking, then, how good is that process? How well does it select the best and avoid the worst from among all the people who, in Benjamin Disraeli's immortal phrase, are struggling to "reach the top of the greasy pole"? Given everything we've learned in the more than two centuries since the Constitution was written, can we improve it? Can we do a better job of evaluating candidates so that we elect better presidents? Perhaps even more importantly, can we avoid disastrous ones?

I've been studying how leaders are selected, with a particular focus on the presidency, for more than a decade. My research reveals that the system we have is not even close to good enough. It's far too easy for someone to be elected who is completely unable to do the job. That possibility has always existed, and the United States has suffered greatly when it's happened. Sometimes it's only barely escaped catastrophe. But the problem may be even worse today, and the vast power of the presidency makes the stakes higher than they have ever been.

Fortunately, we can do much better. This book synthesizes a new way of understanding leader selection with research from political science, management, psychology, and other fields, to provide an objective, nonpartisan way to evaluate presidential candidates that anyone can use and that requires only information about candidates that would be widely available before the election. It's a system that American citizens can use to answer the most important question they are ever asked: should this person be president?

We begin by identifying what sort of candidates are likely to become presidents who will make a real difference if they win. Not all presidents do. Some, despite the awesome power placed in their hands, are surprisingly inconsequential. Then, we'll examine some of the best and worst of the forty-five members of history's most exclusive club, which will help us understand what traits are likely to produce failed and successful presidencies, and how to detect them.

Next, we'll use this lens to examine Donald Trump, the modern president who has perhaps inflamed the most intense passions on either end of the political spectrum, and Joe Biden, the president as this book goes to print. Finally, I suggest some plausible reforms to the way we nominate candidates and changes to the powers of the presidency that might help us improve the quality and performance of future presidents. This quadrennial choice, especially in times of crisis, can have an outsize impact not only on the lives of Americans but on inhabitants of the entire globe. For all our sakes, Americans need to make the right choice, and the framework I lay out here aims to help us achieve that lofty goal.

DO LEADERS REALLY MAKE A DIFFERENCE?

But do presidents actually matter? And, if so, how much? Candidates and partisans certainly care. But if you aren't actively involved in government or politics, does the identity of the president really make much difference in your life? Modern American political parties are far more ideologically distinct than they were even a generation ago, so Republican presidents will enact different policies than Democratic ones, for sure.[2] But does it matter *which* Republican or *which* Democrat holds the office?

For instance, if Hillary Clinton had won in 2008 instead of Barack Obama, wouldn't she have pushed for universal health insurance? If Ted Cruz had won in 2016 instead of Donald Trump, wouldn't he have tried to cut taxes? So how large is the impact of an individual president?

Leaders' impact cannot be understood without understanding how they got the job. Consider what I call the "paradox of leader selection": the more effort you put into picking a leader, the less it matters whom you pick. Let's unpack that. The more important people think leadership is, the more effort they will put into picking their preferred leader. The path to power will become so rigorous that it filters out outliers, and the remaining candidates will all resemble one another. When a selection process is perfect, then *which person* it picks doesn't matter. Only the process does.

Think about it this way. When you're buying a car, you probably put a lot of effort into picking the right one. You'll decide on a budget, pick a few finalists, and take those out for test drives. If you're like me, you'll bore all your friends discussing your options until you finally pull the trigger. But, realistically, how much of a difference will it make which finalist you chose? A luxury SUV and a smart car are very different—but they wouldn't both have been in your final few. Instead, all the cars you seriously looked at were probably pretty similar and, whichever one you picked, your life going forward will be basically the same. Your friends definitely will not care.

The same thing happens when candidates for leadership positions are closely scrutinized and the ones who don't fit what the system is looking for are pushed out. Everyone who ends up close to getting the job will be functionally the same. The square pegs will fall by the wayside, and the remaining pegs will all share a striking resemblance.

Most large organizations have a selection process which ensures that individual leaders are very similar to their likely alternatives, and this effect gets stronger as you move up the organization. As they increase in rank, "the population of managers becomes more and more homogenous . . . At the limit, one [corporate] vice-president cannot be reliably distinguished from another." This makes leaders fungible, like dollar bills. While this doesn't minimize the importance of management as a whole—"It is hard to tell the difference between two different light bulbs also; but if you take all light bulbs away, it is difficult to read in the dark"—it does call into question the importance of individual managers.[3]

To judge a president's impact, then, we need to measure them counter-factually.[4] If Clinton is the equivalent of Obama when it comes to health-care (and other policies), as Cruz is to Trump, then we have a way of understanding any given leader's "unique impact"—the marginal difference between what did happen and what *could have happened* if the next most likely person had been chosen instead. A president can only have a unique impact if the process that selected him or her was *imperfect*, so that the most likely alternative president would have made substantially different choices than the person who got the job.

If you're a baseball fan you've heard of Wins Above Replacement (WAR), which measures the value of players relative to a "replacement player" who could fill their position. Unique impact measures leaders by comparing them to the most likely replacement leader. Unlike WAR, though, unique impact is a double-edged sword. A higher WAR is always better, but a larger unique impact can be good or bad. If the next most likely winner would have a unique impact by, say, engaging in an unjust and unlawful war, that's not a positive unique impact. But if you do something that no one else would have and it works, you're a genius. If it doesn't, you're a fool. Unique impact increases *variance* in performance—the higher the impact, the larger the variance, be it good or bad.[5]

Researchers have generally identified three forces that minimize leaders' unique impact: (1) constraints from the external environment; (2) constraints from the internal dynamics of the organization; and (3) they are selected by a process that tends to homogenize the pool of potential leaders, meaning that outliers who might act differently are not chosen in the first place.[6]

But, under a variety of circumstances, leaders do have significant dis-cretion, despite internal and external constraints.[7] The more powerful the organization (or country, in the case of presidents), the less it is bound by external factors; the more powerful the individual leader, the less he or she is bound by internal constraints. Whether or not leaders will use their discretion to have a unique impact depends on what they do with it.

THE SPECIAL CASE OF THE PRESIDENCY

Although political scientists pay surprisingly little attention to most lead-ers, American presidents are the exception. Just as social scientists debate if individual leaders matter, political scientists debate whether individual presidents do. President-centered research has focused on the ways that the traits of individual presidents matter, while presidency-centered research has concentrated on how the context presidents inhabit explains how they behave.[8]

Perhaps the most influential single scholar of the presidency, Stephen Skowronek, has powerfully made the case for context. He found that the vulnerability or resilience of the era's governing institutions is the crucial factor determining a president's opportunities for leadership. Empirical research supports Skowronek's position that the status of institutions, which he calls "political time," strongly affects presidential performance, far more strongly, in fact, than the traits of individual presidents. This conclusion is supported by findings in fields ranging from psychology, where the fundamental attribution error finds that the effects of situation usually swamp those of personality, to management, where CEO effects are generally relatively small.[9]

What models focused on context cannot do, however, is help us select better presidents. However insightful it may be, a model that is solely about context, by its very nature, is purely descriptive. It does not—and cannot—have a prescriptive component, because other than perhaps pres-idents themselves (and not even most of those), no one has the power to change political institutions enough to improve the next president's odds of success. It removes agency from our politics—that of presidents, and that of voters.

You don't have to believe that context doesn't matter, however, to believe that it's not the *only* thing that matters. Even given situational constraints, it is at least plausible that a more skilled president could perform better—perhaps even vastly better—than a less capable one. To get better presidents, we need to understand how they are chosen, and what individual-level characteristics make someone a successful president of the United States—the driving idea of this book.

Despite the importance of context, researchers, following in the footsteps of James David Barber's book *Presidential Character,* have tried to identify the characteristics that play a role in presidents' successes or failures. Two keep coming up. The first is a president's experience before being elected. This seems logical. Certain jobs (e.g., governor) could be good preparation for the Oval Office. If that's true, then presidents who held those jobs should do better. Surprisingly, however, researchers have found conflicting results on the importance of prepresidential experience, ranging from little to no effect, to weak effects in specific parts of the job, to less experience being superior to more, to experiences similar to the presidency being helpful, while those unlike the presidency hurt.[10]

Other researchers have tried to match presidents' personality traits to their performance. They have examined how certain traits affect willingness to use force, use of executive orders, process for making major decisions, and overall performance. The most influential has been the legendary psychologist Dean Simonton, who found that a trait he called "Intellectual Brilliance" strongly predicted presidential performance. While high intelligence contributes to Intellectual Brilliance, they are not the same. Simonton defines it as "an inclusive cognitive propensity that spans broad and artistic interests, a pronounced curiosity and inventiveness, plus more than average wisdom and idealism." Presidents score as having high Intellectual Brilliance if, based on blinded excerpts from historical studies about their lives, evaluators rated them as having wide interests or being artistic, inventive, curious, intelligent, sophisticated, complicated, insightful, wise, and idealistic, but not dull or commonplace.[11]

Presidents are usually selected by campaigns in which they capture a party's nomination and win a general election—although that isn't the only path. Nine vice presidents have replaced a president, eight due to the president's death and one because of his resignation. That possibility aside, though, capturing a party's nomination and winning a general election may tend to homogenize candidates. Nominations and elections mean that much of the time, those who become president and their counterfactual alternatives are similar enough that many individual presidents have little unique impact. Those are the presidents who make up the belly of the curve spread out between the best and worst. We are more interested in the tails of the distribution.

The System in Theory: The Presidential Elections the Founders Intended

Any well-designed system for selecting presidents has five functions:

(1) minimizing the harmful effects of the pursuit of office by the highly ambitious;

(2) promoting effective executive leadership and constitutional uses of executive power;

(3) securing a capable president;

(4) ensuring a legitimate succession; and

(5) providing for the proper amount of choice and change.[12]

These aren't controversial. Minimizing the dangers of ambitious contenders was a major concern in the United States for a century after the Constitution was first established, so much so that Lincoln's first public speech warned that the ambitions of brilliant men were the greatest threat to American institutions.[13] The need to ensure legitimate accession had been largely obviated by the passage of time, which has strengthened the legitimacy of American institutions, until this was challenged for the first time in American history in 2020 and 2021. The provision of a proper amount of choice and change is perhaps the central issue of politics.

The remaining functions, then, are the subject of this book: how does the system make sure that the United States has a capable president who engages in effective, constitutional executive leadership?

The Founders considered this the *most important* goal of the system they had created. James Madison, the principal author of the Constitution, wrote, "The aim of every political constitution is, or ought to be, first to obtain for rulers men who possess most wisdom to discern, and most virtue to pursue, the common good of the society; and in the next place, to take the most effectual precautions for keeping them virtuous whilst they continue to hold their public trust."[14] This is an elitist view of the presidency, to be sure. Madison assumes that the president must be someone special, that the presidency should be reserved only for the wisest and most virtuous, and that even they should be watched lest they be corrupted.

The Electoral College was the Founders' mechanism for ensuring that only the "best" could become president. Hamilton argued that the electors who made it up would be:

> men most capable of analyzing the qualities adapted to the station, and acting under circumstances favorable to deliberation, and to a judicious combination of all the reasons and inducements which were proper to govern their choice. A small number of persons, selected by their fellow-citizens from the general mass, will be most likely to possess the information and discernment requisite to such complicated investigations . . . The process of election affords a moral certainty, that the office of President will never fall to the lot of any man who is not in an eminent degree endowed with the requisite qualifications.[15]

Hamilton believed that judging presidential candidates takes "information" and "discernment"—and that most Americans so lacked both that the job should instead be delegated to a "small number" of elites who had the judgment to do what they could not.

Despite some highlights, few would argue that Hamilton's unvarnished optimism about Washington's heirs has been borne out. Part of the reason may be that the system has never behaved the way Hamilton intended. The Electoral College has never even attempted to fulfill the role for which it was created. Instead, that task—ensuring that the president was up to the job—fell to the "factions" the Constitution was meant to restrain.[16] Today we call them political parties.

THE SYSTEM IN PRACTICE: THE PRESIDENTIAL ELECTIONS WE HAVE

Presidential elections are the central events of American political life. Students of politics have published endless research on presidential campaigns, what is involved in them, and what it takes to win them. Some, exemplified in political science by Samuel Popkin and in journalism by Theodore White and Richard Ben Cramer, focus on what sort of candidate can win. Other research examines voter preferences, how voters make their choice, and what role candidate characteristics play in their decisions.[17]

A different stream of work has concluded that campaigns and elections are so unimportant they are best understood through a "minimal effects" model, which holds that candidates and campaigns just don't matter that much. Vote share is mostly driven by structural factors ranging from the state of the economy to party registration. While some research has challenged this model, by finding that campaigns have greater effects or by arguing that changes in the tools of political communication make its assumptions no longer valid, in general it remains the dominant view.[18]

Even if the minimal effects model is true in its strongest form, and candidates don't matter much during general elections, they can still make a huge difference in the race for the nomination. American political parties have chosen their nominees in many ways, but whichever they used, the only way to get elected president has been via the nomination of a major party.

How effectively has the system for selecting presidential nominees evaluated and homogenized candidates to ensure that the person who occupies the Oval Office and the most likely alternative president are similar? Does the nominating system create candidates who are as fungible as dollar bills? To understand that question, we'll begin by describing the circumstances in which high-impact leaders can come to power. Then we'll look at the specific case of how American presidents are, and have been, chosen, to see how that general model applies to the specific case of the presidency.

THE LEADERS WHO MATTER: LEADER FILTRATION THEORY

Instead of asking *if* leaders matter, we should ask *which* leaders do. Reframing the discussion that way helps us understand—and even predict—which leaders have a large unique impact.

Predicting unique impact is not just an academic exercise. High-unique-impact leaders can change a country—or even the world. Leaders have a unique impact when they do things that others who plausibly could have been in their shoes would not have. This might be in their choice of policies or the skill with which they are implemented, but unique impact is only possible if the leader has effects that likely alternative leaders would not have.

Unique impact produces *high-variance outcomes*. Most people would not play Russian roulette no matter how high the reward for victory. If you chose to play for stakes of a billion dollars, though, you might end up as one of the wealthiest people on earth. Or you might end up dead. That's a high-variance outcome.

My explanation for which leaders are likely to have a high unique impact is Leader Filtration Theory (LFT).[19] When we think about how a leader got the job, instead of thinking of the winner as being selected from a pool of candidates, we should think of him or her as the product of a filtration process, which lets some kinds of candidates through while blocking others.

Filtration isn't purely random. It works to identify the person who is most like an ideal leader—the kind of leader who will move through the filter. In this context "ideal" doesn't mean "best." It just means the candidate best suited to making it to the end of the process, a hypothetical candidate with the characteristics most likely to pass through the filter. We should think of characteristics in the broadest possible terms. Intelligence and managerial skill help candidates in most filtration processes. But often so does height. When he polled half the Fortune 500, Malcolm Gladwell found that almost a third of their CEOs were men 6'2" or taller, even though fewer than 4 percent of American men are. No one would argue that tall people are better leaders, and companies put enormous effort into CEO selection. Yet American companies seem to implicitly value height. In other words, for most companies, the "ideal leader" is tall.[20]

The ideal leader usually isn't explicitly described, but there is always some set of characteristics that maximizes the odds of passing through the filter. The closer a candidate is to that ideal, the more likely it is that they will stay in the pool. This means that over time the pool of candidates becomes more homogenous. If the filter is tight enough, then the differences between the winner and likely alternate leaders will be negligible, making them fungible.

Such interchangeable leaders are *Modal*. In a statistical distribution, the "mode" is the most common outcome. Imagine if you could replay history a million times over, keeping all the candidate characteristics the same but allowing the random elements (like the weather on Election Day) to change. Some candidates—the ones who are ideal, or nearly so— would win many, many times. They are, or are close to, the mode of possible outcomes. Imagine picking prizes from a bowl, where most of the prizes are packets of M&Ms. A few of them, though, are mystery prizes, one of which is a winning lottery ticket, while the rest are live grenades. The bag of M&Ms is the modal prize, and it doesn't matter which bag you get. But, of course, it matters a great deal if you grab the lottery ticket—or the grenade.

Other candidates might win only once because they are very different from the set of ideal candidates and need lots of lucky breaks to make it all the way. The further they are from the mode, the more luck they need. These leaders are at the extreme of the possible outcomes of the process, so I call them Extremes. While Modal leaders are likely to take actions largely indistinguishable from those of other Modal leaders, an Extreme leader is more likely to take actions that are very different, and because they are different, these Extreme leaders can have a large unique impact— a life-changing jackpot or an explosion.

You can never know with certainty if candidates or leaders are Extremes (especially contemporaneously), but the best way to tell is to see how Filtered they are. Think of this as getting a chance to examine all the different items in the prize bowl and eliminate the mystery prizes before picking. Since most mystery prizes are bad, most people would eliminate all of them, forsaking their chance at the lottery ticket to avoid the grenades, and instead take the small but certain win of the M&Ms. That means that if you were watching the drawing, you could guess the odds M&Ms were going to be picked by knowing how well the prizes were examined first. Filtering candidates is like examining prizes with the goal of eliminating everything that's not a bag of M&Ms.

Filtration has two parts: *evaluation* and *decision*. Evaluation requires gathering information about a candidate. Decision is the use of that information to decide if a candidate can continue in the filtration process. For a candidate (or leader) to be Filtered, both components are necessary.

Evaluation is the process of gathering information about a candidate's true capabilities and intentions to judge what he or she will do if given power. Evaluation is tough. Many characteristics that make people likely to fail are difficult to detect.[21] Candidates have every incentive to seem as close to the ideal as possible. After all, they want the top job.

Before you trust someone with power, you want to know who they really are, not who they appear to be. Once you give them power, after all, they no longer need to pretend to be someone they are not to get it—and if you try to take that power away from them, they can use it against you. Power lets people do what they have always wanted to do and be who they have always wanted to be.

For most people, power's effect is to make them worse—what's called the "power paradox." Power gives most people a false sense of control, increases their self-esteem, and makes them more optimistic and oriented towards taking action. For most of us, power decreases inhibitions and empathy. The powerful are "more likely than other people to engage in rude, selfish, and unethical behavior."[22]

Some people, however, become better when they have power. While people who place low importance on morality become more likely to break rules when they become powerful, people who place acting morally at the center of their identity become less likely to behave poorly. Similarly, people who have community orientations become more likely to help others as they became more powerful, even while those who are low in their focus on community became less willing.[23] Either way—positive or negative—power is a *liberating* force. It gives you the ability to be the person you really want to be underneath, when you no longer have to worry about convincing other people to give you power.

This means that in making the decision to give someone power, it is crucially important to understand who they truly are, not just who they seem to be. On superficial examination all you will see is the face they present to win the approval of those around them—to make it through the filter. The more someone wants power, the more they will be willing to be inauthentic. Only a thorough evaluation can discern their true self.

Thorough evaluation requires extensive knowledge of candidates to assess their capabilities, intentions, and character. Such knowledge comes only from prolonged close contact. It cannot be acquired easily, because "true knowledge of another person is the culmination of a slow process of mutual revelation. It requires the gradual setting aside of interview etiquette and the incremental building of trust ... It cannot be rushed."[24]

Evaluation takes time. It requires close examination of someone when they have power. Leader Filtration Theory inverts our normal view of experience. We usually see experience as a developmental process. We ask, "What did you learn from your experience?" That's important. People should learn from experience. Experience changes them.[25] But experience is also a revelatory process. Just as experience provides you an opportunity to learn, it provides others the opportunity to learn about you.

Filtered candidates are experienced because their experience gives observers—like party leaders—the opportunity to evaluate them. Not all experience, however, is equally valuable. The more someone's past predicts their future, the more relevant that past is to evaluation. It's not always obvious what information about someone's past predicts their future behavior. Research on employee performance has found, surprisingly, that people who do well in one company may do poorly in another, even if the two are similar.[26]

Experience within an organization can tell you a lot about how well someone will perform within that organization. Experience in a similar but distinct organization will tell you much less, both because of the differences between organizations and because the sort of information you want to know is personal. It's basically gossip, and gossip has difficulty crossing organizational boundaries.[27] Experience in a different field tells you almost nothing.

Those two requirements of evaluation, experience within an organization and prolonged close contact with candidates, mean that it is primarily conducted by organizational elites. If a candidate has risen through an organization over the course of years with a career that gives those elites ample opportunity to evaluate him or her, then evaluation can occur. The less elites know about a candidate, the less Filtered he or she is.

The second component of filtration is decision. If a candidate is fully evaluated but the evaluation's results play little part in the choice of leader, then that new leader is still Unfiltered. If you inherit ownership of your family's company, then it doesn't matter what the board thinks. If the president dies, the vice president moves up no matter what. The less elites' evaluation of candidates matters, the less Filtered the leader.

When McKinley made Theodore Roosevelt his vice president, partly in response to pressure from the New York political machine that wanted his reform efforts there stopped, Mark Hanna, McKinley's enormously powerful campaign manager, warned, "There's only one life between that maniac and the presidency." When McKinley was assassinated, Hanna's fear became a prophecy. If he could have stopped Roosevelt from ascending to the White House Hanna would have, but his wishes no longer mattered.[28]

The importance of close contact with organizational elites and, even more, the critical importance of the decision component of filtration, means that *filtration and experience are very different.* Experience is necessary, but not sufficient, for filtration. If experience is viewed as purely developmental, then the linkage between experience and performance would be relatively simple. Enough of the right kinds of experience will predict (and produce) success. If experience is also revelatory, however, we need to add how others have evaluated the president's or candidate's behavior while they were accruing that experience and whether that judgment was incorporated in the candidate's elevation to the presidency.

If leaders are thoroughly evaluated and the results play a decisive role in the choice to give them the top job, then those leaders are highly Filtered and therefore likely to have little unique impact. Their performance will tend to be average or pretty good, but it is unlikely to be great or disastrous. Even if huge events happen while they're in office, Filtered leaders will generally do what likely alternative leaders would have done. They might succeed or fail, but they are unlikely to be distinctive; any other Filtered candidate would have done the same. They're fungible.

A leader who was not thoroughly evaluated, or whose evaluation played little or no role in his or her elevation, on the other hand, is Unfiltered and therefore more likely to be an extreme leader. Such leaders are much more likely to have a large unique impact by taking actions that likely alternative leaders would not have. Note that "much more likely," in this case, does not mean "likely" in absolute terms. The general dominance of circumstances means that most of the choices made by even the most out-of-the-ordinary leader will be identical to those made by a normal leader, and some extremes may never get the opportunity to act in ways that produce a high unique impact. The less Filtered a leader, however, the more likely he or she is to stretch those constraints, or even to simply decide that they are not bound by them in the same way. They are much more likely to do extremely well or poorly. To be the lottery ticket. Or the grenade.

Where does this leave us? Most leaders—even the least Filtered ones—have a relatively low impact most of the time. Conventional theories of leader behavior, particularly those that weight context more heavily than individuals, will usually be the best way to analyze them. Leader Filtration Theory is not in competition with those theories. It is prior to them. They work perfectly well in explaining Modal leaders. But when a filtration process allows an Extreme leader to come to power, those traditional theories no longer apply, because such leaders are so different from the norm that their underlying assumption that leaders are roughly interchangeable is simply no longer true. Those situations might be relatively rare, but when they occur, they are extremely important.

FILTERING THE PRESIDENTS

Just as Leader Filtration Theory attempted to resolve the question of which leaders matter, it can help us understand which presidents, despite the importance of context, really mattered, for better or worse.

This could improve presidential performance in several ways. It could show when a highly or less Filtered president is best suited to the moment. Most importantly, it could improve our odds of preventing disastrous presidents from taking power by allowing us to identify those most likely to do great harm—the grenades. Most hopefully, by synthesizing the insights from Leader Filtration Theory with other research on both presidents and leaders more broadly, it might help select presidents who are likely to succeed once in office.

To apply the theory to presidents, we need to examine how they have been Filtered. Presidential systems create the theoretical (and, in the case of Donald Trump, real) possibility that someone could become president

Table 1 Levels of Filtration

		Political elites had enough information and supported the candidate?	
		YES	NO
Political elites had major	Yes	Filtered	Less filtered
role in choice?	No	Less filtered	Unfiltered

without any time in government or politics, or through some other path that exposes them to virtually no filtration at all.

In assessing a president's level of filtration, we need to begin by identifying if political elites play a major role in the choice of nominee. Since only political elites have enough close contact with candidates to filter them effectively, if they do not have a large say in picking the nominee, even highly experienced nominees will be less Filtered. If elites do play a significant role, then we can assess how much information they had about a president when he was still a candidate, and if he was the preferred choice of those elites or if something forced them to accede to a nominee they did not otherwise want. This handy 2×2 can help assess the level of filtration (table 1).

THE HISTORY OF PRESIDENTIAL FILTRATION

The American system for choosing presidents has little resemblance to the one that existed when the Electoral College voted for George Washington unanimously in 1789. Despite this transformation, one thing has remained constant. Party elites have retained significant influence over the nomination process. For most of American history their influence was extremely strong. Since the 1970s rank-and-file voters have had a louder voice through state primaries and, to a lesser extent, caucuses. Party elites, however, are usually still able to assert their preferences, influencing, but not controlling, whom the party selects.[29]

The framers of the Constitution meant for the Electoral College to choose presidents, with no provision for political parties. This, however,

happened only with Washington.[30] Any filtering by the College was irrelevant. Washington was the only choice for however long he was willing to
serve.

From 1796, upon Washington's retirement, through 1828, nominations
were handled by a caucus of party officials, usually members of Congress.
The caucus, however, never became fully institutionalized, partly because
it excluded state-level politicians, but even more because every president
through 1820 so dominated his party as to render the caucus's formal
nomination largely ceremonial.[31] The presidents of the era were well
known to political elites, who had judged them over the course of tumul-
tuous decades, and those elites chose the nominees—and, after the collapse of the Federalist Party briefly rendered general elections functionally
meaningless, the president—based on those evaluations. During this
period, therefore, every president was highly Filtered.

The legislative caucus system was criticized for violating the separation
of powers, as it gave the Congress a role in selecting the president and was
used by members of Congress in 1812 to pressure James Madison into
declaring war on Britain by threatening not to renominate him if he
didn't. After the election of 1824 between John Quincy Adams and
Andrew Jackson went to the House of Representatives, the modern two-
party system emerged, with Jackson heading the Democratic-Republican
Party. At the same time, the caucus system was collapsing. The fading
Federalists were unable to even nominate a candidate to oppose James
Monroe in 1820, and William Crawford, the treasury secretary, received
the caucus's nomination in 1824 even though he had been paralyzed by a
stroke, simply because none of the more popular contenders bothered to
pursue it.[32]

Starting in 1831, the caucus system was replaced by nominating conventions, a system whose essentials lasted more than a century. The first
convention was held by the short-lived Anti-Masonic Party in Baltimore
in 1831, but its advantages were so apparent that the National Republican
and Democratic-Republican parties followed within months. These
conventions—particularly the Democratic-Republican one, because the
soon-to-be-renamed Democrats continue to be a major party today—set
the template for all the ones that followed. Every president since 1832 has
been nominated by a convention.[33]

Delegates to a convention are the paradigmatic example of party elites. Some candidates could muster so much elite support before the convention that the balloting itself was merely a formality or concluded after the first ballot. Other conventions were so divided they took dozens of ballots before they decided on a winner. In all cases, however, the nominee was chosen by party elites, with the average voter having essentially no voice in the outcome, except to the extent that party elites surmised that one or another candidate would have a better chance in the general election.

Beginning in the early twentieth century in response to pressure from the Progressive movement, both Republicans and Democrats began to select delegates through direct primaries, a change that is probably "the most radical of all the party reforms adopted in the whole course of American history." Primaries might seem to have eliminated party elites' power to control the identity of the nominee, but this was far from true. In 1968, for example, Hubert Humphrey did not enter a single primary, while Eugene McCarthy and Robert F. Kennedy entered every available one. The race culminated with Kennedy's victory in the California primary and his assassination the same day, June 5, 1968. But on that day, despite Kennedy's triumph, it was Humphrey who had captured enough delegates to win the Democratic nomination on the first ballot. Through 1968, primaries were virtually "irrelevant to the outcome of the old-fashioned nominating contest."[34]

Primaries were initially important not because of the delegates they elected, but because they allowed candidates to demonstrate to party elites that they could garner enough popular support to win the general election. The most famous example of this phenomenon is the 1960 Democratic primary, when John F. Kennedy's relatively strong performance in West Virginia convinced the leadership of the Democratic Party that, despite his Catholicism, he could gain the support of Democratic constituencies.[35]

Through 1968, then, party elites had virtually complete control over presidential nominations in both parties. The elites, and only the elites, played a major role in filtration. This control did not mean that all candidates, and therefore all presidents, were thoroughly Filtered. Party elites represent and derive their strength from interest groups within the party.

They will tend to prefer Filtered candidates because interest groups tend to support the electable candidate whose policies most closely match their preferences. Candidates, knowing this, attempt to present a maximally appealing profile to those interest groups, which respond by "try[ing] mightily to judge who is authentically committed to their goals and who is merely pretending to be committed."[36] That judgment is only likely to be reliable if it is made of a Filtered candidate, one whose prolonged time in senior government offices enables an accurate judgment of their preferences and abilities.

The fact that party elites will generally prefer a Filtered president, however, does not mean that they always get what they want. A vice president can ascend to the presidency, of course, and be completely Unfiltered. A candidate could have such overwhelming popularity (e.g., Grant or Eisenhower) that party elites could feel they had no choice but to defer to popular sentiment. The elites could, for whatever reason, have settled on a candidate whose career did not offer them the opportunity to accurately assess him. Or major figures in the party could split elite support and make it impossible for any of them to capture a majority, leaving them to settle on a dark horse candidate whose experience has left them judged to be not of presidential timber, only to be resurrected by the fluke circumstances of a convention deadlock.

The disastrous 1968 Democratic convention, which was marred by riots and saw Eugene McCarthy's antiwar campaign defeated by the power of the party establishment, led party nominee Hubert Humphrey to support revamping the nominating process that he had just won. This resulted in the creation of the McGovern-Fraser commission, which reformed the rules by which the Democratic Party selected its nominee. These reforms were soon effectively adopted by Republicans as well. This moved the choice of nominee from the convention to the primaries. In 1968 only 36 percent of delegates went to either party's convention officially committed to a candidate. Four years later, 58 percent of Democratic delegates were committed before the convention, a figure that increased in the following years.[37]

Primaries created a new path to the nomination. Instead of being forced to gain the support of party elites, a candidate could appeal directly to party voters and win enough primaries to capture a majority of delegates before the convention began. Since meaningful filtration is done primarily by those elites—because only they have the close contact with candidates that allows them to accurately discern their true intentions and capabilities—such a candidate will be less Filtered than his or her political experience might indicate.

The fact that such a path exists, however, does not mean that it is well-trodden. The most influential book on how parties pick their nominees is *The Party Decides,* published in 2008. It argues that despite the major changes in the nomination process:

> parties remain major players in presidential nominations. They scrutinize and winnow the field before voters get involved, attempt to build coalitions behind a single preferred candidate, and sway voters to ratify their choice. In the past quarter century, the Democratic and Republican parties have always influenced and often controlled the choice of their presidential nominees.[38]

Even in the postreform era, parties (construed broadly to include all the political elites who have power within the party) work hard to choose their nominee. They usually succeed via an "invisible primary" in which candidates compete for the support of members of the party coalition based on their ability to unite the party, their ability to triumph in the general election, and their fealty to the agenda of powerful interest groups within the party. *The Party Decides* found that while Carter was able to capture the 1976 Democratic nomination as a party outsider without great support from party elites, by 1980 those same elites had adapted to the post-McGovern environment and learned how to regain control of the nomination process.[39]

Elites were able to regain control because winning a nomination means competing across the country, which requires resources exceeding those of any individual candidate. Instead, they have to win financial resources and staff support in the "invisible primary," which forces them to build alliances with party elites across the country. The candidate who does so most successfully has a large, but not insurmountable, lead in the race for the nomination. In the ten primary contests between 1980 and 1996, party elites' preferred candidate won the nomination every time. Although modern communications technologies may have weakened party elites' control in more recent elections, they retain substantial influence.[40]

Scoring the Presidents—Elites' Information and Choice

While party elites in the postreform era do not have total control over the nomination system, they still retain a very loud voice that is overridden only under exceptional circumstances. This means they can filter candidates, even if their power to do so is limited. But that doesn't mean they always will. Party elites may sometimes choose an Unfiltered candidate for any number of reasons, even if their ideal preference might be otherwise.

Since gathering information about candidates requires proximity to them, we can start our assessment of how Filtered a president is by seeing how much time they spent in offices where political elites could evaluate them—as a member of Congress, senator, cabinet secretary, vice president, governor, national or state Supreme Court justice, or general.[41]

Once we assess a president's level of evaluation, the next step is to see if that evaluation played a decisive role in his assumption of the presidency. The less important that evaluation was, the less we should weight his years in filtering offices. For example, if he became president because he was vice president when the president died, then the evaluation was unimportant, leaving such a president Unfiltered except for under two specific circumstances.

First, if he was made vice president in the knowledge that he would soon replace the president (as in the case of Ford and, as we'll see, Truman). Second, if the vice president replaced a Filtered president and was an equally Filtered alternative who might plausibly have gotten the job, then we are comparing one highly Filtered Modal president to another. Had John Hinckley's 1981 assassination attempt on Ronald Reagan succeeded, for example, he would have been replaced by George H. W. Bush—another highly Filtered Republican. If Reagan had not run for office in 1980, Bush would have been one of the most likely alternative presidents. We should assess Lyndon Johnson the same way—as a Filtered product of the Democratic Party establishment, however tragic his path to the White House.

Similarly, several nineteenth-century presidents were "dark horses"—relatively minor figures whose nomination was a surprise, usually because of a deadlock between more prominent party leaders. Dark horse presidents are less Filtered than their level of experience suggests. Although they were evaluated, the result of that evaluation was that party elites did not consider them a leading contender for the presidency. Because of some set of fluke circumstances, however, usually because they were the only person left when the real contenders knocked each other out, they still won the nomination. Presidential candidates who had towering national stature, usually because of their status as a war hero, are also less Filtered because their popularity can swamp elites' judgment.

The less Filtered a president is, the more likely it is that he performed either extremely well or extremely poorly. When presidential performance was assessed using historians' rankings of presidents—a standard practice in both the political science and psychology literature—and presidents were coded as Filtered or Unfiltered, Unfiltered presidents showed more variance in their rankings (see the appendix). When this test was done using an average of presidential rankings conducted before 2012, this finding was statistically significant at higher than the 99 percent level.[42]

Since the end of the Obama administration, three more broad rankings of presidential performance have been conducted: a 2017 C-SPAN survey of presidential historians, a 2018 survey of members of the American Political Science Association (APSA) who study the presidency, and a 2018 survey of experts on the U.S. presidency by the Siena College Research Institute.[43]

I have adjusted their results to eliminate William Henry Harrison and James Garfield when necessary, because both died so early in their terms that they had little or no opportunity to have an impact, and Donald Trump because his term has ended so recently. This leaves forty-one presidents, beginning with Washington and ending with Obama. Twenty-one are Filtered and twenty are Unfiltered. Table 2 shows the results of these surveys, along with a consolidated ranking of presidents that represents a meta-survey, synthesizing the results of twenty-one rankings of presidential performance.

The results of the three most recent surveys are similar to one another, and to the meta-ranking. The specific ranks (e.g., Theodore Roosevelt at 4) are often the same. If we just look at top- and bottom-quartile presidents, they agree on seven of the top ten (Lincoln, Washington, Franklin Roosevelt, Theodore Roosevelt, Eisenhower, Truman, and Jefferson) and seven of the bottom ten (Buchanan, Andrew Johnson, Pierce, Harding,

Table 2 Presidential Rankings

Rank	C-SPAN 2017	APSA 2018	Siena 2018	Meta-Rank
1	Lincoln	Lincoln	Washington	Lincoln
2	Washington	Washington	F. Roosevelt	F. Roosevelt
3	F. Roosevelt	F. Roosevelt	Lincoln	Washington
4	T. Roosevelt	T. Roosevelt	T. Roosevelt	T. Roosevelt
5	Eisenhower	Jefferson	Jefferson	Jefferson
6	Truman	Truman	Eisenhower	Truman
7	Jefferson	Eisenhower	Madison	Wilson
8	Kennedy	Obama	Monroe	Eisenhower
9	Reagan	Reagan	Truman	Jackson
10	L. Johnson	L. Johnson	Kennedy	Kennedy
11	Wilson	Wilson	Wilson	Polk
12	Obama	Madison	Polk	Obama
13	Monroe	Clinton	Reagan	J. Adams
14	Polk	John Adams	Adams	Reagan
15	Clinton	Jackson	Clinton	L. Johnson
16	McKinley	Kennedy	L. Johnson	Madison
17	Madison	G. H. W. Bush	Obama	Monroe
18	Jackson	Monroe	J. Q. Adams	McKinley
19	John Adams	McKinley	Jackson	Clinton
20	G. H. W. Bush	Polk	McKinley	Cleveland
21	J. Q. Adams	Grant	G. H. W. Bush	J. Q. Adams
22	Grant	Taft	Taft	G. H. W. Bush
23	Cleveland	J. Q. Adams	Cleveland	Taft
24	Taft	Cleveland	Grant	Van Buren
25	Ford	Ford	Van Buren	Hayes
26	Carter	Carter	Carter	Ford
27	Coolidge	Van Buren	Ford	Carter
28	Nixon	Coolidge	Nixon	Arthur
29	B. Harrison	Hayes	Taylor	B. Harrison
30	Taylor	G. W. Bush	Coolidge	Coolidge
31	Hayes	Arthur	Hayes	G. W. Bush
32	G. W. Bush	B. Harrison	G. W. Bush	Taylor
33	Van Buren	Nixon	Arthur	Hoover
34	Arthur	Taylor	B. Harrison	Grant
35	Hoover	Hoover	Hoover	Nixon
36	Fillmore	Tyler	Tyler	Tyler
37	Tyler	Fillmore	Fillmore	Fillmore

Table 2   Continued

Rank	C-SPAN 2017	APSA 2018	Siena 2018	Meta-Rank
38	Harding	Harding	Pierce	Pierce
39	Pierce	A. Johnson	Harding	A. Johnson
40	A. Johnson	Pierce	Buchanan	Harding
41	Buchanan	Buchanan	A. Johnson	Buchanan

NOTE: Shading indicates less filtered or unfiltered

Tyler, Fillmore, and Hoover). Of these fourteen, ten are Unfiltered and four Filtered. These fourteen presidents' performances were so extreme that there is little disagreement about them.

The rankings make it possible to examine every president, not just selected ones. By expanding the sample to all presidents, we can minimize the impact of noise and eliminate selection effects.

We can also assess the impact of filtration by looking at it as a continuous, rather than a binary, variable (that is, we assess presidents by their degree of filtration instead of just as Filtered or Unfiltered). If we give each president a "Filtration Score" reflecting his level of filtration, and then order them by that score, we can compare their position in that order to their distance from the median of performance (that is, both high- and low-ranked presidents have a high distance from median rank). This allows us to measure filtration's ability to predict how far a president's ranking would be from the median (for details, see the appendix).

Filtration Score has a statistically significant effect on ranking across twenty-one of twenty-two different rankings of presidential performance and explains roughly one-third of variance in presidential rankings in the most recent surveys. This is a level of explanatory power equal to or better than other models of presidential performance, including Simonton's, even though, unlike other models, it incorporates only easily accessible data that would be contemporaneously available to any American during any election. This is extraordinarily strong support for both the historical validity and contemporary utility of LFT in assessing presidential candidates.

The rankings are an imperfect but nonetheless valuable tool to use in understanding presidential performance. (The appendix includes a more complete discussion of their strengths and weaknesses and describes how they were analyzed.) I use these rankings because a close analysis of them by the political scientist Curt Nichols shows that "the ever popular presidential ranking game appears to have greater internal validity than many in the academy have assumed" and because they remain the only way to test the theory's crucial prediction that Unfiltered presidents will show more variance in performance than their Filtered counterparts.[44]

If we're picking a president, we should understand that highly Filtered and Unfiltered presidents are different. Highly Filtered presidents will generally be competent but unexceptional. Unfiltered ones are often remarkable—for better or worse. Unfiltered presidents, in other words, are a gamble. Unfortunately, they're generally a bad gamble. They have a unique impact by doing what others, in the same situation, would not do. It's just a sad fact of life that there are many more ways to fail than there are to succeed. The easiest way to be a high-impact president is to make mistakes that would never have been made by someone else, or to execute your policies with far less skill or energy than a different and better president would have. Unfiltered presidents can be Lincolns, but you shouldn't count on it.

If you're a party leader or an American citizen deciding whom to vote for, measuring filtration is just a start. You also want to know which candidates are likely to succeed. Perhaps even more important, you want to know which candidates are most likely to fail. The United States today is the wealthiest society in human history and the most powerful nation on earth. Improvements would be great, but there's also a long, long way to fall. We would *like* to have brilliant presidents, but we *must* avoid disastrous ones. How do we identify candidates who have high odds of being a disastrous or brilliant president?

CALLING YOUR SHOT: PREDICTING
PRESIDENTIAL PERFORMANCE

Leader Filtration Theory allows us to create a framework with four buckets we can use to categorize presidents by how Filtered they were and by

Table 3   Extraordinary Presidents

	Success	*Failure*
Unfiltered	Lincoln	A. Johnson
	Washington	Pierce
	F. Roosevelt	Harding
	T. Roosevelt	Tyler
	Eisenhower	Fillmore
Filtered	Truman	Buchanan
	Jefferson	Hoover

their performance. We can put each of the fourteen outlier presidents into one of these buckets: Filtered Success, Filtered Failure, Unfiltered Success, Unfiltered Failure (table 3). The questions *Picking Presidents* answers are outgrowths of this table. What decides if a president will end up on this table? If he or she does, which box will that president end up in, and how do we use that knowledge to judge presidential candidates?

HOW TO READ THE REST OF THIS BOOK

In each of the following chapters we'll start with the theory and with other research on the performance of leaders in general and presidents in particular to develop a theoretically grounded picture which guides our historical exploration. Then we'll look in depth at one or two presidents. We'll examine their path to the presidency in order to judge how Filtered they were. Then we'll examine how they handled the most important issue of their presidency (except for the hyperactive Theodore Roosevelt, whose presidency addressed so many different issues that no single one defined it), using that close study to explore how the theory helps to explain presidential success or failure in the real world. We'll also briefly analyze one or more other presidents in shadow cases.

So, chapters 2 through 5 each examine one of the four boxes in table 3. Most presidents are, by definition, mediocre, and ample research shows that most leaders have little impact, so the theory is not needed to explain those outcomes. Instead, we want to use LFT and other research to explain extreme events—very successful or unsuccessful presidencies. This means that cases are exploratory and should be chosen based on outcome. The presidents where we will look at one issue of their presidency in depth have been selected from the set in table 3.

Within that set, this book's other goal is to describe how the filtration process for presidents works, and by doing so to helping readers evaluate presidential candidates. This means cases were also chosen to be typical of different ways filtration operates.[45] These in-depth cases are paired with shadow cases of other presidents. These shadow cases are meant to be guides to how to apply the theories in this book, not definitive tests of the theory—they are short and somewhat subjective sketches of how Leader Filtration Theory might apply to other presidents.

The major cases in each chapter are not meant to survey entire presidencies. Except for Theodore Roosevelt, all the deep cases examine the single most important decision or policy of the presidency. In each case we're essentially asking, "What was the singular thing about this president's administration that made historians come to a consensus that he was a success or failure?" No presidency, even the most successful one, is beyond reproach, and even the worst has at least a few redeeming qualities. Leader Filtration Theory, and therefore this book, focus on the rare large decisions that tend to define historical memory of a presidency decades later.

Each president profiled here, even the very best and the very worst, undoubtedly has a mixed record. It is far beyond the scope of this book to conduct a comprehensive assessment of a president, much less all of them, and even further beyond it to attempt to revise the historical consensus on a presidency. Instead, in each of the deep cases we'll take the rankings as a given and focus on the single most important decision or issue of their presidency, examining their actions on that issue to develop the theory.

This approach is suited to developing, testing, and applying Leader Filtration Theory because it is a theory about unique impact, a rare but important phenomenon. For both deep and shadow cases the focus will usually be primarily on foreign policy, as that is the domain in which presidents are least constrained and therefore most likely to have an impact.[46]

In the last chapter we'll apply everything we've learned from the previous four to show how the theory would have evaluated Donald Trump and Joe Biden when they were candidates, and how you can use the theory to do a better job of evaluating presidential candidates going forward. Finally, in the conclusion I'll suggest some practical reforms to both the nominating process and the presidency itself that follow from this research.

TODAY'S DILEMMA: PRESIDENTS IN THE TWENTY-FIRST CENTURY

Picking the right president has never been as important—or as difficult— as it is today. Until the 1940s, the president of the United States was one leader among many. Now the entire world depends on him or her. Until the 1980s, the president's freedom of action was constrained by the pressures of the Cold War. Today the American military straddles the world like a colossus. It has competitors, but no peers. In the 2000s, the United States may have been more dominant than any other nation in history, with seemingly little prospect of any near-future rival for preeminence.[47] Today, China's rapid growth makes it likely that the United States will be the world's second largest economy in 2030.

Finally, the presidency has steadily increased in both its power and the scale of the challenges which its occupant is expected to address. It truly has become, as John Dickerson titled his essential book on the presidency, "the hardest job in the world."[48] Even more than their predecessors, presidents of today and tomorrow will likely have to rely upon their own capabilities and that of their staff, instead of allowing Congress to take the lead or simply declaring that some problems are not part of their job.

The stakes may be even higher. Presidential democracies may be more prone to collapse into authoritarianism than their parliamentary counterparts. Only the United States and Chile have managed to maintain a presidential democracy for more than 150 years, and Chile's democracy failed 40 years ago. Meanwhile, the polarization of American politics has increased to an extraordinary extent, often leaving the government so paralyzed that serious observers argue that the collapse of the American constitutional regime is inevitable.[49] This may increase many Americans' desire to pick an Unfiltered president who could shatter an increasingly calcified status quo. Given the risks of Unfiltered leaders, however, avoiding a disastrous Unfiltered president is critically important.

You don't have to go that far to believe that the American system is today under more stress than it has faced in generations, perhaps even since the end of the Civil War. That supreme test was passed only because the United States elected Lincoln, in my opinion the greatest political leader any country has ever produced, the "one man great enough" to take the United States through its "fiery trial." Lincoln reached the Oval Office through a series of circumstances so lucky they lend credence to Bismarck's (likely apocryphal) quip that "there is a special providence for drunkards, fools, and the United States of America."[50]

Americans should be grateful that at the three supreme crises in American history—the Founding, the Civil War, and the combination of the Great Depression and the Second World War—the American people, through wisdom, luck, or divine intervention, chose George Washington, Abraham Lincoln, and Franklin Roosevelt, three leaders so extraordinary that any one of them would make most countries envious. We all hope that future crises will be met by equally extraordinary leaders. But, as is often said in another context, hope is not a method.

2 Harry Truman and the System at Its Best

Sometimes the system works just the way you want it to. At their best, political elites can accurately analyze the country's situation and realize that their interests align with those of the United States. At their most powerful, those same elites can select the person from their ranks who is best suited to surmounting those challenges and elevate him or her to the presidency, where their chosen president rewards their faith.

Almost half of American presidents are to some degree Unfiltered. This is partly a product of the modern presidential system, which allows candidates to bypass elites and appeal directly to the people. British prime ministers are almost invariably far more experienced, and therefore more filtered, than their American counterparts. If we treat years in Parliament as equivalent to years in a filtering position, then the least filtered modern British prime minister is John Major, who spent eleven years in Parliament before succeeding Margaret Thatcher. Those eleven years would put him in the upper quarter of American presidents.[1]

In British politics, the prime minister needs a majority in Parliament—usually, although not always, by gaining the support of the majority party. That can involve awe-inspiringly baroque negotiations. Usually, the modern American political system is nothing like this. Even when the power of party bosses was at its peak in the nineteenth century, nominees still had to win in the general election. On rare occasions, however, the vice presidency allows the American system to approximate a parliamentary one. Two vice presidents—Harry Truman and Gerald Ford—were chosen with the certainty they would soon become president. Perhaps not coincidentally, just as prime ministers come from Parliament, both came from the legislative branch, Truman from the Senate and Ford from the House. Truman's presidency provides an ideal case in which to examine a highly Filtered and Successful president.

To understand how Truman's story illuminates how Filtered presidents succeed, we're going to dive much deeper into his path to the presidency than we will for other presidents. Vice presidents who become president are usually Unfiltered. To show why we should make an exception to that rule, we need to show why Truman is a special case. Only Ford ever became president the way Truman did—as a vice president who was picked for the ticket largely by party elites, not the party's nominee, in the knowledge that he would soon become president. So we need to see how and why the leaders of the Democratic Party came to believe that he was the best possible successor to Franklin Roosevelt, and if this process allowed those party leaders to both fully evaluate Truman, to then make a judgment to put him in the White House based on that evaluation.

Coding Truman as Filtered *weakens* the statistical support for Leader Filtration Theory, because a president with his high position in the rankings would normally be expected to be Unfiltered. In practice his case is an excellent illustration of the ways in which filtration can operate through unconventional paths.

To use Truman's presidency to help fill out our framework of Filtered/Unfiltered and Successful/Unsuccessful presidents, we need to do two things. First, examine Truman's career to see what Democratic elites knew about him, why they picked him, and who else might have become president. Second, examine the most important decision of Truman's presidency and try to understand if that choice was a product of the characteristics that led to his selection. We want to know if Harry S Truman—on average ranked as the sixth best president in American history—really did what he was chosen to do and succeeded by doing so.

When Franklin Roosevelt died on April 12, 1945, Truman had been vice president for eighty-two days. Roosevelt, out of Washington for most of that time and weakened by heart disease, had met with Truman only twice during that time and had not even told him about the nuclear bomb. A few minutes after 5:15 P.M., Eleanor Roosevelt told him, "Harry, the president is dead." Truman, after a few moments of speechlessness, asked, "Is there anything I can do for you?" She replied, "Is there anything we can do for you? For you are the one in trouble now."[2]

Eleanor Roosevelt spoke more accurately than even she could have known. In just the next four months Truman had to deal with crises and questions whose combination of severity and variety has no parallel in American history, including:

> the collapse of Nazi Germany, the founding of the United Nations, firebombings of Japanese cities that killed many thousands of civilians, the liberation of Nazi death camps, the suicide of Adolf Hitler, the execution of Benito Mussolini, and the capture of arch war criminals from Hitler's number two, Hermann Göring, to the Nazi "chief werewolf" Ernst Kaltenbrunner. There was the fall of Berlin, victory at Okinawa (which the historian Bill Sloan has called "the deadliest campaign of conquest ever undertaken by American arms"), and the Potsdam Conference, during which the new president sat at the negotiating table with Winston Churchill and Joseph Stalin in Soviet-occupied Germany, in an attempt to map out a new world. Humanity saw the first atomic explosion, the nuclear destruction of Hiroshima and Nagasaki, the dawn of the Cold War, and the beginning of the nuclear arms race.[3]

Each item on that astonishing list would, by itself, merit a chapter in a history of most presidencies. For Truman they were piled one atop the other from the instant he was catapulted into the Oval Office, with more and worse to come. Yet Truman's most consequential choice came years later and he, a product of Missouri's corrupt Democratic machine, met the challenge as few ever have.

"GIVE 'EM HELL HARRY": HARRY S TRUMAN

A Failed Haberdasher from Missouri

Harry S Truman (famously, he had a middle initial but no middle name) was born on May 8, 1884, in Lamar, Missouri. He grew up on his family's farm in Missouri, where his father's hard work, inventiveness (he held a patent for one of his inventions), and speculation on wheat futures made his family moderately prosperous. He was a good enough student that he skipped third grade, and in his own words read "everything I could get my hands on—histories and encyclopedias and everything else." Truman applied to West Point for college but was turned down because of poor eyesight. By all accounts he had an exceptionally happy childhood.[4]

In 1901, however, his father's speculations failed catastrophically, wiping out the family wealth and eliminating any chance Harry had of going to college. For the next sixteen years Truman devoted himself to working on the farm with his father and to unsuccessful business ventures, as well as meeting and pursuing Bess Wallace, the only daughter of a far wealthier family. He proposed in 1911 and was turned down. She changed her mind two years later, but they did not announce their engagement until 1917 and did not marry until 1919. In 1905 Truman volunteered for the Missouri National Guard. He initially failed in his attempt to join because of his poor eyesight but passed on his second attempt by memorizing the eye chart. He served until 1911.[5]

In 1917 the United States entered World War I. Truman was thirty-three, and even apart from his vision he had every reason not to volunteer: he was two years above the draft's age limit, he had been out of the Guard for almost six years, he was supporting his mother and sister, and Wilson had asked farmers to remain on their farms because of the importance of American agriculture to the war effort. Truman, however, felt obligated to serve.[6]

Truman's latent leadership abilities were soon recognized by the army. He rejoined his former artillery unit, whose men elected him as a lieutenant. He was soon promoted to captain and given command of a 194-man unit rife with discipline problems. In only a few months, however, Truman transformed it into one of the best units in his regiment and led the men in combat, where he displayed remarkable courage and leadership under fire.[7]

While in the army Truman also established a profitable sideline managing his unit's commissary, which after the war inspired him to partner with a friend to found a men's haberdashery, or clothing store. It failed disastrously, collapsing in 1922 and ruining his finances for two decades.[8]

Truman's other legacy from the army was more fruitful. In training he befriended James Pendergast, the nephew of Tom Pendergast, the legendary head of the Kansas City Democratic machine. In late 1921 Truman was asked if he wanted to run for eastern judge in Jackson County, an administrative position that would give him great influence over patronage. Truman, knowing that his haberdashery was on the point of collapse, immediately accepted.[9]

Truman served with distinction. Although the Pendergast machine was, even by the standard of the era, extraordinarily corrupt, Truman was personally honest (although he likely looked the other way when he became aware of some of Pendergast's corruption), and he managed government spending so efficiently that even the *Kansas City Star* and *Independence Sentinel,* both staunch machine opponents, strongly endorsed his reelection. In 1926 he ran for presiding judge, a position he held for eight years to widespread acclaim.[10]

Truman in the Senate

In May 1934 Pendergast picked Truman as the machine's candidate for the Senate, and the machine delivered Truman a decisive victory in the Democratic primary, which, given the Democratic Party's overwhelming strength in Missouri at the time and particularly the enormous popularity of President Franklin Roosevelt there, virtually ensured his victory in the general election. When Truman arrived in Washington, however, he discovered that his hard-earned Missouri reputation for incorruptibility did not travel to Washington, where he was viewed as just another machine politician.[11]

In the Senate Truman was a steadfast supporter of the New Deal who, unlike most senators, put great effort into building up his expertise. His reputation with his fellow senators and, eventually, the nation, began to rise. In 1937 he gave speeches attacking corporate power and corruption that were covered on the front page of the *New York Times.* Somewhat ironically, even while attacking corruption he was keeping his wife Bess on his Senate office payroll, justifying it by saying that she had helped him with his work. He also began to take positions supportive of civil rights— surprising given his background in Missouri—and in favor of strengthening the military in response to the situation in Europe.[12]

As Truman ran for reelection in 1940, however, he faced a brutal political environment. Anticorruption investigations in Missouri had imprisoned Pendergast and shattered his machine. Most observers believed that Truman had little chance of winning the Democratic primary. Truman's reputation in the Senate was strong enough, though, that other senators made the rare effort of intervening in a primary to help him. Truman ran based on his support of the New Deal and of rearmament, on his advocacy of selling arms to Britain, and, daringly, on his mild support for civil rights. Truman's own connection with voters and the last remnants of the Pendergast machine combined to win him the Democratic primary by barely 8,000 votes out of more than 650,000 cast. He returned to the Senate and took crucially important roles on both the Military Affairs Committee and the Military Subcommittee of the Appropriations Committee.[13]

In February 1941 Truman began the sequence of events that would end with him in the White House. Concerned about corruption and mismanagement in military spending, he proposed a special committee to investigate defense contracts. It eventually held more than four hundred hearings and produced fifty-one reports, every one unanimous. They revealed widespread fraud by defense contractors and incompetence on the part of the government. The committee also convinced the Department of the Navy to adopt the legendary Higgins Boat for amphibious landings, a decision that played a crucial role in the success of American amphibious operations during the war. Truman's contributions were so respected that he was featured on the cover of *Time*, and a poll of Washington correspondents named him one of the ten men in Washington most important to the war effort. He was the only member of either house of Congress on the list. By 1943 Truman was being discussed as a potential replacement for Vice President Henry Wallace, although Truman claimed he wasn't interested.[14]

Truman and the Vice Presidency

In 1944 Roosevelt towered over American politics as few ever have. His dominance of the Democratic Party was so total that he faced no significant opposition for an unprecedented fourth term. All the energies that would normally have focused on the presidential nomination instead turned on the second slot on the ticket. The question of Roosevelt's running mate became a furious and confusing struggle for four reasons.

First, if Roosevelt had expressed a clear preference, he would have gotten his choice. But the Sphinx-like Roosevelt "never . . . pursued a more Byzantine course than in his handling of this question."[15]

Second, Vice President Wallace had enough opposition in the party that his renomination was by no means certain, but not enough to make it impossible. Apart from Truman, possible replacements included Senate Majority Leader Alben Barkley, Supreme Court Associate Justice William O. Douglas, Speaker of the House Sam Rayburn, and the frontrunner, Jimmy Byrnes, a veteran of the House, Senate, and Supreme Court whose power in the administration was so great he was referred to as the "assistant president."[16]

Third, the Republican nominee, New York governor Thomas E. Dewey, was a good enough candidate that a strong vice-presidential nominee might be needed to guarantee Roosevelt's reelection. Fourth, and most importantly, Democratic leaders knew that Roosevelt's health was poor and rapidly declining. There was no chance that he would survive his fourth term. The Democratic National Convention that met in Chicago in late July of 1944 would be doing more than choosing a vice-presidential nominee. Hidden from the public, but widely known among party elites, was that it would be choosing the next president.[17]

Wallace's opponents were united by their belief that he was not aligned with the party establishment, instead drawing his support largely from the Left. This was enhanced by Wallace's own qualities. He was, in the words of Edwin Pauley, the acting treasurer of the Democratic National Committee and a leader of Wallace's opposition, "so much the prophet, an unworldly man of mystical leanings and ideas, that it was obvious to all who knew him that he would only make the country a mighty strange president."[18]

Truman had considerable strengths, including his combination of hailing from a state bordering the North and South and his mild support for civil rights, which meant that he could likely garner southern support without alienating African Americans. He had almost ten years of experience in the Senate, where his contributions to the war effort had been significant and his relationships with other senators (unlike Wallace's) were excellent, which meant he could help get Senate ratification for postwar treaties. Set against that was Truman's age (sixty in May of 1944), only two years younger than Roosevelt, and his virtually nonexistent relationship with the president, especially when compared with Roosevelt's extremely close ties to Byrnes.[19]

But Byrnes had three significant weaknesses. First, he was born a Catholic but converted to Episcopalianism when he married, threatening Catholic support for the ticket. Second, Byrnes was a southerner and a segregationist, which might threaten African American support. Third, Byrnes's management of the economy during the war had alienated labor, which could be problematic if he replaced Wallace, who was by far labor's favorite candidate.[20]

The conspiracy against Wallace made its first move in January 1944 when Roosevelt met with several advisers to discuss alternatives to Wallace. Robert Hannegan, who had helped rescue Truman's reelection in 1940, now served as the commissioner of internal revenue and had a close relationship with Roosevelt. Hannegan was particularly enthusiastic about Truman, but equally supportive of Byrnes. Roosevelt, cryptically, declined to reveal whom he wanted.[21]

In May, Wallace left on an extended trip to China and the Soviet Union. Accounts differ as to whether he went at his own suggestion or whether Roosevelt sent him to get him out of the country. Before, during, and after the trip, Pauley ensured that Roosevelt met a steady stream of Wallace opponents. Just before leaving, Wallace met Hannegan, who told him that Democratic leaders across the country wanted him off the ticket. Wallace refused to withdraw. In June Roosevelt told his assistants that while he still supported Wallace, he believed that the opposition to Wallace was widespread and that other party figures should get his reaction to his new status as a "political liability." By July Roosevelt was, in his typically indirect fashion, asking party leaders to sound out Wallace on leaving the nomination, but refusing to ask him to do so directly. Wallace refused to step aside without a direct request from Roosevelt.[22]

Party leaders met with Roosevelt on July 11, only eight days before the convention, to discuss the vice presidency. The group began going through candidates. They quickly eliminated Rayburn because of his lack of home-state support, and Barkley because of his age. Roosevelt suggested Douglas as a younger possibility, but his political amateur status meant that he was dismissed by the other attendees. Byrnes received significant time and attention, but his political weaknesses were deemed too important. Eventually the discussion moved to Truman, and by its end Roosevelt concluded that he was the strongest candidate, with attendees tasked to push out Byrnes and Wallace. After the meeting Hannegan returned to see Roosevelt and got a handwritten note endorsing Truman, but it was weak enough to leave Roosevelt's intentions ambiguous.[23]

Byrnes and Wallace, both capable and ambitious men, continued to maneuver for the prize that both believed was within their grasp, while Truman himself was largely unaware of what was transpiring. On Thursday, July 13, Byrnes met with Roosevelt and showed him a photograph of Eleanor Roosevelt addressing an African American crowd. He argued that their devotion to the First Lady meant that his presence on the ticket would not alienate them. On Friday Byrnes met with Leo Crowley, who was close to Byrnes and Roosevelt, and Postmaster General Frank Walker, who had been tasked with persuading Byrnes to step out of the race without resigning from the administration. Byrnes, however, would not concede and called Roosevelt who, true to form, refused to tell him to step down. Byrnes seized the opportunity and called Truman. After confirming that Truman did not want to be vice president, he told Truman that Roosevelt wanted Byrnes, and asked Truman to nominate him at the convention. Truman agreed and offered to help rally support for Byrnes in the Missouri delegation.[24]

Later that afternoon Hannegan, now confused as to Roosevelt's wishes, called him and began to believe that Byrnes was Roosevelt's choice. The next day Hannegan visited Roosevelt with two objectives. His overriding goal was to remove Wallace. He would have supported virtually anyone to do that. He also needed to clearly ascertain Roosevelt's real desire. He was joined by Mayor Edward Kelly of Chicago, who called Byrnes afterwards to tell him that he was Roosevelt's choice. Byrnes then took a train to Chicago for the convention. Hannegan left the meeting, however, with a note from Roosevelt:

Dear Bob:

You have written me about Harry Truman and Bill Douglas. I should, of course, be very glad to run with either of them and believe that either one would bring real strength to the ticket.

> *Always sincerely,*
> *Franklin Roosevelt.*[25]

Byrnes, Hannegan, and Kelly had breakfast in Chicago on Sunday morning. Hannegan told Byrnes that Roosevelt had told him to "clear it [Byrnes's nomination] with Sidney [Sidney Hillman, a leader of the Congress of Industrial Organizations, a major labor group]." Labor was crucial to Roosevelt's reelection. Hillman wanted Wallace, but if not Wallace, he was strongly opposed to Byrnes. Truman, meanwhile, was reaffirming his lack of interest in the vice presidency. When a reporter mentioned that the next vice president might well soon become president, Truman replied, "Hell, I don't want to be president."[26]

The behind-the-scenes struggle climaxed on Monday and Tuesday, July 17 and 18. On Monday the convention chair released a letter from Roosevelt about Wallace's candidacy that had been written on July 14. It read, in part:

I have been associated with Henry Wallace during his past four years as Vice President, for eight years earlier while he was Secretary of Agriculture, and well before that. I like and respect him and he is my personal friend. For these reasons I personally would vote for his nomination if I were a delegate to the convention.

Roosevelt, however, was *not* a delegate, nor did he urge the delegates to vote for Wallace. It is difficult to imagine a weaker endorsement. The attendees could read between the lines. Wallace wasn't done, but he was gravely wounded.[27]

On Tuesday afternoon Edward J. Flynn, a New York Democrat with a long relationship to Roosevelt, arrived. He met Hannegan, who told him "It's Byrnes!" Flynn rejected that and insisted on a meeting of the party leadership that included Hillman, but not Byrnes. There he reaffirmed the possibility that Byrnes would cost the ticket African American votes and demanded that they call Roosevelt and get a direct answer. Frank Walker was the last man to speak to him and Roosevelt's instructions were, finally, clear. "Frank," the president ordered, "go all out for Truman." Byrnes called Roosevelt the next day in a last-ditch attempt to resurrect his candidacy, but by noon on Wednesday the 19th, the convention's opening day, he was convinced to withdraw.[28]

Anticipating this decision, Democratic Party leaders had already begun working to convince Truman to accept the nomination. Truman had spent much of Saturday, Sunday, and Monday morning rallying support for Byrnes and working on his nominating speech. On Monday night Hannegan called to tell Truman he was the president's choice. While Truman reaffirmed his support for Byrnes, he likely understood that in Byrnes's absence conservative delegates would rally around him to stop Wallace. The next morning he breakfasted with Hillman, who told him that labor supported Wallace, but he was their next choice.[29]

Truman continued to have qualms about the vice presidency and consulted friends and party leaders, all of whom urged him to accept. Byrnes formally withdrew Wednesday morning. That afternoon, party leaders, including Hannegan, Walker, and Flynn, met with Truman and called Roosevelt. When Hannegan informed Roosevelt of Truman's continued reluctance, the response was immediate and unequivocal: "Tell him if he wants to break up the Democratic Party in the middle of a war that's his responsibility." The president then slammed down the phone. Truman, not knowing that Hannegan and Roosevelt had orchestrated the call, exclaimed either "Jesus Christ!" or "Oh, shit!" Either way, the man who had volunteered for World War I at thirty-three could never say no to that. He was in. Now it was between him and Wallace.[30]

Wallace arrived in Chicago Wednesday afternoon with a window of opportunity. Byrnes was out and Truman not yet a candidate. At least 290 of the 529 delegates needed for the nomination backed Wallace and, according to a recent Gallup poll, so did 65 percent of Democratic voters. Wallace's strategy was simple. He would take advantage of his strength and the disorganization of the opposition to stampede the convention in his favor.[31]

The next morning Hannegan released Roosevelt's letter endorsing Truman, but its inclusion of Douglas (who was on a camping trip and unaware that he was being mentioned) limited its effect. Later that day

Truman, when a reporter commented on his good mood, replied "Yes, I am going to be nominated for vice president." Although his confidence was likely partly for show, he and his supporters had no idea what Wallace's team had brewing.[32]

Thursday night saw Roosevelt's renomination and acceptance speech, which he delivered via radio. Wallace seconded Roosevelt's nomination with a speech so powerful that even a Truman organizer described it as "the most inspiring talk he had ever given." This became important because unbeknownst to Truman's backers, they had made a near-fatal error. The convention's ticket takers and ushers were Chicago police controlled by Mayor Kelly, who was nominally supportive of Truman but who may have been hoping to deadlock the convention so that it would turn to his ally, Illinois Senator Scott Lucas. Fifteen thousand convention tickets had been printed and distributed but, crucially, they were handed out in booklets that contained tickets for each day and session of the convention, and every ticket was the same color. This allowed tickets to be used to flood a specific session (e.g., by using tickets for the Friday session on Thursday). Wallace's team seized on the error and filled the hall with his supporters.[33]

After Roosevelt's acceptance speech ended at 10:35 P.M., Wallace's team made its move. The crowd burst into deafening chants of "We want Wallace!" The convention organist, either suborned or caught up in the moment, began playing Wallace's (and his home state of Iowa's) anthem, "Iowa, Iowa, That's Where the Tall Corn Grows." Roosevelt-Wallace banners were unfurled. They even appeared in the Alabama delegation, which hated Wallace because of his support for civil rights. Wallace supporters paraded on the convention floor. As the hall filled with the sound of Wallace supporters singing "We are from I-o-way, I-o-way . . ." Truman's team realized they were on the verge of defeat.[34]

They tried to stem the tide by ending the session. Hannegan screamed to Kelly for help. He replied, "We have fire laws!" realizing that he could have the convention adjourned if the already overcrowded hall was declared in violation. He went to the entrance and opened the doors, allowing hundreds more to pour in. Pauley turned to his second-in-command, Neale Roach, and ordered him to "Stop that organ!" This was easier said than done. The organist could only be reached by telephone, but his telephone had a light instead of a bell and could be easily ignored. Repeated calls were going unanswered. "Tell me how?" Roach asked, "He won't answer the phone." Pauley, at this point desperate, told him to "get an ax" and, if necessary, cut the cables. One of Roach's aides grabbed a fire ax and made his way to the organ.[35]

On the floor, Florida senator Claude Pepper, one of Wallace's most powerful backers, stood on his chair and saw many states included in the Wallace parade. He knew that "chairmen would not allow their delegates to parade for a candidate they objected to strongly [indicating that Wallace had broad support and weak opposition on the floor among the delegates themselves]. Emotions ran high. I was convinced that if a vote could be taken that evening, Wallace could be nominated . . . I shouted at the top of my lungs and waved my standard violently, to no avail." His microphone had been turned off. With the Florida standard in his hand, Pepper began jumping up and down on his chair to get the attention of Jackson, the convention's chairman and a Wallace supporter. Hannegan, however, had told Jackson that "he was Hannegan's chairman and, by God, not to forget it!" Jackson ignored Pepper.[36]

Pepper knew that this was the moment. He began forcing his way through the crowd to the podium. Most of the delegates and reporters recognized him and immediately realized what he was attempting. If he could get to the podium he could nominate Wallace immediately, instead of waiting for the next night when the vice-presidential nomination was supposed to be decided. The excitement on the floor was so great that if he could force an immediate vote, Wallace would likely win. At the edge of the platform he reached a gate that blocked the entrance. The gate was manned by a union representative who recognized Pepper and waved him through. He climbed the steps to the stage in full view of Hannegan, his allies, and the mass of reporters and delegates.[37]

Hannegan chose Mayor David Lawrence of Pittsburgh to move for an adjournment and ordered Jackson, "You get up there right now and I mean now and recognize Dave Lawrence, or I'll do it for you!" Jackson demurred, "This crowd is too hot. I can't." Hannegan, enraged, thundered, "You're taking orders from me, and I'm taking orders from the President." Pepper was one step from the podium. Wallace may have been one step from the presidency.[38]

He got no closer. Hearing Kelly's yells about violations of the fire codes Jackson, barely audible over the screams of the crowd, said, "This is getting serious. People may be injured. We are packed in these aisles until it may become dangerous." He recognized Lawrence, who moved to adjourn. Jackson heard ayes and nays from both sides and ruled that the ayes had it. At 10:54 P.M. the convention was adjourned until 11:30 A.M. the next day. To eliminate any further disturbances the party leaders cut off the mics and the platform spotlights.[39]

That night and the next morning Hannegan's team went to work. After hearing of the tumult, Roosevelt himself called to ask, "What the hell's going on there? Are you letting this thing get out of hand?" Although they reassured him that everything was under control, the night had been fraught. Adjourning, however, had bought them time. Every state delegation was informed that Truman was Roosevelt's choice. This was the key argument. Added to it may have been the full arsenal of the party establishment, ranging from patronage to outright bribes. Truman was uninvolved. Instead he spent most of the night finding and sobering up his fellow senator from Missouri, Bennett Clark, whom Truman wanted to nominate him.[40]

The result was that on Friday the balance of power in the convention was radically different. Although the nominating speeches backing Truman were weak (a barely sober Clark gave a particularly poor one) while those supporting Wallace were powerful, it no longer mattered. Truman's backers had decided on a brilliant strategy. Instead of trying to win on the first ballot (likely impossible given Wallace's support), the Truman forces encouraged state delegations to run "favorite son" candidates. These candidates would receive their home state's votes, but no other ones, on the first ballot. If enough ran, they would deny Wallace an immediate victory. Additionally, the speeches supporting each nominee would delay the voting for hours, giving the Truman team more time to pressure wavering delegates.[41]

Their plan succeeded. Sixteen people were nominated for vice president while Truman spent hours in a room below the speaker's platform meeting delegates. The first ballot did not begin until 4:30 P.M., five hours after the day's session had begun. Five hundred eighty-nine votes were needed for a majority. When the first ballot was over Wallace had 429 and Truman 319. The rest were split among favorite sons. Wallace's team had held some votes in reserve to create an impression of momentum on the second ballot and thought he still had a chance. They were wrong.[42]

The plans of Truman's backers had been kept so secret that even after the first ballot Interior Secretary Harold Ickes, one of the most important figures in the party, was unaware of them. After the first ballot's results were announced, Ickes rushed to Frank Walker and in a panic repeated several times, "It's going to be an impasse. We've got to do something, Frank. I'll see you after this ballot." Walker, however, was so confident that after calming Ickes, he left the convention for his hotel without even waiting to see the outcome.[43]

By Friday Hannegan had solidified his control over Jackson, if it had ever wavered, and as soon as the results from the first ballot were announced, he used it to finish Wallace. Instead of breaking for dinner, Jackson moved immediately to the second ballot, denying Wallace's team any chance to negotiate for more support. Wallace's strength began to increase during the second vote, getting as high as 489 delegates, only 100 short of what he needed.[44]

Then Hannegan's plans kicked into action. Maryland governor Herbert O'Connor, one of the favorite-son candidates, withdrew, throwing his delegates to Truman. Senator Bankhead of Alabama then did the same. Assistant Attorney General Noman Littell, a Wallace supporter, described Hannegan's mastery:

> I could see Hannegan at the front edge of the platform motioning excitedly to this delegation and then to that. For all the world he was like an organ player pulling great stops on a giant organ. First to the left, then to the right and then in the center, as one delegation after another, through its speaker, rose to the microphone standing by the aisle and announced its vote.

Hannegan later said that he wanted "Here lies the man who stopped Henry Wallace from becoming President of the United States" on his tombstone. Wallace's defeat was so total that the Iowa state chairman motioned to make Truman's nomination unanimous. Even that request was denied as a final way of driving home the extent of the party establishment's dominance. The final vote was 1,031 votes for Truman and 105 for Wallace. Even Wallace, recognizing the inevitable, cast his vote for Truman.[45]

The 1944 general election was almost anticlimactic. Roosevelt's health problems remained unknown to the public and his popularity, even after twelve years in office, remained a formidable asset. With Roosevelt physically unable to do much campaigning and primarily focused upon the war, Truman became his chief surrogate. The Roosevelt-Truman ticket won the popular vote by three million and won the electoral vote of thirty-six of the forty-eight states. On January 20, 1945, Roosevelt was reinaugurated and Truman was sworn in as vice president.[46]

Assessment: Truman, the Filtered Vice President

Normally, vice presidents who ascend because of the president's death are Unfiltered. Vice presidents are usually chosen for idiosyncratic reasons ranging from convention floor compromises to the whim of the nominee, almost always with the overriding goal of maximizing the ticket's odds of victory. Little thought is given to the potential vice president's ability to step into the presidency. Recent vice-presidential nominees—Sarah Palin is far from the only example—highlight this.

Harry Truman, however, represents the opposite end of the spectrum. Roosevelt may have been unwilling to contemplate the implications of his declining health, but every Democratic Party leader knew that he would not survive his fourth term. Given that, they considered both the electoral implications of the vice-presidential nominee and what he would do as president. The three most likely nominees were all enormously experienced politicians who were well known to party elites. Wallace had been secretary of agriculture and vice president. Byrnes had served in all three branches of government. Truman had done well in the Senate for ten years.

Party leaders simply decided that Wallace was too far to the left and persuaded Roosevelt to replace him, then selected Truman, who was acceptable on policy (like Byrnes) and a political asset (unlike Byrnes), as that replacement. Roosevelt's extended—and cruel—dangling of the vice presidency in front of Byrnes may have been meant to ensure that Wallace's supporters would rally behind Truman to avoid getting Byrnes.

Truman, however he reached the Oval Office, was clearly one of the more Filtered presidents, with his Filtration Score of 10 putting him in the upper half. Party elites knew Truman well. They'd had ten years to evaluate him in the close confines of the Senate. They were just as familiar with Wallace and Byrnes. They filtered out Byrnes and Wallace and chose Truman who, just as expected, succeeded Roosevelt. The only thing that surprised them was likely how fast that happened.

If Truman was Filtered, we should expect his most important decisions to be in accord with the mainstream of elite Democratic Party opinion. Since Wallace was filtered out because of his left-wing views, if there was a difference between Truman and Wallace (the most likely alternative candidate), Truman should take the more conservative (but also more representative of party elites) position. If he and Wallace agreed, however, and particularly if they agreed on a decision where Truman took a conservative position, then this would be particularly strong evidence that Truman's decision was a product of the system, as even the too-left-for-party-elites Wallace would have made the same choice.

Truman and the Korean Decision

As I noted above, the first months of the Truman administration were among the most consequential faced by any president. A complete analysis of all of Truman's almost eight years in office is beyond the scope of this book. Instead we're going to drill down on the most important action of his presidency. Of all Truman's decisions, one from his second term stands above the rest. Truman himself said it was "the most important in my time as President of the United States:" entering the Korean War.[47]

Truman was not alone in this assessment. John Lewis Gaddis, the dean of Cold War historians, has said that the Korean War was "quite possibly the most important event since World War II" because it "intensified and militarized" the Cold War. Defending South Korea was a heavy burden. Chairman of the Joint Chiefs Omar Bradley told President Truman that deploying American ground troops would make it impossible for the United States military to meet its other commitments without mobilization. Over the next three years more than thirty thousand American soldiers died in the fighting.[48]

THE ROAD TO WAR

The five years between the end of the Second World War and the beginning of the Korean War were marked by steadily increasing tensions between the former allies of the United States and the Soviet Union, now the world's dominant powers. From the American perspective, one broken agreement and Soviet provocation followed another, predisposing almost everyone in the American government to interpret any actions by Communist states as the product of Soviet aggression.

At the Yalta Conference in February 1945 Churchill and Roosevelt had gotten Stalin's agreement to hold free elections in countries occupied by the Red army, including the Baltics, Poland, and the rest of Eastern Europe. Stalin never had any intention of following through. At the Potsdam Conference, which followed in July and August, Truman revealed the existence of the nuclear bomb to Stalin (who already knew thanks to his extensive spy network within the United States) and agreed on a jointly occupied and demilitarized Germany.[49]

Following Potsdam Stalin continued the occupation of Iran that had begun in 1942 and pushed for the cession of Turkish territory to the Soviet Union, which would have given it control of the Turkish straits. Truman and Clement Attlee (who had replaced Churchill as England's prime minister) pushed back. They rejected his demands and took the issue of Iran to the newly created United Nations. In early 1946 George Kennan, then a Foreign Service officer in the Moscow embassy, presented an explanation for Soviet behavior in his legendary "Long Telegram." Kennan argued that Soviet aggression was an inevitable product of the nature of the Soviet "dictatorship" and that it could be deterred only by "containment," which would require the United States to counter Soviet attempts at expansion.[50]

In March 1947 Truman announced the "Truman Doctrine," which committed "the United States to support free people who are resisting attempted subjugation by armed minorities or outside pressures . . . to work out their own destinies in their own way." In June Secretary of State George Marshall announced the Marshall Plan, an enormous commitment to aid in the rebuilding of Europe to create a bulwark against Communism. Marshall, cleverly, made this assistance available to

Soviet-dominated states as well as those of Western Europe. Stalin responded by forbidding their participation.[51]

In early 1948 Stalin approved a Communist coup in Czechoslovakia that overthrew the only democratic government in Eastern Europe. Later that year he announced a blockade of West Berlin, which lasted until May 1949. The Western Powers responded by committing to supply West Berlin by air and creating NATO. In August 1949 the Soviet Union detonated its own nuclear weapon, stunning an American government that had been comfortable in its belief that its nuclear monopoly guaranteed its superiority over its former ally. October 1949 saw another shock to American confidence with Mao's announcement of the formation of the People's Republic of China and the revelation of major spy rings in the United States and Great Britain. The combination spurred on rising anti-Communist hysteria in the United States.[52]

American Cold War strategy was codified by NSC-68, presented to Truman in April 1950. NSC-68 argued that the Soviet Union had a vast military superiority over the United States and that American security could be threatened by anything that convinced other nations to ally with the winning (Communist) side. Although this estimate of American weakness is now known to have been severely mistaken, at the time it had broad support within the government.[53]

Tensions were increasing on the Korean Peninsula. The peninsula had been occupied by Japan, and Japan's surrender led to its partition between the United States and the Soviet Union at the 38th parallel of latitude. Although this had been meant to be temporary, Cold War tensions made unification impossible. The Soviet Union established a Communist dictatorship in the North under Kim Il-Sung, while in the South Syngman Rhee, a leader of Korean opposition to the Japanese occupation, established an American-backed authoritarian government.[54]

Korea, however, was peripheral to American interests and attention. NSC 68 had stated that America's primary interest was ensuring that major concentrations of industrial power (e.g., Western Europe and Japan) did not fall into Communist hands. In January of 1950 Secretary of State Acheson (who had replaced Marshall) delivered a speech outlining American policy in Asia. It emphasized that the United States would fight to defend Japan and the Philippines but left ambiguous whether it would use force to defend South Korea.[55]

DAYS OF DECISION

The Korean War began at 4:00 A.M. (Korean time) on June 25, 1950, with an artillery barrage followed by a massive ground attack. Truman was on vacation in Independence, Missouri, when Acheson called. Acheson told him that he had already asked for a meeting of the U.N. and urged him not to risk a night flight to Washington. Truman arrived in Washington the next evening. He immediately proceeded to Blair House (the White House was undergoing extensive renovations) to meet with his top advisers. During the flight Truman had concluded that the invasion was akin to Hitler and Mussolini's actions before the Second World War. He believed that defeating the invasion was necessary to both preserving the authority of the United Nations and averting a third world war. Over dinner and during the discussions afterwards Truman found that this view was shared by all the attendees, including the secretaries of state and defense, the service secretaries, and the Joint Chiefs. He wrote in his memoirs of the "complete, almost unspoken acceptance on the part of everyone that whatever had to be done to meet this aggression had to be done. There was no suggestion from anyone that either the United Nations or the United States could back away from it."[56]

Truman issued his first public statement the next day. He declared that the United States would "vigorously support the effort of the Security Council to terminate this serious breach of the peace." This was met by criticism from Republicans who felt that Truman was appeasing a Communist attack. Bad news from Korea kept flowing back to Washington, all of it highlighting that a rapid North Korean victory was inevitable without a major commitment of American forces. At Acheson's suggestion Truman convened a second Blair House evening meeting. There Bradley presented Douglas MacArthur's assessment that American air and naval forces had to be deployed to Korea. Acheson suggested doing this, further shoring up America's position in Asia, and getting a U.N. Security Council resolution calling on all members to aid in the defense of South Korea. Truman concurred. Once again there was no significant disagreement from any of the attendees.[57]

American air and naval forces entered combat on June 27. That morning Democratic and Republican congressional leaders unanimously expressed support for American intervention, as did Thomas Dewey, whom Truman had, famously, barely defeated in the 1948 presidential election. That evening the U.N. Security Council (which the Soviet Union was boycotting) approved a resolution calling on all powers to aid South Korea. It had taken less than three days for Truman to commit American forces, consolidate bipartisan support, and build an international coalition.[58]

On Thursday the situation in South Korea had continued to deteriorate. MacArthur left Japan to personally examine the fighting. He determined that South Korea could only be saved by immediately committing American ground troops. That evening, even before MacArthur's report had arrived, Truman had already decided to deploy American ground troops in support roles. At 1:31 A.M. the next morning MacArthur's recommendation finally reached Washington. Shortly before 5 A.M. Truman agreed to commit a single American regimental combat team but deferred deciding on a larger commitment. Truman met with the same advisers at 8:30 A.M., where they again unanimously agreed to give MacArthur the authority to use all ground forces under his command to defend South Korea. Less than five days after the invasion began the United States was, once again, fully committed to war.[59]

Assessment: The Skillful Implementer of the Mainstream View

Korea was no Pearl Harbor. Truman could have chosen differently. The United States had withdrawn its occupying forces from South Korea by 1949, and Acheson had not included Korea in the American defensive perimeter. The Truman administration, however, was united in its belief that the invasion of South Korea needed to be defeated to prevent the formation of a Communist "bandwagon."

American strategy before the Korean crisis was obsessed by the danger of pro-Soviet bandwagons. Kennan stated in 1947 that "a given proportion of the adherents to the [Communist] movement are drawn to it . . . primarily by the belief that it is the coming thing, the movement of the future." Kennan was not alone. Acheson too believed in bandwagons.[60]

Policymakers focused on the psychological dangers from perceived defeats. NSC 68, for example, declared that "in the absence of affirmative decision on our part, the rest of the free world is almost certain to become demoralized. Our friends will become more than a liability to us; they can eventually become a positive increment to Soviet power."[61]

The focus is not on objective shifts in power. The focus is on perceptions, on the confidence of American allies that they were on the winning side. In fact, NSC 68 identifies bandwagoning as the greatest danger facing the United States, arguing that "the risk that we may thereby be prevented or too long delayed in taking all needful measures to maintain the integrity and vitality of our system is great. The risk that our allies will lose their determination is greater."[62]

Once the crisis began, these beliefs drove actions. The State Department intelligence estimate used at the first Blair House meeting reviewed the impact of the invasion on various regions of the world. In Japan it argued that "failure of the United States to take any action in Korea would strengthen existing widespread desire for neutrality . . . the failure of the US to assist the ROK [Republic of Korea] would add force to the argument that alignment of Japan with the United States would, while inviting Soviet aggression, in no way ensure American protection of Japan against such aggression." In Nationalist China, "the tendency for flight or defection to the Communists would increase." In Southeast Asia, "leaders will lose whatever confidence they may have had in the effectiveness of US aid to combat Communism." Finally, in Western Europe, "the capacity of a small Soviet satellite to engage in a military adventure challenging . . . the might and will of the US, can only lead to serious questioning of that might and will. In occupied Germany . . . neutralist pressures . . . may be expected to increase."[63]

Acheson wrote on June 28 that failing to repel the invasion "would encourage 'new aggressive action elsewhere' and demoralize 'countries adjacent to [the] Soviet orbit.'" President Truman himself felt that if the invasion was rewarded "the scale of violence and the number of participating states would gradually increase to global dimensions."[64]

The entire government believed in the possibility of pro-Soviet bandwagons. That belief made support for entering the Korean War virtually unanimous. Republicans were more hawkish than Democrats, which strongly argues that a Republican victory in 1948 would not have changed the outcome, as does Dewey's support for Truman's decisions.

The other Democrat who might have been president was Wallace (assuming he could have been reelected in 1948). Wallace's greater sympathy for the Soviet Union might well have resulted in a more accommodationist American foreign policy, at least temporarily.[65]

Revelations from American decryptions of Soviet messages suggest that party leaders' concerns about Wallace were not entirely misplaced. Wallace had said that if he became president, his preferred candidate for secretary of the treasury was Harry Dexter White, then director of the International Monetary Fund. Both the decryptions and opened Soviet archives make it virtually certain that White was a Soviet spy.[66]

Wallace himself, however, was not. And his views in 1950 were very different from those he had expressed earlier. He had left the Democrats to run for president in 1948 on the Progressive Party ticket, only to be defeated badly. On July 6, 1950, the Progressive Party met to determine its response to the invasion of South Korea. All of its leadership, save Wallace, opposed American intervention. Wallace split with them and issued a statement:

> I want to make it clear that when Russia, the United States and the United Nations appeal to force, I am on the side of the United States and the United Nations. Undoubtedly the Russians could have prevented the attack by the North Koreans and undoubtedly they could stop the attack any time they wish. I hold no brief for the past actions of either the United States or Russia but when my country is at war and the United Nations sanctions that war, I am on the side of my country and the United Nations.[67]

In 1952 Wallace published "Where I Was Wrong" in which he sought to explain "the circumstances which have caused me to revise my attitude [on the Cold War]." He explained that conditions in Czechoslovakia following the Communist coup there, along with what he had learned of the real extent of suffering within the Soviet Union, had convinced him that "Russian Communism in its total disregard of truth, in its fanaticism, its intolerance and its resolute denial of God and religion is something utterly evil."[68] It seems likely that Wallace, like Truman, would have been willing to intervene in a war that was almost universally seen in the United States as a pure example of Communist aggression.

Truman did not get the credit he deserved from his contemporaries (arguably, in their eyes he could never escape FDR's long shadow), but his retrospective esteem seems secure. His decision to enter the Korean War was the most important among many and it captures the essence of what made him a Filtered Success. Truman did what virtually any president in his situation would have done—albeit extraordinarily well. Truman mustered virtually unanimous support from Democrats, Republicans, NATO allies, and even the U.N. Security Council *in less than five days*. This is a level of political and diplomatic virtuosity that any administration would be proud to claim.

Truman may not have been impactful, but he leaves a remarkable legacy nonetheless. He was far from perfect. For example, recent revelations from his papers show clearly that he pocketed his presidential expense account and illegally evaded taxes on it, making himself a wealthy man in the process. His corrupt choice to put his wife on his Senate payroll clearly presaged this behavior in the White House.[69] But from the creation of NATO to the desegregation of the military (an act which becomes less surprising when we remember that Truman triumphed over Byrnes in part because of his greater acceptability to Black American voters), at the critical moments that marked the end of the Second World War and the beginning of the Cold War the United States could have done far worse.

Truman's elevation to the White House was the system at its best. It identified key challenges facing the United States and chose someone who, based on an extensive record in politics, was more than capable of meeting them.

SHADOW CASES: SNAPSHOTS OF SUCCESSFUL
FILTERED PRESIDENTS

Truman and Jefferson are the two highest-ranked Filtered presidents, but other Filtered presidents have also performed well, even if they did not reach the same heights. These snapshots can help us fill out our picture of successful modern Filtered presidents.

John F. Kennedy

Kennedy, famously the youngest man ever elected president, might not seem Filtered, but despite his youth, Kennedy had a long political resume before he entered the White House. The son of a spectacularly wealthy father, Kennedy was educated at Choate, then Harvard. He served in the navy in World War II and received the Navy and Marine Corps Medal for his actions saving members of his crew after the torpedo boat he commanded was rammed and cut in half by a Japanese destroyer. In 1947 he ran for Congress and, buoyed by his father's support, won handily. He served in the House for three terms before defeating the Republican Henry Cabot Lodge Jr. for the Senate. Kennedy was reelected in 1958 and declared for the presidency in 1960. His Catholicism was a significant handicap in the race, but he won several primaries and entered the convention in the lead. His campaign was well-organized and financed enough to win the nomination on the first ballot, and he narrowly defeated Richard Nixon in the general election.[70]

If you ignore Kennedy's youth, this is a conventional political story. Kennedy served thirteen years in national political office before he became president, making him more, not less, Filtered than most presidents. In fact, his Filtration Score of 13 puts him in the upper third of most-Filtered presidents. When viewed through this lens, the Kennedy administration, despite its tragic abbreviation, looks familiar. For example, Kennedy's policies with regard to Cuba followed the broad outlines established by the Eisenhower administration, while his skillful management of the Cuban Missile Crisis seems like exactly the sort of bravura performance you'd expect from a seasoned politician who was nonetheless gifted enough to rise so far at such a young age.[71]

George H. W. Bush

Bush, like Truman, is the model of what an American parliamentary system might produce. The son of Prescott Bush, a banker and senator, George H. W. Bush joined the navy after graduating from Philipps Academy six months after the United States entered the Second World War. He became the youngest-ever naval aviator and received the

Distinguished Flying Cross. After the war he graduated from Yale Phi Beta Kappa in two-and-a-half years, then moved to West Texas, where he launched a successful career in the oil industry. In 1966 he won election to the House, where he served for four years until giving up his seat for a failed run for the Senate. He became ambassador to the United Nations, then chairman of the Republican National Committee. He was then made the American envoy (equivalent to ambassador) to China for two years and then served as director of the CIA. In 1980 he ran for president but was defeated handily in the primaries by Ronald Reagan, who selected him as his vice president. In 1988 he beat a crowded field of Republicans for the presidential nomination and won the general election in a landslide.[72] His Filtration Score of 13 ties him with Kennedy.

Bush only served one term before being defeated by Bill Clinton, but that one was eventful. Although Bush was initially skeptical of Reagan's embrace of Gorbachev, he soon adapted his views and successfully navigated the reunification of Germany, the collapse of the Warsaw Pact, the dissolution of the Soviet Union, and the Iraqi invasion of Kuwait. He assembled a massive international coalition and then led it in a war that crushed the Iraqi military in one of history's most lopsided military victories. Bush and his national security adviser Brent Scowcroft's book *A World Transformed* remains a masterpiece description of the conduct of foreign policy.[73]

In domestic policy, Bush's record also includes the passage of the Americans with Disabilities Act, the renewal of the Clean Air Act, and a 1990 budget deal that broke both his own campaign promise and Republican Party orthodoxy to raise taxes and substantially cut the budget deficit. His presidency was certainly not without failures, ranging from the savings and loan crisis to his dilatory response to the HIV epidemic, but overall, it presents a picture of solid Filtered competence rising to occasional virtuosity.[74]

William Jefferson Clinton

As with any recent president, any evaluation of Clinton can only be tentative. Clinton, like Kennedy, was young for the presidency and often characterized as inexperienced. Like Kennedy, however, he had a long political

career. Clinton was educated at Georgetown, then Oxford on a Rhodes
Scholarship, then Yale Law School. He returned home to teach at the
University of Arkansas, then ran unsuccessfully for Congress. In 1976 he
ran for state attorney general and won, then was elected governor in 1978.
He was, at thirty-two, the youngest governor in the country. He was
defeated for reelection in 1980, but then won again in 1982. He served as
governor for ten years, eventually running for the White House in 1992,
where he triumphed over a crowded Democratic field to face and defeat
incumbent president George H. W. Bush and independent candidate H.
Ross Perot.[75] His Filtration Score of 12 puts him well into Filtered territory, only a notch behind Kennedy and H. W. Bush.

Perhaps the most striking takeaway from Clinton's two terms in the
presidency is, compared to both his predecessors and successors, how
relatively benign the international environment was. Despite conflicts in
the former Yugoslavia and the 1997 Asian financial crisis, the international environment was relatively placid during his two terms compared
to that faced by his predecessor and successor.[76]

Clinton himself acknowledged this, once remarking, "9/11—I wish I'd
been there." Similarly, Rahm Emmanuel, one of his closest advisers, commented that Clinton was not a "transformative president" because the
requirements "that make up what would be a transformative president
weren't there for Clinton." There was no crisis he could have used as a
catalyst. Although historians will likely judge Clinton harshly for his part
in the deregulation of the financial sector, its power and influence were so
vast that these policies were bipartisan, and it is unlikely that any
Democrat representing the moderate wing of the party, as Clinton did,
would have opposed them.[77]

The scandal that resulted in his impeachment, while serious, also
seems, with some distance, minor compared to Watergate or Iran-Contra.
Given the extent to which Clinton's compulsive infidelity and willingness
to lie were revealed during the campaign, his behavior in both regards in
office is hardly surprising. The Clinton presidency is, in some ways, a fun-
house mirror of Truman's. Both centered on an experienced president who
had risen from poverty to the Oval Office. Truman combined personal
character (despite his financial misdeeds) with an era that presented him
with almost unmatched opportunities to secure a historical legacy.

Clinton, on the other hand, matched deep character flaws with an almost uniquely stable global environment. His presidency lacked the self-inflicted policy disasters that an Unfiltered president might have suffered, but equally lacked any of the signal triumphs that might have overshadowed or forestalled his impeachment.

THE STEADY HAND OF FILTERED PRESIDENTS

As we'll see in the next chapter, not all Filtered presidents succeed. This chapter shows, however, that they're usually a pretty good bet. Even the luckiest president will face a wide variety of difficult problems, and Filtered presidents have been judged by their peers as suited to handling them. Filtered presidents are unlikely to be brilliant, both because they are reflections of the elite consensus (and genius is, necessarily, at variance with the consensus) and because brilliance is not necessarily what political elites are looking for. They are, however, likely to be competent. They will understand the world and the government. They will know how to deploy the vast resources of the United States and the presidency to achieve their ends.

There is unlikely to ever be a Filtered Lincoln, but given the right opportunities, a Filtered president can deliver enormous benefits, as Truman did. The United States is the wealthiest, most powerful country in history. It is far from perfect, but avoiding disaster is perhaps the most important goal of its political system. Competent, stable, and effective may seem to be a low bar for presidents. It is not a bar, however, that every president has crossed. As we evaluate presidential candidates, we should keep in mind the overriding importance of picking a president we are *certain* can do the job. Most of the time, Filtered presidents are the closest we can get to that level of assurance. We'll examine the circumstances in which they can fail, despite that seeming guarantee, in the next chapter.

3 James Buchanan and the Collapse of the System

Harry Truman was an example of the American political system working as well as anyone could reasonably hope. That was good for the United States and the world in the second half of the twentieth century. But we shouldn't be surprised. Political systems are supposed to work. In a competitive world, systems that don't work must fix themselves or die. A country that was governed so badly that it was repeatedly led at moments of crisis by disastrously poor leaders would likely not be independent for long. Adam Smith's theories about competition and Charles Darwin's of survival of the fittest apply to countries too. If you disagree, ask the rulers of South Vietnam or the Confederate States of America.[1]

What's more, the United States has done much more than survive. Since the Constitution took effect in 1789 it has thrived in a way that no other country can even approach. Measured by wealth and power, it has few rivals and no equals. Measured by longevity, the American government is not just older than those of China, France, and Italy—it is older than all of them combined. None of this means that American society or government is perfect. That's far from the case. But it does mean that the American political system has probably been doing something right. If that's true, then we should expect Filtered presidents to generally do well.

If Filtered presidents are usually at least adequate, though, that makes the situations when they fail even more interesting. Filtered presidents generally do what the system wants them to do—as was the case with Truman and the U.S. intervention in Korea. Their failure, then, may tell us more about the system than the person. Why would the system be so wrong? Anyone and any group of people can be wrong, of course. The future is hard to predict. Even experts struggle to do better than chance.[2]

The sort of mistake that drops a president down to the bottom of the rankings, though, isn't just a one-off. Even catastrophes may not suffice. George W. Bush presided over the worst terrorist attack in American history, a grossly mismanaged war of choice in Iraq, the devastation of a major American city by a hurricane, and the worst economic downturn since the Depression. Whatever responsibility for those failures you attribute to him, they happened on his watch. But even that string of disasters leaves him far from the bottom in every ranking.

A failed presidency isn't just about one mistake, or even a series of mistakes. It's about a catastrophic policy pursued past the point of no return. How could a Filtered president, someone who is presumably competent, experienced, and capable, someone who does what the system wants, follow such a path? Looking at the presidents in this chapter, it seems likely that the answer is that Filtered presidents are an example of the system getting what it wants—but what you want isn't always good for you. Filtered presidents who fail catastrophically do so when what the system wants and what the system needs are radically different.

We can understand how this happens by situating Leader Filtration Theory's application to presidents within Yale professor Stephen Skowronek's theory of political time. Skowronek showed that the strength of political institutions was a major factor in explaining successful and failed presidencies. He said that failed presidencies were the product of "disjunctive" political environments. These are situations where a president is "affiliated with a set of established commitments that have in the course of events been called into question as failed or irrelevant responses to the problems of the day." He describes this as an "impossible" leadership situation. Although presidents in this situation may have some ability to salvage some victories from the wreckage, they are generally remembered as failures.[3]

It is possible for a president to succeed when the political environment is dominated by outdated commitments. In fact, the best presidents are those elected at such a time—Skowronek terms them "reconstructive" presidents who create a new order. If it is possible to succeed in this environment, Leader Filtration Theory's question becomes, why didn't the system find someone who could? The question, in other words, isn't what's wrong with the president, it's what's wrong with the system that makes it choose the wrong one?

Looking at the presidents profiled in this chapter, we'll see that the answer to that riddle lies in the fact that all political systems, including the American one, must balance the interests of many different groups. However they divide—across regions, industries, ethnicities, income, or something else entirely—the interests of these groups will inevitably conflict. The groups use their power to pursue their own interests, sometimes at the expense of other interest groups. That conflict is the essence of most politics.

One of the most effective ways interest groups can pursue their agendas is by influencing who gets a party's nomination for president.[4] In other words, they seek to exert their preferences via the leader filtration system. If a group is concentrated in one party or has disproportionate influence over political elites, then its political power may outstrip its basic societal strength. If that group became strong enough to gain veto rights over a party's presidential nomination, it could vastly decrease the odds of a president from that party pursuing an unfavorable policy, and even use it to secure policies that benefit itself at the expense of other groups.

What's more, the competition among candidates to gain the support of this group means that the policies favoring it will become steadily more extreme, and therefore more harmful to other groups. If a single interest group becomes so powerful that it can dominate key questions of national policy through multiple presidencies, then those demands may create a crisis that threatens the survival of the system. The dominant interest group can drag policy in its direction through the party it controls even if the underlying distribution of power in the United States is changing against it.

In other words, institutions don't just become "failed or irrelevant"; they become so because of the power dynamics within the system. Politicians respond to an interest group's disproportionate power by distorting institutions in its favor. This stresses those institutions until they no longer reflect the society as a whole and are stretched to the point of failure. Even as institutions weaken, however, the interest group's disproportionate power within the party means that it will be able to continue selecting Filtered presidents who are still committed to furthering its particular interests. The failure of a Filtered president, in other words, is far more about the system than the individual.

If Harry Truman is an ideal example of the Filtered successful president, James Buchanan is the exemplar of one who failed. To understand Buchanan's position in our Filtered/Unfiltered, Successful/Failed framework, we need to analyze his presidency as we did Truman's.

THE OLD PUBLIC FUNCTIONARY: JAMES BUCHANAN

A Solitary Journey

James Buchanan was the most qualified president since at least John Quincy Adams, and no president since matches his breadth of experience. Buchanan was America's only unmarried president and to this day he remains one of the oldest. He was a plausible presidential candidate in 1844, 1848, and 1852 before finally being elected in 1856. He was a major political figure for so long his nickname was the "Old Public Functionary." [5]

Buchanan's career is virtually a caricature of filtration. It was exactly what you'd hope for in the man who was leading the United States as sectional tensions escalated to the point of crisis. Instead, he failed so catastrophically that he is routinely judged the worst president ever.

Buchanan, one of eleven children, was born in a log cabin in Pennsylvania on April 23, 1791. His father was a well-off businessperson and farmer. He attended Dickinson College and, despite being almost expelled for misbehavior, graduated with honors in 1809 and moved to Lancaster, Pennsylvania, then the state capital. He served as an apprentice to an attorney there, joined the bar, established his own practice, and soon became one of the state's most successful attorneys. [6]

Buchanan launched his political career in 1814 at the age of twenty-three with a run for the state legislature. He began as a Federalist—the party of Washington and Hamilton that favored a strong central government and opposed Jefferson's Democratic-Republicans (soon to become simply the Democrats). This was the first of eleven consecutive successful campaigns. He harshly criticized Madison's performance during the War of 1812 but served in it as an enlisted man. His political career was briefly interrupted by the death of Anne Coleman, a former fiancée who is the only definite romantic entanglement of his life.[7]

In 1821 Buchanan reentered politics with a successful run for Congress. The collapse of the Federalists led to a shift in Buchanan's party and political principles. In 1824 he accurately assessed Andrew Jackson's rising popularity and moved to the Democrats. He became entangled in the presidential contest between Jackson, Adams, and Henry Clay that year, and although he backed Jackson, who went on to dominate American politics for a generation, Buchanan permanently alienated him. Nevertheless, in 1829 he became chairman of the House Judiciary Committee.[8]

Buchanan's rise was interrupted by a failed Senate race in 1830, but Jackson, motivated by his dislike of Buchanan, made him ambassador to Russia. He told his biographer, "If I could have sent him further away, I would have." Buchanan, however, succeeded beyond all expectations, charming Czar Nicholas and securing the first commercial treaty the czar signed with any country. He returned home a year later but continued to annoy Jackson.[9]

Buchanan's return left his political path uncertain. Ironically, Jackson inadvertently cleared his way back into the Senate. When Jackson appointed Pennsylvania senator William Wilkins to fill Buchanan's old position in Moscow out of revenge for Wilkins's opposition to Jackson on the recharter of the Bank of the United States, it opened the Senate seat for Buchanan, who filled out the remaining two years of Wilkins's term. In 1836 Martin Van Buren, Jackson's handpicked successor, won the presidency and Buchanan rode to reelection on his coattails.[10]

In Washington Buchanan roomed with his closest friend, Senator William R. King of Alabama. The two may have had a romantic relationship, although there simply is not enough evidence to conclude one way or the other. King, a wealthy Alabama slaveholder, also brought Buchanan into his Southern and proslavery social circle. This likely played a role in his steady move towards becoming a "doughface"—a northern politician with southern principles. Buchanan had not previously expressed strong views on slavery. He had even purchased the freedom of two enslaved persons owned by his brother-in-law. By 1836, however, he was committed to "states' rights" and by the 1840s he was opposed to any attempt to restrict slavery, saying, "Touch this question of slavery and the Union is from that point dissolved."[11]

Buchanan thrived in the Senate, where he was appointed to the Judiciary and Foreign Relations Committees, the latter of which he chaired. Realizing that the Senate was the ideal platform from which to advance his career, he turned down Van Buren's offer to become attorney general. Instead, Buchanan distinguished himself as the foremost Democratic proponent of Manifest Destiny. This was a popular position, but one with far more support in the South than in the North or Mid-Atlantic. With expansion came conflicts over the spread of slavery. Buchanan was already eyeing the presidency (he declined the offer of a Supreme Court seat in 1844), however, and recognized that his principal support came from the South, so despite a lack of support in Pennsylvania, he closely aligned with southern Democrats.[12]

Buchanan made his first bid for the presidency in 1844. In February the secretary of state was killed in an accidental gun explosion, which allowed President John Tyler (William Henry Harrison's vice president who was elected on the Whig ticket but was in practice a Democrat) to appoint South Carolina senator John C. Calhoun to the position of secretary of state and annex Texas, beginning a war with Mexico. This rallied southern support to Tyler, who was hoping to be nominated for reelection as a Democrat. Former president Martin Van Buren, however, opposed the war and entered the race for the Democratic nomination, rallying both northern Democrats and antiwar Whigs. The combination of southern support for Tyler and northern support for Van Buren threatened to squeeze out Buchanan.

At the convention, Buchanan cleverly used his control of the Pennsylvania delegation to move that capturing the Democratic nomination would require two-thirds of the delegates, arguing that this would ensure that the nominee had broad-based, instead of purely sectional, support. This functionally gave the South a virtual veto over the Democratic nominee until the 1940s. It also eliminated both Van Buren and Tyler, leaving Buchanan a likely compromise candidate. At this point, however, the seventy-seven-year-old Jackson intervened to get his long-awaited revenge for Buchanan's supposed perfidy in 1824. Once Van

Buren's campaign stalled, Jackson threw his support behind his fellow Tennessean James K. Polk, who quickly gained the nomination. Once he won the presidency, Polk made Buchanan secretary of state.[13]

Buchanan nearly took himself off the path to the Oval Office by dithering over an offer to join the Supreme Court. His time as secretary of state was eventful, including the Mexican War and a settlement with Britain over the boundary between Canada and the United States in the Oregon Territory. Polk's assessment of Buchanan memorably sums him up: "Buchanan is an able man, but is in small matters without judgment and sometimes acts like an old maid."[14]

Buchanan made his second bid for the presidency in 1848 when Polk chose not to run again. Buchanan was the most experienced candidate and the only one who had never criticized slavery, which gave him southern support. This was even more of a leg up because there were no major southern candidates. At the convention, however, Senator Lewis Cass took the lead on the first ballot and swayed Virginia, which was less committed to the proslavery cause than states in the Deep South, allowing him to capture the nomination. Whig nominee Zachary Taylor ended up riding his victories in the Mexican War to the White House, leaving Buchanan again out of office.[15]

Buchanan returned to Pennsylvania and began hosting politicians at his home in Wheatland to prepare for a presidential run in 1852. American politics centered on struggles over slavery expansion. Every time a new state entered the Union it threatened the balance in the Senate between free and slave states. Since 1820 this had been managed by the Missouri Compromise, which declared that states south of Missouri's southern border were slave states and those north of it free. California threatened to disrupt the Compromise. Clay negotiated the Compromise of 1850 in which California was admitted as a free state, but the South got a stricter Fugitive Slave Law.

Buchanan had to take a position on the Compromise. He chose to solidify his southern support. The new Fugitive Slave Law outraged the North, as it allowed owners tracking slaves who had escaped to the North to seize their slaves without due process, penalized anyone who helped an enslaved person escape, and legally required citizens to help slaveholders recapture their slaves. Buchanan supported it strongly and went even further than that. He argued that the only reason slavery was a problem was because of the opposition to it. Buchanan declared that opposition to slavery actually "deprived the slave of many privileges which he formerly enjoyed, because of the stern necessity thus imposed upon the master to provide for his personal safety and that of his family."[16]

Buchanan was disappointed again in 1852. The convention split between Buchanan, Cass, Illinois senator Stephen Douglas (nicknamed "The Little Giant" for his combination of short stature and powerful oratory), and William Marcy from New York. Buchanan went into the convention believing that southern support left him positioned to win. Buchanan, Cass, and Douglas each captured the lead for some ballots, but none was able to secure two-thirds support. Buchanan held states in the Deep South but was unable to secure support from border or northern states, which meant no one else could win the nomination either. After thirty-three ballots the Buchanan delegates split. While Pennsylvania, Georgia, and Alabama continued to back him, others swung to Marcy, while Virginia voted for Franklin Pierce, one of the heroes of the Mexican War. They intended to show that no candidate could secure the necessary two-thirds and convince the convention to turn to Buchanan as a compromise candidate. Instead, the fatigued delegates turned to Pierce, who won on the forty-ninth ballot.[17]

After Pierce enjoyed a landslide victory in 1852, he offered to make Buchanan the minister to Great Britain. Although this was a step down from secretary of state, Buchanan, who could never bear to be out of public life for long, accepted. Buchanan's posting in England ended up benefiting him in the most unlikely way imaginable. American ministers were required to wear simple clothing befitting the representative of a republic. They even had the title minister, not ambassador, because ambassador smacked too much of royalty. British protocol, however, required formal attire to attend court or the opening of Parliament. Equally important, socializing with the British elite—an essential part of any ambassador's duties—required more elaborate attire. Buchanan chose to wear standard American dress embellished with a sword, which at least ensured that he would not be taken for one of the servants. The British press was outraged, but his decision won him acclaim in the United States, where it cast the stuffy Buchanan in the supremely unlikely role of ordinary American.[18]

The other major incident of Buchanan's term as ambassador was his participation in the writing of the Ostend Manifesto, which argued that the United States should purchase Cuba from Spain and that it should go to war if it could not. The Manifesto's most important effect was on domestic politics. Southerners wanted Cuba in part because they feared that instability there could set off an American slave uprising. Northerners, on the other hand, saw it as another attempt by the slave power to expand its reach, just as it had with the Mexican War.[19]

The other favor Buchanan's time in Britain did for him was to keep him uninvolved in the political tumult over the Kansas-Nebraska Acts. The territory that made up the present-day states of Kansas and Nebraska was north of the Missouri Compromise line. States made from it should have become free states. Senators from slave states, however, were strongly opposed to this outcome, as it would further swing the Senate's balance towards free states. Douglas proposed that the Kansas and Nebraska territories be organized under a doctrine of "popular sovereignty," where the residents of the territories could vote on allowing slavery. This would also repeal the Missouri Compromise. Franklin Pierce threw his full weight behind the bill, which passed. Pro- and antislavery settlers began to pour into Kansas to gain control of the territory, triggering the guerrilla war known as "Bleeding Kansas."[20]

In the 1854 and 1855 elections Democrats were crushed throughout the North. Lincoln, who had abandoned politics, was so outraged by Kansas-Nebraska that he reentered them. The collapse of the Whig Party led opponents of the Acts to coalesce under the new banner of the Republican Party. Pierce, meanwhile, was so weakened by his support of the Acts that he was not guaranteed renomination. Buchanan, safely ensconced across the Atlantic, was suddenly the Democrat least tarred by the party's political catastrophe.[21]

Just before the convention, three more events further inflamed sectional tensions. First, Massachusetts senator Charles Sumner was beaten unconscious while he sat defenseless at his desk on the floor of the Senate by South Carolina congressman Preston Brooks in retaliation for his speeches attacking slavery. Second, the town of Lawrence, Kansas, which had been founded by antislavery activists in the hope of making Kansas a free state, was sacked by proslavery activists. Third, in retaliation for the first two acts, the antislavery crusader John Brown killed five proslavery settlers in a raid that came to be known as the Pottawatomie Massacre.[22] The combination hugely increased fears of a civil war, increasing pressure within the Democratic Party to conciliate the South by nominating a pro-southern candidate on a proslavery platform.

The convention began in Cincinnati on June 2. Pierce hoped to take the nomination, as did Douglas. Its platform matched Buchanan's preferences perfectly, endorsing the Fugitive Slave Law, noninterference in slavery, and further American expansion in the Gulf of Mexico, while condemning antislavery (but not proslavery) protests. A more prosouthern platform is hard to imagine.[23]

Buchanan took the lead on the first ballot with 135 votes, followed closely by Pierce at 122. His managers had control of the convention and no other candidate passed him even once. Douglas had only 33, while the aged Lewis Cass took 5. Pierce had strength in New England and the South, while Buchanan's support ranged from Virginian and Louisiana to Maryland, Ohio, Indiana, and his home state of Pennsylvania. Pierce held steady for the next four ballots while Buchanan slowly crept further ahead. Pierce then started to decline as some of his support switched to Douglas, likely as part of a coordinated strategy between the two campaigns to keep Buchanan from gaining the nomination. The next morning Douglas surged into second place with 121 votes, while Buchanan maintained his lead, moving up to 168. Buchanan's managers then promised Douglas that they would support him in 1860 if he withdrew. When he did, Buchanan took the nomination unanimously on the seventeenth ballot.[24]

The general election was a three-way contest between Buchanan, former president Millard Fillmore for the nativist American, or "Know-Nothing," Party, and explorer John C. Frémont for the newly formed Republicans. The Democrats' advantages included the collapse of the Whigs, a sectional split of the Know-Nothings, and the Republicans conducting their first national campaign. Buchanan carried every slave state except Maryland (which was the only state that went to Fillmore) along with five free states, including his home state of Pennsylvania. Although he would become a minority president, capturing only 45 percent of the popular vote in one of the highest-turnout elections in American history, he decisively captured the Electoral College with 174 votes to 114 for

Frémont and 8 for Fillmore. Buchanan had, finally, seized his long-sought prize.[25]

Assessment: A Mainstream President

Describing Buchanan as Filtered seems to understate the case. He was about as filtered as a president can be. His Filtration Score of 24 ties him with Gerald Ford as the second most Filtered president. Over the course of an enormously long career, he had made his capabilities and views as clear as anyone could ask. He came close to the presidency three times before going all the way. No one ever accused Buchanan of genius, but he had succeeded in the Pennsylvania state legislature, in the U.S. House of Representatives, in the Senate, as minister to Russia and to Great Britain, and as secretary of state. Everyone in the American political system knew who he was. What did they see?

For most of Buchanan's career the central issue, one that subsumed almost every other, was slavery. Except for Abolitionists, who were a relatively small group, people across the political spectrum saw the central dilemma of American politics not as how to handle slavery, but how to handle sectional conflict over its expansion. As the proslavery movement gained strength in the South and the Democratic Party, it also gained the power to ensure that the system would only select presidents who would support the South as much as possible.

James Buchanan was the ultimate product of that filtration system. He was the quintessential "doughface." Buchanan was a northern man with southern principles. At every key junction of his career, Buchanan hewed to the southern line. Although he claimed to personally oppose slavery, nothing in his public life up to the moment of his election even hinted at any desire to restrict its power or spread. Whether it was his southern social circle, his repeatedly expressed desire to never touch slavery, his stance on the Fugitive Slave Law, his involvement with the Ostend Manifesto, or his complete inability to understand why anyone objected to slavery in the first place, Buchanan never missed an opportunity to secure his southern flank. That is *why* he was finally selected as the Democratic nominee in 1856. If it had not been Buchanan, it would have been someone else with similar views.

The Democrats were not purely sectional. They still had a formidable presence in the North. It is clear, however, that particularly after the imposition of the two-thirds rule the Democratic Party no longer had the option of nominating a presidential candidate who was anything but subservient to the South.

In Buchanan, the system got what it wanted.

"General Jackson Is Dead": James Buchanan and the Cleavage of the Democratic Party

Buchanan used the four months between his election in November and inauguration in March to assemble his cabinet. Instead of putting together one that consolidated the Democratic Party behind him, however, Buchanan chose one with which he was personally comfortable and that reflected his views. This meant that it was entirely prosouthern, with no representation from Democrats who had backed Douglas or anyone sympathetic to the antislavery movement. This isolated Buchanan from any real understanding of the passion aroused by the struggle over slavery in Kansas, a tendency that was further reinforced by his exclusively prosouthern circle of intimates and unofficial advisers.[26]

BUCHANAN AND *DRED SCOTT*

Buchanan set the stage in his inaugural address. He strongly endorsed the Kansas-Nebraska Act and popular sovereignty. He never mentioned the violence that had flared in Kansas throughout 1856, instead declaring that slavery in the territories was "happily, a matter of but little practical importance." He punted the question of slavery in the territories to the Supreme Court, which the entire country knew was currently deciding *Dred Scott*. Buchanan stated, against all legal and historical precedent, that slavery in the territories was a "judicial question, which legitimately belongs to the Supreme Court of the United States" and that he, "in common with all good citizens," would "cheerfully submit" to the Court's ruling.[27]

Dred Scott was a Missouri slave whose master had taken him into a free state for several years. Scott sued, claiming that residing in a free state had emancipated him. The case had wound its way through the courts for years and finally reached the Supreme Court. The chief justice, the pro-southern Roger B. Taney, had already drafted a decision containing two enormous victories for slavery. Taney held, despite ample precedent otherwise, that African Americans could never be citizens of the United States and so Scott had no standing to sue. Additionally, in the first use of the Supreme Court's power of judicial review of federal legislation since it had been established fifty-four years earlier, he declared that Congress had no power to regulate slavery in the territories and that the Missouri Compromise was therefore unconstitutional.[28]

Buchanan already knew what the Court was going to decide. Even before his inauguration, two justices—John Catron of Tennessee and Robert Grier of Pennsylvania—had corresponded with him, and Catron had solicited his help in lining up votes for Taney's ruling. Although the Court had a southern majority, Taney felt that the decision would have more impact if a northern justice concurred. Buchanan, in a gross violation of judicial independence, lobbied Grier to join the majority. This liberated Taney to write a broader and more prosouthern opinion. Proslavery forces were overjoyed by this seeming vindication, but *Dred Scott* inflamed antislavery forces and weakened the Democratic Party in the North, where it was committed to popular sovereignty.[29] Buchanan did what he had always done, what he was chosen to do by the filtration system of his era and, even before he became president, struck his first blow for the South.

BUCHANAN, DOUGLAS, AND KANSAS

The next major issue facing Buchanan was Kansas. By 1857 violence there had largely ended, but the political struggle over how it would enter the Union had just begun. Proslavery radicals were agitating for Kansas's admission as a slave state, while northern Democrats had campaigned in 1856 on popular sovereignty. They had assumed that since most Kansas residents were in favor of it being a free state, it would be admitted as one. There were only a few hundred slaves in the territory, and more northern settlers were expected to arrive. The territory's legislature and constitutional convention, however, were the products of fraud by radical proslavery forces so extensive that antislavery interests were boycotting them.[30]

After complex political maneuverings, the convention met in September 1857 in Lecompton, Kansas. It was dominated by proslavery forces that produced a proslavery wish list. It explicitly legalized slavery in the state and adopted the slave codes (that is, the laws governing slavery without which it was impossible to maintain, regardless of its formal legal status) of Kentucky and Missouri. Although many of the delegates, including the convention chair, John Calhoun, had promised while campaigning that they would submit the constitution to the voters for ratification, this was before the decisive free-state victories in the most recent legislative elections. A clear majority of the delegates at Lecompton now opposed submitting their constitution to the people, knowing that it would be overwhelmingly defeated in any remotely fair election.[31]

Outnumbered moderates, with secret help from Buchanan, persuaded the convention to superficially compromise by putting the constitution's article on slavery to a popular vote. The constitution, however, also required that the powers of the territorial governor and legislature be transferred to Calhoun before the vote, creating the possibility of another rigged election. It also declared that even if the vote went against slavery, slaves already in the territory would remain enslaved. Furthermore, the constitution could not be amended until 1864, and even then, no amendments interfering with slavery were allowed. Lecompton attempted to ensure that Kansas would remain a slave state no matter what the voters chose.[32]

With the completion of the Lecompton Constitution the focus switched back to Washington. Republicans and northern Democrats were united in their opposition to ratifying the Lecompton Constitution without an honest vote from Kansas residents. All agreed that Buchanan should live up to his promise of exactly that. Although southern radicals urged that Lecompton simply be accepted, some prominent southerners, including the governors of North Carolina and Virginia, felt otherwise. A united North and divided South presented Buchanan with an opportunity. Rejecting Lecompton would strengthen his position and that of the Democratic Party in the North, while the sheer transparency of the fraud in Kansas and the clear antislavery majority there had deprived southern radicals of grounds for complaint. Buchanan had already committed himself to popular sovereignty on the question of slavery. All he had to do was decide if he would keep his word.[33]

Douglas was initially uncertain about his own stand. As the author of the Kansas-Nebraska Acts, he was committed to popular sovereignty. He soon heard from constituents that Kansas's admission as a slave state would be politically devastating. Of fifty-six Illinois newspapers, fifty-five denounced Lecompton. He reviewed the proceedings of the Lecompton convention and concluded that the Lecompton Constitution was a "fraud." He declared, "We will nail our colors to the mast and defend the right of the people to govern themselves against all assaults from all quarters."[34]

Buchanan, however, decided to reverse course. He concluded that since the only important question in Kansas was slavery, the partial submission of Lecompton to the voters was enough. The proslavery radicals in Kansas had presented him with a choice. He could keep up with his career-long pattern of aligning with the South or break with it to keep his promise. It's not surprising that the highly Filtered Buchanan did exactly what he was chosen to do and stuck with the South.

On December 3 Douglas came to the White House to discuss Kansas. The two already shared a strong mutual dislike that had been enhanced by Buchanan's decision to completely cut Douglas out of patronage and deny him any voice in his administration. Tempers soon flared until Buchanan angrily told Douglas, "Mr. Douglas, I desire you to remember that no Democrat ever yet differed from an administration of his own choice without being crushed. Beware the fate of Tallmadge and Rives [two Democrats whose careers had been destroyed by Andrew Jackson]." Douglas, flashing the wit that would allow him to go toe-to-toe with Abraham Lincoln a few months later, replied, "Mr. President, I wish you to remember that General Jackson is dead!" and walked out.[35]

Buchanan and Douglas were now at open war. The struggle between the Little Giant and the Old Public Functionary would be decided in Congress, where the terrain favored Buchanan. Thirty-seven of the 61 Senators were Democrats, 25 of them from slave states, with another 5 Whig-Americans from the South. The House had 128 Democrats, 75 from the South, with another 14 Whig-Americans, all of them from the South, and 92 Republicans.

On December 8 Buchanan used his State of the Union to lay down his position. In his typical turgid style, he declared that the election of delegates to Lecompton that had been boycotted by free-state voters was "in the main fair and just" and described free-state settlers as adherents to a "revolutionary organization." He did not condemn the rampant electoral fraud by proslavery forces, or indeed criticize any actions by proslavery settlers. He further argued that even if the voters of Kansas rejected the slavery article of Lecompton, the rights of property in slaves now in the Territory are reserved." Buchanan was staking out a proslavery position even more extreme than any of his previous ones. He argued that Kansas should be admitted to the Union as a slave state no matter how its people voted because "the relation between master and slave . . . [is] entirely distinct from institutions of a political character."[36]

Buchanan, seemingly incapable of understanding why anyone would object to slavery, blamed antislavery forces for any difficulties resulting from struggles over slavery and wanted to remove it as a focus of political debate. To achieve that goal, he was willing to back the South even at the cost of splitting northern Democrats.

Douglas replied the next day. He had no more sympathy for enslaved persons than Buchanan did. During the debate on the Kansas-Nebraska Act he had used an ethnic slur on the Senate floor, only to be rebuked by Republican senator (and later Lincoln's secretary of state) William Henry Seward: "Douglas, no man will ever be president who spells Negro with two g's." His authorship of the Kansas-Nebraska Act, however, made him more closely identified with popular sovereignty than any other politician. Douglas was a master orator who always drew a crowd when he spoke. Now he had a packed gallery eager to see the rare spectacle of a no-holds-barred attack on the president by a member of his own party.[37]

Douglas took a tone of slashing sarcasm:

> That would be as fair an election as some of the enemies of Napoleon attributed to him when he was elected First Consul . . . "If you vote for Napoleon all is well; vote against him, and you are to be instantly shot." That was a fair election. This election is to be equally fair. All men in favor of the constitution may vote for it—all men against it shall not vote at all . . . if they allowed a negative vote the constitution would have been voted down by an overwhelming majority, and hence the fellows shall not be allowed to vote at all

. . . I care not what they have in their constitution . . . I do hold that the people of Kansas have the right to be consulted and to decide it, and you have no rightful authority to deprive them of that privilege.[38]

Douglas won the argument but not the Senate battle. Buchanan unleashed the full arsenal of powers available to the White House to pass Lecompton and crush his hated rival.[39]

On December 21, Kansans voted on the Lecompton Constitution in an election that was again boycotted by free-state voters, resulting in a 6,143–569 victory for the constitution with slavery. More than 2,000 of the votes were fraudulent. In January free-state voters held their own election and 10,266 voted against slavery, while only 162 voted for.[40]

On February 2, 1858, Buchanan sent the Lecompton Constitution to Congress. His accompanying message was as generous a gift to southern proslavery forces as they could possibly have hoped for. In a scathing assault on the free-state residents of Kansas, he declared that they were "mercenaries of Abolitionism" and that their attempts to oppose the slave-state legislature had, "with treasonable pertinacity," created a "revolutionary government" in Kansas. Buchanan threw his full support behind Lecompton, declaring that "Kansas is therefore at this moment as much a slave state as Georgia or South Carolina."[41]

The Senate voted in March, where Buchanan's pressure on Democrats was effective enough that only three joined Douglas in opposition, allowing Lecompton to pass there with an eight-vote margin. The House, where the North had a far stronger presence, was much more difficult terrain. Although Democrats had a 22-seat majority, only 75 of their 128 members were from the South. The debate was so heated that when a Republican from Pennsylvania and a Democrat from South Carolina came to blows, more than 30 other representatives joined in a brawl on the House floor.[42]

Buchanan was undeterred, declaring that he would drive Lecompton "naked" through the House. The spring saw Democrats take crushing defeats in elections in New England and Michigan. During the Senate debate John Crittenden, a Whig-American senator from Kentucky, introduced a bill that proposed admitting Kansas only after the constitution was approved in a fair election. It was rejected in the Senate, but on

April 1 it passed the House as northern Democrats defected from the administration's position.[43]

Democrats, scrambling to save their position, managed to get a tie vote for a conference committee, which was broken in the administration's favor by the Speaker of the House. This committee cobbled together a compromise bill that offered Kansans a federal land grant (normal for new states) and had them vote on accepting Lecompton and receiving the grant and statehood immediately or, if they rejected it, waiting for statehood until the state's population had grown substantially. This was meant to allow Buchanan to save face so that Kansans appeared to be voting on the land grant instead of on Lecompton, and they had the carrot of immediate admission to the Union to vote his way.[44]

The bill passed, but the inducement failed. In a carefully watched vote in August, Kansans rejected Lecompton again with 1,788 voting for and 11,300 against. On the most important issue Buchanan would face until secession began following the election of Abraham Lincoln in 1860, he had been decisively defeated.[45]

Assessment: Walking the Path to Civil War

It is difficult to overstate the consequences of Buchanan's choices on *Dred Scott* and Lecompton. By aiding Taney, he emboldened the chief justice to attempt to resolve slavery through judicial fiat, enraging slavery opponents and convincing them of the existence of a proslavery conspiracy in the highest levels of the American government. *Dred Scott* convinced antislavery advocates that proslavery forces could never be appeased.

If Buchanan's intervention in *Dred Scott* was damaging, his choices on Lecompton were catastrophic. By favoring the South at every opportunity Buchanan split the Democratic Party and crippled it in the North. In the words of his biographer Jean Baker, he followed "a suicidal course that led to a traumatic division in the Democratic party, thereby ensuring the election of the Republican Abraham Lincoln ... Buchanan consistently acknowledged his party as one of the few surviving mechanisms available to keep the nation intact. So why did he destroy it?"[46]

The answer is that while his actions led to that outcome, his actions were also a product of the system. Buchanan made the choices that he was chosen to make by a system that had catastrophically failed. The Civil War did not happen because of Buchanan, even though his hand was on the reins when the last steps were taken. The path had been set long before he finally won the presidency. Buchanan was not stupid, lazy, or incompetent. He was every bit as capable as you'd expect one of the most qualified presidents in American history to be. With the advantage of hindsight, though, we can clearly see that he was just *wrong*—a simple fact that turned his (significant) virtues into vices. But he was wrong in exactly the way that the system demanded of him, as it would have of anyone else who became president at that moment in time.

Just as we'd expect from a leader as Filtered as Buchanan, everything he did was a product of the context. Buchanan was not forced to devote himself to the proslavery cause. That was what he wanted to do. Douglas, in Buchanan's place, would never have conceded everything to the South. That is why Douglas was not in Buchanan's place. Southern Democrats would never have accepted someone unwilling to give in to their demands; they proved that by leaving the party when Douglas was nominated in 1860, ensuring Lincoln's election and triggering the Civil War.

This completes our picture of Buchanan's failure. No leader as highly Filtered as Buchanan is likely to be incompetent or ineffectual unless his faculties have diminished for medical reasons. Buchanan was a determined and skilled president who used those skills to favor the South to such an extent that the country suffered for it. Buchanan spent his entire lengthy career catering to the interests of slavery—and the system rewarded him for it. He did the same as president. He did what he was chosen to do by a system that was so broken that its fundamental contradictions could only be resolved by the Civil War. James Buchanan did not cause the Civil War. He was chosen by a system whose failures made the war inevitable.

In one of the longest political careers in American history, Buchanan's north star was giving the South what it wanted. He did this because it advanced his career and because—as southern leaders knew—his southern sympathies were genuine. Buchanan made his choices because they were what he wanted to do. If he had wanted to do anything else, the filtration system would never have allowed him to become president. The system was looking for a president who would give proslavery activists everything they asked for. Yet it was that appeasement which inflicted a catastrophe on the United States so gargantuan that only Lincoln's towering genius could save it.

SHADOW CASES: HERBERT HOOVER AND THE GREAT DEPRESSION

Herbert Hoover's position as a failed president is, in some ways, unfair, and under spirited attack by conservatives seeking to rehabilitate him. He certainly suffers in part simply from not being Franklin Roosevelt, who was perhaps an even more difficult act to precede than he was to follow. Even if you agree with the harshest assessments of Hoover's presidency, any fair evaluation of his prepresidential career would conclude that no president between Grant and Eisenhower made greater contributions to the welfare of the world before being elected. After his death it was said that Hoover had "fed more people and saved more lives than any other man in history."[47] It isn't necessary to believe the statement is literally true (Norman Borlaug, the father of the Green Revolution, surely holds that title today, if Hoover ever did) to believe that the fact that it was plausible is an astonishing tribute to a man generally reviled for his failures during the Great Depression.

Hoover was the quintessential self-made man. He was orphaned at eleven and worked his way through Stanford, once crossing eighty miles on foot in three days to get a job during the summer of his junior year. He trained as an engineer and worked in Australia and China with such success that by twenty-seven he was one of only four full partners in the world's foremost mining syndicate. He struck out on his own and built a substantial fortune, while still anonymously donating significant portions of his income to support friends, family, and boys who were struggling as he once did.

Hoover was in London when the First World War broke out and brilliantly organized efforts to return Americans home. He became chairman for the Commission for Relief in Belgium and was credited with saving that country from starvation. At its peak the commission fed nine million people a day. He returned home and was put in charge of managing

American agriculture to support the war effort. He again succeeded dazzlingly and became an international hero of such stature that when the Wilson administration feared that postwar privation would trigger the spread of Communism in Europe, Hoover was dispatched back to Europe in the belief that his sheer presence would give Europeans hope.[48]

Hoover aspired to the Republican nomination in 1920, but his failure to declare himself a Republican until after World War I made that impossible. Harding made Hoover his commerce secretary, where Hoover played such a central role in the administration that he was referred to as the "secretary of commerce and under secretary of all other departments." He continued to oversee the American Relief Administration (ARA) while in the cabinet, and from 1921 to 1923 the ARA fed fifteen million people in Europe every day. Hoover's status was further elevated by his response to catastrophic Mississippi River flooding in 1927, which made him so widely admired that he captured the Republican nomination by a huge margin on the first ballot. He won the 1928 election in a landslide despite a lack of charisma so notable that a common joke was that "his hair parts in the middle and his Christian name is Herbert."[49]

Hoover spent eight years either as secretary of commerce or in the temporary cabinet-level position of food administrator. Given the prominence of his positions before serving as food administrator, however, and those he took after, it seems reasonable to add them to his time in filtering positions. The combination gives him a Filtration Score of 13, putting him in the upper third of all presidents.

If anyone seems suited to the job of responding to the Great Depression, surely it's the man who saved Europe from starvation. Why, then, are his efforts generally seen as inadequate? The popular shorthand of him as a president who did nothing to combat the Depression is mistaken. In 1932 Hoover urged the creation of the Reconstruction Finance Corporation (RFC) to loan the then-staggering sum of $2 billion to companies to jumpstart the economy. He pushed to subsidize mortgages and got Glass-Steagall, a bill meant to increase the provision of credit, through Congress. Each of these was an enormous increase in the role of the government in the economy that would have been unthinkable at any other time.[50]

The Great Depression, however, was not another time. It was a blow to the country like none other. Hoover was tied to the traditional approach of self-organizing efforts by private-sector entities, the model he had advanced so brilliantly during World War I, instead of larger exertions by the government. So he refused to support direct relief or jobs programs for the public, a striking contrast to the approach his successor would adopt during the New Deal.[51]

Even more important was Hoover's continued attachment to the gold standard. Hoover was not captive to Wall Street. He probably did more than any other major figure to curb financial speculation before the collapse and even commented that "the only trouble with capitalism is capitalists. They're too damned greedy."[52]

Hoover was nevertheless an exemplar of his era's business and political elite. His commitment to the gold standard, an article of faith among those elites, was almost certainly the single policy mistake most responsible for the severity and length of the Great Depression. It took a popular revolt that culminated in Franklin Roosevelt's election to break that elite consensus and take the United States off gold, one of the many actions Roosevelt took that were strongly opposed by business leaders of his era.[53]

However much Hoover differed from elite consensus, it was not by enough. In the face of the greatest economic disaster in American history, for example, he retained Andrew Mellon, the banking titan who had served as treasury secretary for all of Harding and Coolidge's administrations. Mellon and the Federal Reserve "made essentially no effort to prevent the wave of bank failures that paralyzed the financial system." Hoover, in fact, reported that Mellon's advice on dealing with the Depression was to "liquidate labor, liquidate stocks, liquidate the farmers, liquidate real estate . . . It will purge the rottenness out of the system."[54]

Even if Hoover disagreed, he failed to replace Mellon, the man who, after all, had been treasury secretary for *more than eight years* before the collapse. It is hard to imagine a worse performance by a treasury secretary than the Great Depression happening on his watch when he had eight years to prevent it. But even that did not convince Hoover that Mellon, and the approach he took and represented, had failed.

Hoover's extraordinary life story and achievements before he was elected leave little doubt that he was one of the most capable men ever to become president. If the Great Depression had never happened, he likely would have been remembered as a success, even if he lacked a temperament suited to democratic leadership (the 1928 election was the first, and only, election Hoover ever won).[55] Under the pressures of the Great Depression, however, the business-dominated elite consensus of which he was the paradigmatic product was simply insufficient to the moment.

Hoover was no Buchanan. Buchanan's failures both reflected and were a product of the moral failures of the elites who governed the American leadership filtration process in the 1850s. They had no objections to slavery and so chose a president who shared their convictions. They misidentified the problem, thinking that it was the antislavery movement when the problem was slavery.

Hoover was often far too willing to underplay the human suffering caused by the Great Depression, but he, like the elites of his era, understood that Americans were suffering and wished to help. Their problem was a technical failure, not a moral one. Hoover and those who selected him correctly identified the problem, but not the solution. The elite consensus view on economic policy was inadequate to the crisis of the Great Depression, and only breaking with that consensus allowed the Great Depression to be addressed. Hoover was by most standards an admirable man, Buchanan far from it. But neither bears true responsibility for the failure of his presidency. They were in the White House because the filtration system that selected them, however effective it might have been a generation or two earlier, was simply unable to adapt to the country's new needs.

SHADOW CASES: THREE FILTERED PRESIDENTS AND FINANCIALIZATION

Leader Filtration Theory is mainly meant to provide insight on the overall success or failure of presidencies. Asking it to have insight on the outcome of individual issues is stretching the theory to its limits. Nonetheless, the idea of a single concentrated interest that has massive influence over the political system, uses that influence to sway the government in its favor, and thus stresses the system to a breaking point has such contemporary relevance that it seems worth exploring further.

Over the course of twenty years, Ronald Reagan, George H. W. Bush, and Bill Clinton—three Filtered presidents (they have Filtration Scores of

8, 13, and 12 respectively, putting all three in the upper half of presidents by filtration)—chose, in cooperation with Congress, to largely remove the constraints on the American financial system put in place after the Great Depression. They did so not out of personal corruption, but simply because the power of the financial sector was so great that, as with Buchanan and the South, the only way for a Filtered candidate to reach the presidency was to demonstrate loyalty to this single, overwhelmingly powerful interest. The power of the American financial sector had become so great that it has "cognitively captured" American elites in both parties. From prestige, to offering public-sector officials lucrative postgovernmental careers, to the sheer financial resources devoted to lobbying, the American financial sector exerted a power over the government unrivaled by any other interest group.[56]

The choice to deregulate was supported by both Democrats and Republicans. Bill Clinton and George H. W. Bush were both discussed as Filtered presidents in the previous chapter. Ronald Reagan clearly was one as well. His professional background as an actor may have been unique (up to that point in time) in American politics, but he was also a two-term governor of California who didn't just easily capture the Republican nomination in 1980, he came quite close to unseating an incumbent president of his own party in 1976.[57] Reagan was a known quantity who was clearly acceptable to the Republican Party elite.

Key events in financial deregulation included the deregulation of thrifts in 1982 (under Reagan), the elimination of restrictions on interstate banking in 1994 (Clinton), and the repeal of Glass-Steagall by the passage of the Gramm-Leach-Bliley Act in 1999 (Clinton again).[58] Deregulation was the elite consensus, and supporting the elite consensus is the sine qua non of passing filtration.

The consequences of this generation of Filtered choices were catastrophic. They culminated in the 2008 Global Financial Crisis. It is difficult to overstate its impact. By one estimate, in 2016 per capita GDP in the United States remained *15 percent* below what it would have been in the absence of the crisis—a shortfall of as much as $4.6 trillion. The financial crisis cost the United States government more than $2 trillion in foregone tax revenues from 2008 to 2010. A study by the Federal Reserve has found that on average it cost *every single American* $70,000.[59]

The financial crisis was only the most obvious harmful effect of a broader change in the American economy. That change is known as *financialization*. The finance and insurance industries are critical to the functioning of a modern economy. If they become too large, however, they can slow growth and increase inequality and the danger of financial crises. In 1950 finance and insurance accounted for 2.7 percent of U.S. GDP. By 2017 that number was almost three times as high. In 1970 the profits of the finance and insurance industries accounted for 24 percent of all other sectors combined. By 2013 that number was 37 percent, despite shrinking substantially after the financial crisis. In 1980 the total value of all U.S. financial assets was five times the country's GDP. In 2007 it was ten times GDP. Domestic credit supplied to the private sector in the United States grew from 71 percent of GDP in 1970 to 192 percent in 2017, even though an IMF study has found that private-sector credit slows growth and increases volatility when it exceeds 80–100 percent of GDP. This increase in economic power was reflected by an increase in political power, with the finance, insurance, and real estate industries spending almost $6 billion on lobbying between 1998 and 2013, second only to healthcare.[60]

Financialization is not an inevitable product of economic development. The American economy was (not coincidentally) similarly financialized before the Great Depression, and the regulatory reforms pushed through in response by Roosevelt (and, to a lesser extent, Hoover) accounted for finance's supporting role in the postwar American economy. Starting in the late 1970s, however, and particularly during the 1980s and 1990s, the American government deregulated the sector, allowing finance to climb back into a lead role in the economy.[61] Financialization was a choice, one that the elites who dominate the American filtration system ensured a generation of presidents and Congresses would make.

GOING WRONG WITH CONFIDENCE: FILTERED PRESIDENTIAL FAILURES

Looking at the presidents examined in the last two chapters, we can conclude that Filtered presidents are a safer bet than Unfiltered ones, but they are far from a certain one. Filtered presidents are likely to be competent and able to perform the basic tasks of the presidency. They are, however, inevitably representative of the preferences of the system of elites that permitted their rise. If those elites are basically correct in their assessments of the needs of the nation, then future historians will likely judge the Filtered presidents that they produced to have been successful. If those elites are wrong, then the same skill that allowed someone to pass through the filtration system will be turned to policies—like Buchanan's—that inflict enormous harm. The failure here is that of the system, not the person it chose, but the consequences of that failure can be vast. Historically the American system has usually been more right than wrong, as reflected by the United States' current dominant position on the world stage. That does not mean it always was, or that it will always be in the future. When the system is wrong, the Filtered leaders it selects can steer the ship of state into disaster.

4 Unhappy in Their Own Way

FAILED UNFILTERED PRESIDENTS

While Filtered presidents fail in consistent ways, Unfiltered presidents fail distinctively. Variation, after all, is the hallmark of being Unfiltered.

This chapter, like the previous two, starts with Leader Filtration Theory to understand what insights it might have about Unfiltered leaders. Here I'll pair the theory's insights with research from political science, management, and psychology to identify characteristics that are both likely to help a candidate pass evaluations and hinder their performance in office. Then we'll look at a set of failed Unfiltered presidents to try to flesh out that abstract picture.

Unfiltered failed presidents are perhaps the greatest danger of the American political system. No other major power chooses unfiltered leaders nearly as often as the United States. This danger is compounded by our presidential system, in which it is far harder to dethrone an unfit leader than in parliamentary systems.[1] By using Leader Filtration Theory as our guide to disastrous Unfiltered presidents, we can identify some of the warning signs that should steer us away from future presidential candidates.

INADEQUACIES

Historians' judgments of presidents can be unsparing. The presidency is a brutally hard job. One way to understand how hard is to look at life spans. Higher social status generally leads to a greater life expectancy. This effect is so strong that winning a Nobel Prize increases life expectancy by more than a year over being nominated for one, even though nominees also have high status.[2] A longer life is surely one of the sweetest fruits of victory.

The presidency, however, is the great exception to this rule. The winners of presidential elections surely have higher status than the vanquished. Across seventeen countries, however, democratically elected heads of government are outlived by those they defeated.[3] The stress of the presidency isn't just metaphorically lethal, it is literally so. In assessing men who by the common judgment of historians were overmatched by the demands of the Oval Office, it's worth remembering how harsh those demands can be.

The sheer difficulty of the presidency means that not anyone can do it successfully. Any native-born American over thirty-five can be president, but that doesn't mean that just anyone *should*. In general, as the last two chapters showed, the American filtration system, when it can fully evaluate candidates, usually removes those who are unintelligent, incompetent, or have unacceptable views. We know, however, that the filtration system doesn't always get that chance. Almost half of American presidents have been Unfiltered, and when that happens, the odds of a failed or even a catastrophic presidency go up substantially. One reason this can happen with Unfiltered presidents is that some candidates are simply not up to the job, and the superficial filtration process they underwent failed to detect it.

Any rational filtration system is going to select for traits that make leaders more likely to succeed and against those that make them more likely to fail. Because of that selection process, Filtered candidates will be more likely to possess those traits than Unfiltered ones. For the presidency, the two most important requirements for the job are intellectual brilliance and managerial ability. We don't need to look at Filtered candidates too closely to see if they have the intelligence and managerial skill necessary to be president, because the filtration system has done it for us. But Unfiltered candidates who are not up to the necessary standards may not have been removed from the pool, so we shouldn't have the same confidence about them.

Research on leadership in a wide variety of fields finds that intelligence is the single most important trait for predicting leader success. Intelligence is a strong predictor of performance across jobs, and the more complex the job, the more important it becomes. This is true for all types of leaders, including political ones. Even studies that question this finding conclude that intelligence is an important factor.[4]

In the case of the presidency, the legendary psychologist and expert on performance Dean Simonton created the standard model explaining presidential performance decades ago. He found that when the impact of circumstances is removed, *Intellectual Brilliance* is by far the most important trait linked to presidential success. Intellectual Brilliance combines measures of intelligence with related but distinct factors such as curiosity, sophistication, and inventiveness.[5]

Intellectual Brilliance is the only personality factor that correlates with presidential performance after accounting for context. Intellectual Brilliance is not enough for success, but brilliant candidates are far more likely to make successful presidents than their less gifted rivals, and very low Intellectual Brilliance is likely to be a crippling handicap.

Additionally, the presidency is an unrivaled managerial test. A modern president is responsible for a federal government that dwarfs every company on earth but has far more limited powers over employees and budgets than almost any CEO. Managing any government is hard; managing the United States' government verges on impossible.[6] Unfiltered presidents may simply lack the managerial ability to implement their preferred policies even if their ideas are good ones, because their good ideas may founder on that ineffectiveness.

CAMOUFLAGED CANDIDATES

Beyond simply not being up to the job, though, Unfiltered candidates may be camouflaged in ways that make their flaws hard for superficial evaluation to detect. A favorite quote from Shakespeare is useful here. In *Macbeth*, Malcolm remarks that "Angels are bright still, though the brightest fell. / Though all things foul would wear the brows of grace, / Yet grace must still look so."[7] Filtration processes try to sort the angels from the devils. The problem is that devils will use their powers to look like their unfallen brethren—they present with brows of grace. Similarly, ambitious people who desire the presidency will do everything they can to seem like someone who should be president.

Setting external factors aside, Unfiltered presidents, like any other president, can fail because the policies they enact are poorly executed, or because the choices that they make and the policies they pursue are fundamentally poor ones. These two categories are not mutually exclusive. This means that we're trying to identify candidate traits that hide these flaws from a superficial examination. Any trait that makes it harder to evaluate a candidate and discern their true intentions and capabilities will make it more likely that the candidate, if chosen, will fail in one of those two ways.

Some traits—I call them *intensifiers*—disguise potential flaws without necessarily hindering performance. Others—*façades*—are more dangerous. Their presence makes someone look more capable upon first impression but hinders long-term performance. Intensifiers make it more difficult to accurately evaluate a candidate. They broaden the spectrum of possible outcomes without necessarily making them better or worse. Intensifiers are a yellow light—an indicator that a candidate may be crucially flawed and deserves closer scrutiny. Façades, on the other hand, make candidates seem highly capable but are actually very likely to cause failure or disaster in office. Façades are a red light—a sign that the candidate is very likely to fail. Unfiltered candidates often shine like stars. What we are trying to do is distinguish falling stars from rising ones. Both burn brightly, but only one burns out (table 4).

INTENSIFIERS

Intensifiers are traits that can cloud evaluators' judgment but are not necessarily harmful in office. They increase the variance in outcomes without directly affecting the average outcome (although they may decrease average outcomes indirectly) by making it possible for leaders who could never

---

Table 4   Intensifiers and Façades

Intensifiers	Charisma
	Fame
	Ceremonial positions
	Unearned advantages
Façades	Dark Triad personality traits
	Excessive risk-taking
	Radical or simplistic ideologies

---

otherwise have become president to enter the Oval Office, for better or worse. Intensifiers and façades both draw their power from one of the most important and prevalent cognitive errors: the tendency to believe that all good things tend to go together. For example, we tend to assess attractive people as intelligent, whether or not that's true. Psychologists call this a "halo effect," where one positive trait (e.g., good looks) can skew our perceptions about completely unrelated traits.[8]

Halo effects can make it more difficult to evaluate candidates. An intensifier can be something as simple as height. Recall Gladwell's finding that most American CEOs are over six feet tall. Height makes you more likely to pass through the filtration system, but no one would argue that it is particularly important in determining a leader's success or failure while in office. Height increases the spread of possible outcomes (by enabling candidates who would otherwise be eliminated to make it to the top) but has only an indirect effect on average outcomes. Tall managers and short managers have equal skills, so height doesn't directly affect performance. Height does allow less capable tall candidates to beat out more qualified shorter ones, though, so it likely decreases average performance indirectly.

Looking at the presidents profiled in the rest of the chapter, four important intensifiers for presidents that we'll discuss are charisma, fame, ceremonial or peripheral positions, and unearned advantages.

Charisma can be the product of something as basic as good looks. Better-looking people are advantaged by their looks in virtually every interaction they have with another person, from the dating market to negotiating loans. Charisma's role in politics was first analyzed by the great sociologist Max Weber. Some researchers argue that charisma is just something we attribute to leaders retrospectively to explain their success. More broadly, charisma is a relationship, not just an attribute of a candidate. Even leaders who are broadly considered charismatic are generally not appealing to everyone, and some leaders whom most find completely unappealing are intensely charismatic to small subsets within the population. If you've ever met someone who generates a powerful charismatic effect in you—Bill Clinton is the classic example—its reality is palpable. A truly charismatic personality is a force of nature. Charismatic leaders are judged more effective than their noncharismatic counterparts. Charisma can be learned to some extent, but whether learned or innate it can inspire followers to extraordinary devotion and obedience.[9]

Charisma can be hard to define, but I think it is best thought of as the ability to get people to do things through force of personality that you could not persuade them to do through rational argument. Charisma comes in many forms, from looks to rhetorical skill to interpersonal charm. It is a powerful asset for political candidates. It can deceive party leaders into supporting candidates who lack more fundamental requirements for success.[10]

Charisma is the paradigmatic intensifier. If the charismatic leader's ideas are good, this can produce extraordinary success. If they are bad, charisma enables disastrous failures. In either case, charismatic leaders can, through force of personality, rise more quickly and blur evaluations of their performance. We should treat a presidential candidate's charisma as at least as much of a warning sign as an asset.

A second likely intensifier is extraordinary fame or status. Becoming a national figure, or even a national hero, because of military success, like Grant or Eisenhower, or reasons unrelated to politics (e.g., in business) does give us information about a candidate. But it provides far less than you'd guess. Research shows that skills are usually not portable. A star performer in one company who moves to another very similar company is unlikely to remain a star.[11] Skills that made someone famous outside politics tell us little about his or her skills in it.

Fame from outside politics can trigger a halo effect, as evinced by the devoted following of even seemingly talentless celebrities. Extraordinary status gained in one arena—even when it was earned—may blind evaluators to defects in another. Great fame, particularly from nonpolitical successes, is therefore a significant warning sign about an Unfiltered candidate.

A third likely intensifier is ceremonial or peripheral positions. Some offices have far more prominence than power. Others are so remote from political elites that performance in them may escape scrutiny. Either can give evaluators false confidence in their judgment of candidates by providing those candidates with the veneer of a presidential resume. The governor of Texas, for example, is formally the chief executive of the nation's second largest state, but in practice in many ways has less real power than the state's lieutenant governor. This makes a Texas governor seem far more thoroughly evaluated than he or she actually is.

A fourth likely intensifier is unearned advantages, like coming from a wealthy and powerful family. Such a family can help a candidate compile an impressive resume. That resume, however, provides less information about the candidate's true capabilities than it would for one without inherited advantages. Unearned advantages deprive observers of the ability to fully evaluate candidates, boosting their (perceived) performance with assets that will be useless once they're in the Oval Office.

FAÇADES

Some Unfiltered leaders fail because of bad luck or circumstances. Beyond that, however, one of the prime advantages of filtration is its ability to block leaders with characteristics that make them nearly certain to fail. Some such characteristics—façades—make candidates seem more appealing on superficial evaluation despite their harmful effects. Unfiltered leaders are more likely to have such façades because they have not been subjected to rigorous scrutiny. Façades become particularly dangerous when they are matched with intensifiers that might have allowed a candidate to escape the negative consequences of the façade earlier in their career and magnify their impact once in office. A president who wishes to pursue disastrous policies is bad enough but becomes much worse if he or she also has the charisma to overcome the objections of others inside and outside the government.

Façades are different from intensifiers because, while both make evaluations more difficult and can enable a candidate who will do great harm to gain power, façades have overwhelmingly negative effects in the long term. Thinking about façades as tradeoffs is the key way to understand them and to differentiate them from intensifiers. Intensifiers just increase spread. Façades shift rewards in time, by generating short-term benefits but creating long-term costs. If a characteristic makes you look good in the short term but creates the potential for long-term disaster, then it's a façade. At least three types of façades are likely to be especially important in presidential politics: "Dark Triad" personality traits, excessive risk-taking, and radical or simplistic ideologies.

The Dark Triad is three related but distinct personality traits that often appear together: narcissism, Machiavellianism, and psychopathy. Hitler and Mussolini, for example, are classic examples of Dark Triad personalities. Leaders with the Dark Triad often leave wreckage in their wake. Under the right circumstances each component of the Dark Triad can help elevate candidates even though they hurt leaders' performance.[12]

Narcissism is the classic façade. Narcissists have immense self-confidence and are often perceived as natural leaders. In power, however, narcissists tend to be disastrous.[13] Imagine a narcissist—with all their potential for uncontrollable rage when their self-image is threatened— trying to negotiate a nuclear standoff to get an image of the full scope of potential disaster.

Narcissists are so common in politics that "if individuals with significant narcissistic characteristics were stripped from the ranks of public figures, the rank would be perilously thinned." Presidents with high grandiose narcissism (grandiose narcissists are flamboyant and dominant, while vulnerable narcissists are withdrawn and hypersensitive) do better in historians' rankings but were also more likely to face impeachment resolutions and engage in unethical behavior.[14]

Narcissists are often impressive on first encounter, so much so that others assess them as the best leaders in a group. And while, yes, a narcissist's bold vision, risk-taking, and charisma can make him or her very successful, more often narcissistic leaders are a very bad bet. Their falsely positive self-images make them more likely to be self-serving, dishonest, and to alienate their followers over time. Companies with very narcissistic CEOs tend to have much more variance in performance than those with less narcissistic ones.[15]

Machiavellianism is "a personality trait characterized by cunning, manipulation, and the use of any means necessary to achieve one's political ends." In other words, Machiavellian personalities tend to lie to and manipulate others for their own benefit. Machiavellians are particularly likely to rise in unstructured settings, and some level of Machiavellian traits in a leader can even be helpful. Machiavellian presidents, for example, tend to have more legislative successes. Very Machiavellian leaders, however, tend to engage in manipulations that hurt their organizations and deprive subordinates of meaning in their work.[16]

Psychopathy, despite its popular association with serial killers, can boost careers, so much so that psychopaths are substantially overrepresented in the ranks of senior executives. Psychopaths often have enormous superficial charm and can be extraordinarily decisive, among other traits that serve them well in settings like job interviews. But psychopaths also tend to harm their organizations. Their skill at manipulation and their indifference to the harms they inflict means that power enables them to do enormous damage.[17]

Psychopathic traits can be divided into two sets that can appear independently, so a single individual can have one or both: *Fearless Dominance* and *Impulsive Antisociality*. Fearless Dominance is made up of traits like boldness, charm, and physical fearlessness. It is likely to be mostly an intensifier, often helping candidates rise to the top, but having both positive and negative effects on their performance in office. Impulsive Antisociality, on the other hand, is made up of traits like poor impulse control, self-centeredness, and a tendency to blame others. It is likely to have purely negative effects on leader performance.[18]

On average, presidents exhibit high levels of Fearless Dominance, but they exhibit Impulsive Antisociality at the same levels as the general population.[19] Impulsive Antisociality may go undetected in an Unfiltered candidate or masked by that candidate's psychopathic charm. It may even help a candidate pass through a loose filtration process if it makes him or her more likely to engage in violations of rules and norms in pursuit of career success. It is, however, likely to have a substantially negative effect on presidential performance.

People with Dark Triad traits are often risk-takers, though risk-taking is also a trait that stands on its own. Successful leaders must take risks. Britain's elite Special Air Service has the motto "Who Dares, Wins" for a reason.[20]

Risk-taking unleavened by prudence, however, is the domain of the reckless. Leaders may often be tempted to take more risks than is good for their country. Leaders who have faced policy reverses and fear being deposed, for example, may "gamble for resurrection" by taking even larger ones in the hope of saving their position, even if the best interests of their country require cutting their losses instead. Think of Hitler gambling for a victory at the Battle of the Bulge, for example, instead of trying for a negotiated peace with the Western Allies in the hopes of getting better terms for Germany.[21]

Risk-taking is a special type of façade, one that may be particularly common in Unfiltered leaders. A short run of brilliant successes is far more likely to be a product of luck instead of skill than a long one is, but without (and often even with) that long baseline, it can be very difficult to differentiate between the truly brilliant and a gambler on a hot streak.[22] An Unfiltered candidate who has repeatedly taken great risks—even if they worked out—is displaying a major warning sign.

A third façade is a radical or simplistic ideology. Presidents' ideology clearly impacts their behavior. For example, presidents' belief in whether the threat posed by other states is driven by their internal domestic institutions helps to determine their choices about when and how to intervene militarily to influence them. Eisenhower, for example, tended to believe that the threat posed by other states was primarily a product of their foreign policy, while John F. Kennedy saw it as produced by their internal institutions. Consequentially, Eisenhower was less interested in changing other states' domestic institutions.[23]

Ideologies can be simple or complex. H. L. Mencken famously remarked that "there is always a well-known solution to every human problem— neat, plausible, and wrong." This is more than just a witty comment. Leaders who think about the world in complex ways are more successful. Generals who display high degrees of cognitive complexity, for example, outperform those who do not. Presidents with high degrees of integrative complexity are more likely to prevent war during an international crisis and to be less drawn to extremist ideologies.[24]

Simple and extreme ideologies can have great appeal, however. They may draw some of their strength from the Dunning-Kruger effect, or the tendency of those who don't know much about a subject to be most prone to *overestimating* their competence in it. A large fraction of Americans know surprisingly little about how their government works, and the voters who know the least are actually more confident in their understanding than the ones who know much more.[25]

Candidates who offer these falsely confident voters simple solutions may be buoyed through the filtration process, but that very simplicity means that their solutions are likely to fail. Prolonged filtration would have allowed those failures to stop these candidates' progress, but Unfiltered candidates might never have put their ideas to the test.

A final façade is a false appearance of health. Most presidents serve out their terms. Anyone would change at least somewhat over that time, particularly given the stress of the office. Health issues, however, can vastly exacerbate these changes and make them far more negative. Advanced age, for example, can have severe effects on leadership skills.[26]

Aging decreases energy levels and makes people more vulnerable to illness. A high energy level is crucial to meeting the demands of the presidency, while illness can have crippling effects on executive abilities. Aging changes personality by enhancing underlying tendencies. Far from mellowing with age, most people's personalities become exaggerated, essentially turning them into exaggerated versions of themselves. Aging can enhance crystallized intelligence—the ability to accomplish routine tasks. But it diminishes fluid intelligence, the ability to solve new problems, which begins declining at twenty, and is crucially important in handling crises.[27]

Other underlying medical issues can be even worse. Amphetamine addiction, for example, crippled Anthony Eden's decision-making during the Suez Crisis and was widespread in the Nazi leadership. Alcoholism and other forms of substance abuse are surprisingly common among national leaders, with the best estimate suggesting that 15 percent of democratically elected leaders are clinically diagnosable as alcoholics. Similarly, psychological conditions are more common among political leaders than you might expect. Even the leaders of established democracies are classifiable as clinically paranoid about 3 percent of the time, or about twice as often as this condition exists in the general population.[28]

Façades share a tradeoff between the short and long term.[29] Leaders with Dark Triad characteristics, ones who take unwise risks, those who propose simple solutions to complex problems, or those who pretend to good health are boosting their short-term success at the cost of harming their long-term prospects. In a sufficiently superficial filtration process, this short-term boost might carry a candidate through to victory. In the United States, it might even make one the most powerful person on earth.

Bluntly, electing someone with a façade is an incredible gamble, and almost always an unwise one.

UNFILTERED FAILED PRESIDENTS

Of the five lowest-ranked Unfiltered presidents, three—John Tyler, Millard Fillmore, and Andrew Johnson—were vice presidents elevated by the president's death. We'll examine Johnson, the embodiment of the worst-case vice-presidential succession, in this chapter, as well as Pierce, a dark horse president. Each is a striking illustration of a way in which Unfiltered presidents can go wrong.

Shadow Cases: Franklin Pierce

Franklin Pierce was born with every advantage anyone could ask for. He had a famous name, political connections, and was so handsome (with all the charisma that entails) that he is still often called one of the best-looking presidents. Despite those legs up, his presidency was a disaster. He had many virtues useful for gaining the office, but few that were useful once in it. His presidency was crippled by divides in the Democratic Party and destroyed by his deference to the South and likely also his severe alcoholism.

Born November 23, 1804, in Hillsborough, New Hampshire, he was the seventh child of General Benjamin Pierce, a Revolutionary War hero. In college he was an indifferent student who seems to have put much more effort into his social life. The heavy drinking that eventually killed him and dogged his political career may have begun then. He became a lawyer and compensated for his lackluster legal abilities with his extraordinary memory for names and faces, personal charm, empathy, and skill at public speaking. Bolstered by his father's reputation, he entered politics and in 1832, at only twenty-seven, was elected to Congress.[30]

His legislative career was undistinguished and marked by intense hostility to Abolitionists. In 1837 he was elected to the Senate, but he served for only five years before resigning in frustration over his position in the minority and his desire to increase his income. By the end of his time in the Senate, however, he had secured complete control over the New Hampshire Democratic Party, which he used to enforce a ban on any opposition to slavery or hostility to the South. Pierce served as a brigadier general in the Mexican War, during which he performed competently but without distinction, and suffered a knee injury severe enough that it hobbled him for the rest of his life.[31]

By 1852 the fractures in the Democratic Party that would split it in 1860 were already apparent. The front-runners for the nomination—Cass, Buchanan, and Douglas—so hated one another that party leaders feared it would be impossible for any one of them to achieve the two-thirds vote necessary to gain the nomination. Normally Pierce would have had no shot as his own state's party had endorsed Levi Woodbury, a Supreme Court justice. Woodbury died in November 1851, however, making Pierce New Hampshire's favorite son. New Hampshire congressmen began to suggest Pierce as a compromise who could garner support from the North because of his roots there and from the South because of his opposition to the antislavery movement. When the convention deadlocked, Pierce was nominated on the forty-ninth ballot. When he was told, it was such a shock that he looked stunned and his wife fainted. Even Pierce's most sympathetic modern biographer, who describes him as someone who was "an unknown person" to the general public, notes that "the amazing thing about Pierce's nomination is that to the last moment it remained totally unanticipated by all of the leading candidates."[32] It's hard to imagine a better description of a dark horse. This, in combination with his relatively brief national political career, gives him a Filtration Score of 2.5, making him one of the least Filtered presidents.

Pierce campaigned on the platform that the Compromise of 1850 had forever ended sectional disputes over slavery. He was opposed by Winfield Scott, who was one of the heroes of the Mexican War but had no aptitude for politics and agreed with Pierce on this critical issue. Pierce won twenty-seven of the thirty-one states in the largest landslide since the 1820s.[33]

Pierce's presidency was tragically marred even before it began. In January, he and his wife were on a train with their son Benny when the car derailed and fell more than twenty feet, landing on its roof. Pierce and his wife were badly bruised, but Benny, sitting right behind them, had the back of his head sheared off and died in front of his horrified parents.[34]

The dominant issue of the Pierce administration, and the one that cemented his position as one of the worst presidents, was the struggle over the Kansas-Nebraska Act. Pierce's decision to endorse the act and thus overturn the Compromise of 1850, despite the role of the Compromise in his campaign, was disastrous. Why Pierce chose to go back on his campaign promises and support the Kansas-Nebraska Act remains a matter of historical debate, one for which there is no clear answer. Explanations range from Pierce's needing southern senators for his foreign policy agenda, to his hostility to Abolitionism, to his simply being persuaded that it was the right policy, to his desire to maintain the unity of the Democratic Party as the Whigs collapsed.[35]

Pierce's support of Kansas-Nebraska, however, "had precipitated a political crisis over slavery that could not be resolved except by civil war."[36] Although it seems virtually certain that some other issue would have eventually ignited the tinder of sectional conflict, Pierce's choices likely accelerated that process.

In the end, Pierce's reasons are immaterial. His choice was an enormous unforced error. His own party so completely repudiated him that he had virtually no support for a renomination in 1856. When Pierce left the White House, he is said to have remarked that "there's nothing left but to get drunk." He spent his remaining years doing just that. Pierce opposed the northern war effort during the Civil War and died of cirrhosis of the liver in 1869.[37]

Pierce fits well with predictions of how Unfiltered presidents can fail. Unearned advantages boosted him into an office for which he was completely unsuited. Because he occupied that office at a moment when even a tremendously gifted leader would have struggled, the consequences were disastrous for him and for the country.

Andrew Johnson: Squandering Victory

Andrew Johnson, like Harry Truman, had the misfortune of succeeding a titan. Unlike Truman, he catastrophically failed to rise to the challenge. Lincoln was struck down on April 14, 1865, at the Union's moment of triumph. That day was Good Friday, so across the North sermons two days later, on Easter Sunday, spoke of Lincoln dying for the sins of the Union. The North's victory assured Lincoln of a towering position in history, but his assassination resulted in his virtual apotheosis.[38] Even the best and most able leaders would have struggled to step into such extraordinary shoes. Johnson, though, was neither good nor skilled.

FROM A LOG CABIN TO THE VICE PRESIDENCY

Johnson was born in a log cabin on December 29, 1808, in Raleigh, North Carolina. His father died when he was three as the result of a heroic attempt to save the passengers of a capsized boat. When he was nine poverty forced his mother to apprentice him to a tailor, a position he was obligated to stay in until twenty-one. At fifteen he fled his apprenticeship and moved to Tennessee, where he settled in Greeneville and married his wife Eliza when he was eighteen. The ceremony was, oddly enough, performed by a cousin of Lincoln's father. In Greeneville he discovered that he was a skillful debater and was elected an alderman in 1829, running as representative of the town's lower-class whites, the constituency whose interest he championed for his entire career. He was elected Greenville's mayor and, in 1835, to the state legislature, where he split his votes between Whigs and Democrats. He staunchly opposed spending on internal improvements, and his constituents punished him for this by defeating him when he ran for reelection.[39]

In 1839 Johnson returned to the legislature as a Democrat and supporter of South Carolinian John C. Calhoun's proslavery and pro–states' rights position. In 1841 he was elected to the state senate. His personal financial situation also improved enough that he bought several slaves. In 1843 he became a member of Congress, where he voted largely with southern Democrats. In 1846 he introduced the first-ever version of the Homestead Act, which was meant to give federal lands to white Americans willing to move west to live on them. Although the bill failed, pushing it would be a focus of his political career and a break with the South, which opposed it because of its limited benefits for slaveholders and the decrease in federal revenues from the sale of western lands. In 1852 Tennessee Whigs used their control of the state legislature to gerrymander his district into a safe Whig seat, making it impossible for Johnson to win reelection.[40]

Instead of accepting defeat, Johnson ran for governor of Tennessee and won a two-year term. The office was largely ceremonial, but Johnson used it to consolidate his support among poor whites in the state. He was reelected but chose not to run for a third term, instead getting the state legislature to make him a U.S. senator. There he pushed the Homestead Act and was again stymied by Southern opposition. As the 1860 election neared he hoped to be the Democratic nominee as a compromise between the northern and southern wings of the party, but Douglas captured a majority of the votes, although not the two-thirds needed. The result was a split in the Democratic Party, which ran both northern and southern candidates, virtually guaranteeing that Lincoln, the Republican nominee, would win.[41]

The Civil War vastly elevated Johnson's northern reputation. Johnson was the only senator from a seceding state to stay with the Union. In a speech that won him acclaim across the North and condemnation across the South, he declared in typically melodramatic language that if the Union were destroyed, he would ask for "no more honorable winding sheet than that brave old flag, and no more glorious grave than to be interred in the tomb of the Union." After Lincoln's inauguration Johnson returned to Tennessee and, despite serious threats to his life, campaigned against secession. He helped produce a decisive victory for Unionists in East Tennessee in the statewide election on secession, even as prosecession forces carried the state on the back of large margins in its center and west. Johnson returned to Washington, where he continued to serve as a senator. He used his position there to lobby Lincoln to take military action in Tennessee and to build a railroad to the state to facilitate military operations there. In early 1862 he departed the Senate when Lincoln made him military governor of Tennessee. He was harsh enough on Confederates and their sympathizers that he demanded a loyalty oath from all public officials there, but his most notable act was convincing Lincoln to exempt Tennessee from the Emancipation Proclamation.[42]

The first half of 1864 presented Lincoln with very unfavorable terrain for reelection. The war was dragging on with mounting casualties and no end in sight. Lincoln was so concerned that in August he wrote a memorandum:

> This morning, as for some days past, it seems exceedingly probable that this Administration will not be re-elected. Then it will be my duty to so co-operate with the President-elect as to save the Union between the election and the inauguration; as he will have secured his election on such ground that he can not possibly save it afterwards.[43]

After sealing it in an envelope, he asked every member of his cabinet to sign. Any election is a fraught prospect. It must have been much more so for Lincoln, who feared that his defeat would spell the end of the Union.

One tool Lincoln had to improve his odds was the vice-presidential nomination. Hannibal Hamlin had served well, but he was a Republican from Maine who added nothing to the ticket's chances. A prowar Democrat, however, might get support from pro-Union Democrats who would normally not vote for a Republican. If Lincoln maneuvered Hamlin off the ticket and Johnson onto it remains unclear. Lincoln and his secretaries all stated that he left it to the convention. He had, however, sent an emissary to speak with Union general Benjamin Butler, a prowar Democrat, about joining the ticket, and he may have sent one to Nashville to meet with Johnson. He may have expressed a preference for Johnson to friends.[44]

As is often the case with Lincoln, his political maneuvering was so skillful that historians are left with an impossible puzzle. It is certain, however, that Johnson was chosen solely for political reasons. No one thought Andrew Johnson would be the next president. Had anyone even proposed him, his well-known flaws, ranging from alcoholism to temperament, would surely have excluded him from the conversation. Lincoln's health, however, appeared excellent, and no American president had ever been assassinated, so the possibility was likely never even discussed. This, combined with Johnson's elevation via assassination, makes him an entirely Unfiltered president with a Filtration Score of 0, putting him in a seven-way tie for least Filtered president. When Lincoln, buoyed by Sherman's victory at Atlanta and Farragut's at Mobile Bay, swept to victory, Johnson was a heartbeat from the White House.[45]

Any reservations Lincoln had about his running mate were likely exacerbated by Johnson's performance on Inauguration Day. Johnson arrived in Washington the night before and, although in poor health, celebrated with a great deal of whiskey. The next day he visited Hamlin and asked for more. Hamlin, a teetotaler, had to send out for some, and Johnson had at least three more glasses. When he delivered his inaugural address, he was obviously drunk and humiliated himself before everyone of importance in Washington. Johnson and Lincoln did not meet one on one until more than a month later, the day Lincoln made his fateful trip to Ford's Theater. When John Wilkes Booth assassinated Lincoln, he replaced a man whose very last speech had proposed extending the vote to Black Americans with Johnson, who proclaimed that "this is a country for white men, and by God, as long as I am President, it shall be a government for white men."[46]

WINNING THE WAR AND LOSING THE PEACE

Johnson kept Lincoln's cabinet and told Radical Republicans, "I hold this: Robbery is a crime; rape is a crime; *treason* is a crime; and *crime* must be punished." In fact, however, his desire to punish individual Confederate leaders obscured his opposition to changing the South's racial hierarchy. He moved to bring Confederate states back into the Union under his own authority, without Congressional involvement. Johnson argued that since the states had no right to secede, their secession had no legal force and they should be brought back into the Union quickly, with the abolition of slavery the only change in their domestic arrangements.[47]

Johnson acted while Congress was out of session. Only six weeks after he became president he issued proclamations that granted amnesty and restored voting rights to all Confederates except those in small exempted classes (primarily the Southern rich whom Johnson had hated and envied for his entire life), who would have to personally request a presidential pardon. He rejected any federal efforts to guarantee voting rights to freed slaves.[48]

This was just the beginning. Johnson authorized the return of property in the hands of freedmen that had been seized from wealthy slaveowners. The state governments that sprang up under his aegis were dominated by former Confederates, so much so that Georgia chose Alexander Stephens, the former Confederate vice president, as one of its senators. Southern states passed "Black Codes" designed to keep African Americans subordinate to whites. The codes denied them the right to vote, serve on juries, or testify in court against whites. They even banned African Americans from hunting and fishing, two activities they had been allowed under slavery. Southern whites, encouraged by their belief that the president was on their side, began to engage in horrific violence against freed slaves, killing hundreds or thousands and preventing any attempts to punish the murderers. Southern whites, northern Democrats, and conservatives were pleased, but Republicans were outraged.[49]

Once Congress returned to session, Republicans struck back. Both the House and Senate refused to seat former Confederates. They passed a bill to continue the Freedmen's Bureau, which Lincoln had created to protect former slaves, and one to overturn the Black Codes and give the formerly enslaved the same civil rights as whites. Johnson vetoed the first bill. He ignored the violence in the South and declared that there was nothing "in the condition of the country . . . to justify" the bureau. He said that freedmen who were unhappy with their treatment in the South were free to leave. The Senate was unable to overturn his veto and Johnson, feeling his victory and possibly drunk, gave a speech in February condemning Republicans who opposed him as enemies "opposed to the fundamental principles of this Government." Johnson then doubled down and vetoed the civil rights bill as well. His attacks on Congress grew so heated that Grant became concerned that Johnson would launch an armed takeover of the government.[50]

Radical Republicans won a massive victory in the 1866 congressional elections. They soon began to consider impeaching Johnson. The displaced Hamlin made the case, asking "Did we fight down the rebellion to give the South more power?" Ascendant Radical Republicans passed Reconstruction Acts that superseded Johnson's actions, divided the South into five military districts, and made approving the Fourteenth Amendment and giving the franchise to freed slaves a requirement for readmission to the Union. Johnson responded by sabotaging the Freedmen's Bureau and instructed his attorney general to issue legal opinions that limited the powers of the military governors and restored the vote to former Confederates. He then issued a proclamation pardoning almost all southerners of treason.[51]

The war between Congress and the president continued to escalate into 1868, culminating with Johnson attempting to remove Secretary of War Stanton without the congressional approval required by the dubiously constitutional Tenure of Office Act. Johnson was finally impeached by the House and spared conviction in the Senate by a single vote.[52]

The impeachment limited Johnson's ability to further sabotage Reconstruction and he would be replaced by Grant in 1869, who took a leading role in the passage of the Fifteenth Amendment, which was meant to guarantee the franchise without regard to race, even though its provisions would go unenforced. By then, however, the damage had been done. Even Hans Trefousse, Johnson's sympathetic biographer, acknowledged that "Johnson had made any effective Reconstruction impossible . . . he reanimated Southern resistance and fatally undermined efforts to integrate the freedmen into society."[53]

In 1865, shattered by defeat in the Civil War, southern whites would have agreed to almost any peace terms, including land reform and a full extension of the franchise to freedmen. When Johnson offered them the chance to maintain their prewar social structure, with African Americans facing an only slightly reduced level of oppression, they adopted the policy of total resistance to civil rights that defined life in the South for another century.[54]

ASSESSMENT: SQUANDERING THE FRUITS OF VICTORY

Johnson was clearly Unfiltered. No one considered him a potential president, and his elevation to the White House was as random an accident as can be imagined. Did he have an impact? How Lincoln would have handled Reconstruction is unknowable. There is no question, however, that Johnson took a radically different course than he would have. It is impossible to imagine Lincoln cooperating with and even encouraging Southern whites to reverse their military defeat through political victories. Equally, the supremely adroit Lincoln would never have found himself so at odds with Congress.

Johnson is our model disastrous Unfiltered leader. His alcohol usage was likely pathological. His ideology was both simplistic and far out of the Republican mainstream. Johnson viewed the relationship between whites and Blacks as purely competitive, arguing that any improvements in the condition of African Americans should be matched by equal improvements for whites to ensure that they maintained their dominant position. Johnson, bizarrely, believed that planters and their former slaves were working together to oppress poor whites and responded to a Frederick Douglass–led delegation petitioning for universal suffrage by raging, "Those d——d [sic] sons of b——s [sic] thought they had me in a trap. I know that d——d [sic] Douglass; he's just like any n——, & he would sooner cut a white man's throat than not." The contrast with Lincoln, who called Douglass "my friend" and asked him to evaluate the Second Inaugural, saying "There is no man in these United States whose opinion I value more than yours," speaks for itself.[55]

Without Johnson some combination of Lincoln, Hamlin, and the Radical Republicans would have run Reconstruction. A version of American history in which they redistributed southern lands to freedmen and guaranteed them the vote, followed by eight years of Grant doing the same, is a very different and, I believe, a vastly better one. Johnson demonstrates just how much damage the wrong Unfiltered leader can do.

Although historians rank Buchanan below Johnson, Johnson had a unique impact. Buchanan's choices were the choices of the system. The Civil War may not have been inevitable for all of American history, but by the 1850s it's hard to see how it could have been averted. Either way, only a war could have ended slavery by 1865. If someone other than Buchanan had been elected in 1856—Franklin Pierce, for example—the Civil War would almost certainly still have happened. Buchanan was a faithful representative of his party, the dominant one in the American political system at the time.

Johnson's record has no such defense. His combination of weakness, rigidity, and racism was exceptional even by nineteenth-century standards. The South was able to successfully win the peace after losing the war because Johnson inspired recalcitrant southerners to keep up the fight longer than a war-weary North was willing to maintain the pressure. In the words of the historian Annette Gordon-Reed:

> Johnson's actions breathed new energy and life into white southerners, who in the words of one southern newspaper editor would have been "willing to acquiesce in whatever" Johnson decided to do after war's end. Christopher Memminger, the Confederate secretary of the treasury, later admitted in the

1870s that in the immediate aftermath of the war and Lincoln's assassination, the white South was so devastated and demoralized that it would have accepted almost any of the North's terms. But, he went on to say, once Johnson "held up before us the hope of 'a white man's government,'" it led "[us] to set aside negro suffrage" and to resist northern plans to improve the condition of the freedmen.

Even Trefousse agreed with this assessment. Johnson threw away the opportunity to reset race relations in the South—not through incompetence, but because he was in favor of continuing the oppression of America's Black citizens.[56]

If, instead, southern Blacks had been sheltered by an assertive federal government—as Radical Republicans desired—southern whites might well have accepted this new social order. A century of unyielding and often violent resistance happened, in other words, because of Andrew Johnson. He squandered most of the fruits of the Union's victory in the Civil War and set back civil rights by a century. For example, Hiram Revels of Mississippi was elected as the first Black senator in 1870, with Blanche K. Bruce joining him five years later. The next Black senator was Edward Brooke, from Massachusetts, who would not be elected until 1967. Johnson's selection as vice president in 1864 was Lincoln's greatest mistake. Given the scale of Johnson's damage, Lincoln's assassination may be the greatest tragedy in American history.

Shadow Cases: Jimmy Carter and George W. Bush

Jimmy Carter and George W. Bush might seem to have little in common. One was a Republican, one a Democrat. Both were from wealthy families, although Carter inherited little while Bush, the son of a president and grandson of a senator, is from arguably the most prominent family in the United States. Carter graduated in the top 10 percent of his class at the Naval Academy and served in the navy before returning to Georgia to rescue his family peanut farm. Bush, a self-described alcoholic, drank heavily in college and afterwards, served in the National Guard during the Vietnam War, and returned to Texas, where he started an unsuccessful oil drilling company. Carter served in the Georgia legislature before running for governor unsuccessfully in 1966 and successfully in 1970. Bush used family connections to assemble investors to purchase the Texas Rangers, eventually making over $15 million from an initial investment of under $1 million. He ran unsuccessfully for the House of Representatives in 1978 and successfully for governor of Texas in 1994. He was reelected in 1998, making him a leading contender for the Republican nomination in 2000 even though the Texas governor has far less power than most state governors, and arguably even less than the state's lieutenant governor. Along the way he became a teetotaler.[57]

Carter served one term as governor before running for president in 1976. Although he was initially considered a marginal candidate, his devout Christianity appealed to religious voters and his home state of Georgia gave him a base in the South. The combination of these two factors with his status as a Washington outsider in post-Watergate America brought him victory in the general election. Bush used his unmatched family network and his position as governor of Texas to consolidate a position as the overwhelming front-runner in the 2000 Republican primaries and, after beating back a primary challenge from Arizona senator John McCain and buoyed by the various scandals of the Clinton administration, he won perhaps the narrowest electoral victory in American history in the 2000 general election.[58]

But two things unite these two presidents. First, both are clearly Unfiltered. Carter had a single term as governor, while Bush had little more than one and was enormously boosted by his family name and network. It is difficult to imagine how, say, George W. Smith, with the same capabilities and resume, could ever have been a plausible candidate for governor of Texas. Carter's Filtration Score is 4 and George W. Bush's 6, putting both in the bottom half of presidents.

The second thing is that all but the most dedicated partisans would agree that their presidencies were crippled by their failures as managers. Carter's presidency was far less eventful than Bush's, but this was clearly an issue for him. James Fallows, a former speechwriter of Carter's and an admirer of his, said that:

> Carter and those closest to him took office in profound ignorance of their jobs. They were ignorant of the possibilities and the most likely pitfalls. They fell prey to predictable dangers and squandered precious time . . . Carter often seemed more consumed with taking the correct position than

with learning how to turn that position into results . . . Carter was not alert to bureaucratic perils.

Carter is one of the most admirable people ever to become president, but he was simply not a skilled enough manager to effectively implement his agenda.

Bush's managerial failures were far larger in scale and consequence. Their sheer scope makes summarizing them challenging. There was Iraq, a war of choice launched based on faulty intelligence that, years later, even many of its proponents acknowledge was catastrophically bungled. Failures ranged from invading with too few troops to maintain postwar order, to having essentially no plan on how to govern the country once it was occupied, to disbanding the Iraqi army immediately after the invasion, to assembling a Coalition Provisional Authority to run the occupied country that was not even remotely capable of the task.[59]

Iraq would be enough to render most administrations a failure in historical judgment. Add to that, however, other episodes from the administration that were almost equally disastrous, including the mismanagement of the war in Afghanistan and the relief effort for New Orleans after Hurricane Katrina, and the failure to both anticipate and effectively respond to the 2008 financial crisis. Even if you agree with Bush's general policy choices and approach, his failures of execution and implementation are virtually undeniable and cost, literally, trillions of American dollars and thousands of American lives.

THE RISKS OF UNFILTERED LEADERS

Unfiltered leaders are different from the norm, and those differences are what drive their enormous potential for both good and ill. This chapter's set of failed Unfiltered presidents suggests that the ones who fail may do so, in part, because of the very same characteristics that allowed them to rise to power without being fully evaluated in the first place.

Unfiltered presidents are not guaranteed to fail, however, as we'll see in the next chapter. Even so, they remain an enormous, and predictable, risk.

5 Five Stars and a Bull Moose

THE TRIUMPH OF UNFILTERED PRESIDENTS

Unfiltered presidents are the greatest vulnerability of the American political system. But they are also its greatest potential strength. That seeming conflict is the hallmark of high variance and the essence of Unfiltered leaders, which creates the potential for both disaster—as we saw in the previous chapter—and for triumph. No rational political system would ever have made Lincoln—a one-term congressman with only a few months of formal education and no significant track record on the major issues of the day—president for the supreme crisis in American history. We won't plunge deep into Lincoln's story here because I've covered it elsewhere, but he is the paragon whose enormous shadow drapes any discussion of great Unfiltered presidents. His successor squandered much of what he had achieved. When the highs are that high and the lows are so low—and Andrew Johnson is far from the worst-case scenario—then ending up on the good side of the spectrum becomes critically important.

In this chapter we'll complete our tour of the presidential types set out in the introduction by examining successful Unfiltered presidents. Here we'll look at Theodore Roosevelt and Dwight Eisenhower, two Unfiltered but highly ranked presidents.

We'll start by synthesizing insights from Leader Filtration Theory and other research from across the social sciences to get some ideas of what to look for in successful Unfiltered presidents. Then we'll look in depth at two presidents who both had an enormous impact—Theodore Roosevelt, who reshaped the presidency around his gargantuan personality, and Dwight Eisenhower, who used the titanic stature he gained from commanding the Allied armies on the Western Front to solidify American commitment to the Cold War structures and strategies developed by Truman.

PICKING UNFILTERED WINNERS

Chapter 4 described a variety of negative indicators about Unfiltered candidates. The biggest positive indicator for an Unfiltered candidate is simply their absence. An Unfiltered candidate without façades is a far better bet than one who has any, and an infinitely better bet than one who has several. That's our starting point, but we'd like to do better. Façades and intensifiers are false signals of quality that can lead us astray. We'd like to identify *true* ones.

Filtered candidates have moved through the system. They have held powerful positions and been assessed. Unfiltered candidates come with no such assurances. What we're looking for are indicators of capabilities so broad they suggest the ability to succeed in the White House. These are identifiable candidate traits that suggest they can perform well even in a job that remains unique. We should assess Unfiltered candidates' potential to succeed as president both directly, by looking at their characteristics, and indirectly, by examining their careers.

When we assess Unfiltered candidates, though, it's important to remember that none of these indicators are even close to enough to guarantee success. Most important, of course, is the ever-present importance of context. Franklin Roosevelt might have succeeded in many environments, but he became the towering figure he is today because of his leadership during the combination of both the Great Depression and the Second World War, two contexts that he managed ably but for which he bore no responsibility. Beyond that, however, we should think of both positive and negative traits for Unfiltered leaders as existing in a constellation, not in isolation. Many candidates are likely to have some of both, and the pluses and minuses of these traits should be weighed individually.

CHARACTERISTICS

We can begin by looking at the façades and inadequacies identified in chapter 4 and see if they have opposites that might produce success. Simonton's model found that Intellectual Brilliance was the most important individual trait linked to presidential success, so if its absence is a warning sign, its presence is a positive indicator.[1]

Mild depression might be the most surprising potential positive indicator of presidential performance. Major clinical depression can be debilitating, and no one's image of the ideal leader includes depression. Depression, however, is complicated. Chronic depression may have been one of the key ingredients in Lincoln's greatness.[2] It is precisely because no one's image of the ideal leader includes depression that mild depression might identify someone who could do well as president. Mild depression is a handicap, so a candidate with it likely has countervailing strengths powerful enough to elevate them to the final levels of the filtration process.

Just as ill health and age can cripple a presidency, resilience and energy are crucial strengths. The modern presidency has enormous physical and emotional demands.[3] Candidates who are vigorous enough to handle the demands of the presidency and young enough to avoid age-related decline are far more likely to succeed than those whose capabilities may be impaired by stress and the passage of time.

The last true signal of candidate quality is really a set of signals. It is any characteristics that made it harder to become a plausible contender for the Oval Office but that would not harm performance in the presidency. The classic example is being a "self-made" man or woman. Just as coming from a wealthy and powerful family makes a resume less informative, coming from a poor one makes a resume *more* informative, because everything on it was obtained without even the baseline advantages given people at the median of American society. For this reason, the American preference for "self-made" men (and women) seems wise. Climbing the ladder of American society is not a guarantee of ability, but it is a better assurance than having been born at the top.

Other handicaps are similar. There is extensive evidence that it is much harder for women than men to succeed in politics. Men are perceived as better leaders than women and female elected officials are perceived as less competent than their equally qualified male rivals. If people have doubts about a candidate's competence, they are more likely to evaluate female candidates harshly than male ones, they are less likely to respond to appeals across party lines when those appeals are made by a woman than by a man, and they are more vulnerable to attacks from their opponents that invoke gender stereotypes.[4]

These effects extend beyond gender. They certainly include race, and likely extend to any other group that faces prejudice in American society. However much progress the United States has made on civil rights, the discrimination faced by African Americans remains powerful. An African American job applicant, for example, has a lower chance of getting a job interview than a white applicant with an otherwise identical resume with a *felony conviction*.[5]

Any plausible Unfiltered candidate with such a trait has been running the race to the White House against a headwind and yet is still leading the pack. This suggests that they have stronger underlying capabilities than a similar candidate who had been boosted by advantages they did not earn, or even than a candidate with a neutral background.

CAREERS

Indirect assessment is about whether candidates' careers suggest that they will perform well in the Oval Office. Anyone who is a plausible contender for the White House is in the highest stratum of the American elite, many members of which simply inherited the position. Others, though, have a track record that can be judged. Because the presidency is unique, broad success is the key positive indicator. A second is the ability to build a team of able followers.

A candidate who had extraordinary successes in one field outside politics (e.g., business) may be perfectly optimized to that field but not suited to politics. Notable success in several fields, however, is a much more encouraging sign. The difficulty with imputing broad capabilities to a candidate who performed spectacularly in a single field is the problem of overoptimization. The best way to perform extremely well at a set of tasks is to specialize in them, but the more any person (or any organization) focuses on maximizing performance at one task, the worse they will get at others.[6]

In examining an Unfiltered candidate for the presidency, one who has succeeded—even spectacularly—in a single area may be overoptimized for success there. Performance usually struggles to transfer between organizations and fields.[7] This may hurt their performance in the presidency. At the least, it should give us little confidence that their previous success will translate to the Oval Office. If they've succeeded in several different fields, though (even if they haven't reached stratospheric heights in any of them), then we should think of that as a very strong sign that they have broad capabilities that might transfer. They might be decathletes, in other words, instead of sprinters or marathoners.

A second indicator—one related to the first—is a candidate's demonstrated ability to gather able supporters. The modern presidency is not a solo sport.[8] Even the most gifted individual leader needs a team filled with capable people to achieve his or her goals. A candidate who can attract able followers is far more likely to succeed as president than one who cannot. If those followers stay with the leader over prolonged periods, it's an even better signal, because they know their leader better than almost anyone else does and have decided to stay on board.

UNFILTERED SUCCESSFUL PRESIDENTS

Of the five highest-ranked Unfiltered presidents, Washington took office in a situation with no modern parallels. Lincoln was covered in my previous book. Franklin Roosevelt steered the country through two of the greatest crises in its history, a combination of circumstances that is unlikely to recur, and was elected four times. All three men have much to teach us, but all three are also so exceptional that it's difficult to draw lessons from their careers that apply to modern presidents. Instead, I want to focus on two others: Theodore Roosevelt and Dwight Eisenhower. We'll also take a shorter look at Barack Obama. All three were Unfiltered presidents who had an enormous impact. Together, they offer ample insights into how we should go about assessing future Unfiltered candidates for the White House.

The "Bully Pulpit": Theodore Roosevelt

If they weren't so well substantiated, many stories from Theodore Roosevelt's life would seem drawn from folk tales. TR was barely forty-three when he succeeded the assassinated William McKinley to become the youngest president ever. By then he had already been a rancher, a best-selling author, police commissioner, assistant secretary of the navy, hero of the Spanish-American War, and governor.

Of the great presidents, TR may be the most magnetic. If Washington's titanic reserve and self-control often make him seem like a marble statue, Lincoln's wisdom, grace, and suffering like a secular saint, and FDR's sphinxlike ambiguity and callousness towards those around him almost unreachably distant, TR was a tornado of energy and drive and boyish enthusiasm, so much so that a British diplomat quipped, "You must always remember the President is about six."[9]

"HASTEN FORWARD QUICKLY THERE": THEODORE ROOSEVELT'S RISE

Theodore Roosevelt was born on October 27, 1858, to one of the most prominent families in New York. His father, also named Theodore but known as Thee, was a successful businessman with an active career in the Republican Party. TR idolized his father. There was only one choice in Thee's entire life that TR did not admire. In response to the demands of his pro-Southern wife, Thee hired a substitute to fight in his place during the Civil War. Although he spent the war working to improve the welfare of soldiers and their families, Thee never forgave himself and the choice shaped TR's life.[10]

TR suffered from life-threatening asthma as a child, and, despite his self-created myth that he defeated it through force of will, it plagued him throughout his life. The asthma kept him isolated from his peers and sufficiently weak that he was often bullied by them on those rare occasions when he did encounter them. His father's commitment to "Muscular Christianity," a philosophical movement that focused on physical self-improvement, led TR to begin a rigorous program of weightlifting that soon segued into other sports, particularly boxing, that he continued for the rest of his life.[11]

TR went to Harvard in 1876. While TR was there Thee was nominated to be the collector of the Port of New York (a position whose opportunities for corruption made it crucial to machine politics) but was rejected because of his commitment to government reform. Thee died of stomach cancer shortly thereafter, devastating his worshipful son. TR inherited enough wealth to ensure a comfortable life. After college he started Columbia Law School but grew bored and ran for the legislature, winning a seat at twenty-three. That same year he published his first book, *The Naval War of 1812*, to such acclaim that a copy was placed on every ship in the United States Navy and even British reviewers called it a classic of military history.[12]

TR made his mark in the Assembly by fighting corruption. He became leader of the Republican minority in his second term but was denied the speakership when Republicans took control of the Assembly in 1883. In February of 1884 his wife died of Bright's disease two days after giving birth to their daughter Alice, and his mother died of typhoid on the same day in the same home. An understandably devastated and depressed TR threw himself into his work in the legislature, but the combination of his psychological state and his loss of support from reformers when he decided to support the corrupt James Blaine after he won the Republican nomination convinced him to leave politics.[13]

TR spent much of the next two years in the West, where he established a cattle ranch that failed so badly it cost him half his fortune. It was, none-theless, a valuable experience. TR came from enormous wealth and privi-lege and spoke with the grammar and accent of his class. He once amused his employees by ordering some of the cowboys working for him to "hasten forward quickly there!" But he won their respect through a combination of brutally hard work (he routinely spent forty or more hours in the saddle) and remarkable courage, including knocking out with his fists an armed drunk who threatened him in a bar and chasing a trio of boat thieves down flooded and frozen rivers, capturing them, then single-handedly bringing them to the nearest sheriff. This required escorting all three, by himself and on foot, across the Dakota badlands for thirty-six hours, a task he undertook even though the norms of the time and place were that he could have simply executed them out of hand rather than take such a risk.[14]

In 1886 TR married his childhood sweetheart and reentered politics. At the request of party leaders, he ran for New York mayor despite having no chance. After his defeat he wrote *The Winning of the West*, a history of the frontier that was instantly acclaimed a classic by reviewers around the world and whose sales helped restore his diminished fortunes.[15]

Roosevelt supported Benjamin Harrison in the 1888 presidential election and was rewarded with a position on the U.S. Civil Service Commission. Although the position was usually considered a poorly paid sinecure, TR used it to crusade in favor of civil service reform. At the time most government positions were filled by the winner of the presidency and government employees were expected to contribute a portion of their salary to the party, filling its coffers for the next election. This, inevitably, led to both rampant corruption and gross incompetence. Opposing this practice had cost Thee his spot at the Port Authority, and TR did not miss the opportunity to take up his father's cause. Although he had little formal authority, he used his mastery of publicity to expose scandal after scandal, elevating himself to national prominence and doing so well that Democrat Grover Cleveland kept him on after his victory in the 1892 election even though TR had campaigned for the defeated Harrison.[16]

In 1894 a proreform Republican became mayor of New York and offered TR a position as one of the four members of the Board of New York City Police Commissioners. He quickly recruited two soon-to-be-legendary reformist journalists, Jacob Riis and Lincoln Steffens, to chronicle his efforts. He was immediately elected president of the board and set to work reforming the police force. The police chief, Thomas Byrnes, was a towering figure of enormous power and corruption. TR forced him to resign in nine days. TR and Riis soon went on a midnight patrol in disguise, surprising policemen who were supposed to be on their beats and discovering that most were ignoring their duties.[17]

TR pushed to improve standards throughout the force. He imposed merit appointments instead of choosing officers based on politics, mandated annual physical inspections, cracked down on corruption, and began the practice of giving medals for meritorious service. He became so popular that street vendors sold costumes of his distinctive glasses and buck teeth. He chose to rigorously enforce the state's law banning the sale of alcoholic beverages on Sundays and won national acclaim although he was met by protests in New York City. Instead of hiding, he attended demonstrations against him, even dancing polkas with girls in attendance, and left to cheers from the crowd.[18]

By 1896, however, opposition from Democrats and machine politicians had stymied TR's progress on the commission and soured the experience for him. When William McKinley became the Republican nominee for president, TR seized the opportunity, met with Mark Hanna, McKinley's enormously powerful campaign manager, and was sent crisscrossing the country on the heels of William Jennings Bryan, the Democrats' charismatic candidate. When McKinley won decisively, TR was able to leverage his hard work into the position he coveted and which his first book had prepared him for—assistant secretary of the navy. Although his appointment was delayed by a combination of opposition from machine Republicans and an (accurate) fear that he was eager to start a war, New York Republicans eventually persuaded McKinley to choose him at least in part because they felt he would be far less of a headache for them in Washington than he would be if he remained in his home state.[19]

As assistant secretary TR campaigned for increases in naval strength and, true to his unabashed and (even by the standards of the era) extreme imperialism, for the United States to seize Cuba from Spain. He was so vociferous on this subject that he once accosted Hanna at a reception, haranguing him so violently that he frightened Hanna's guests and caused Hanna to express his gratitude that TR had not been made assistant secretary of state, for if he had been, "we'd be fighting half the world."[20]

McKinley, a Civil War veteran, worked hard to avert war, enraging TR. When the USS *Maine* exploded in Havana Harbor (almost certainly by accident, although TR and most other Americans blamed Spain), public furor reached a crescendo and TR sent orders to American naval forces to prepare for war without authorization from McKinley or the secretary of the navy. When diplomacy failed, TR, then thirty-nine, resigned and worked with Leonard Wood to create the First U.S. Volunteer Cavalry

Regiment under Wood's command. His peers saw his choice to fight on the front lines as an act of madness. The regiment came to be known as the "Rough Riders" and was made up of volunteers from across the country, ranging from eastern elites to cowboys and Native Americans. It was a collection that only TR could have assembled. Soon after they arrived in Cuba, sickness amongst senior American officers led to Wood's promotion to commander of the Second Brigade and TR's to full colonel and command of the Rough Riders.[21]

The Rough Riders performed well in combat, including a charge up Kettle Hill on July 1, 1898 (part of the larger battle of San Juan Hill). TR was the only man on horseback and constantly exposed to enemy fire as he led his men up the hill under heavy fire, taking it while suffering heavier casualties than any other cavalry regiment. He personally killed at least one Spanish soldier. Once he had seized Kettle Hill's summit, he ordered his men to join the battle for San Juan Hill, contributing to the victory there as well.[22]

TR considered this battle the high point of his life, and friends would refer to him as Colonel Roosevelt ever afterwards. He was nominated for the Medal of Honor for his actions but the army, unhappy with the prominence of volunteers instead of career soldiers in the fighting, blocked him from receiving it despite his lobbying. He received it posthumously in 2001, making him the only recipient of the Nobel Peace Prize to also receive his nation's highest military honor, and one of only two father-son pairings to receive the Medal of Honor (his oldest son received it, also posthumously, for his heroism on D-Day).[23]

Fighting in Cuba continued for months, but as it bogged down into skirmishing the Rough Riders were demobilized. When the unit disassembled, TR's men surprised him with the gift of a Frederic Remington sculpture. The men then walked past their colonel in single file, many weeping as they said goodbye. They returned to their everyday lives while TR prepared to run for governor of New York.[24]

TR's heroics during the fighting and mastery of publicity had built on his already substantial public image to catapult him to national hero status. When he returned to New York Republicans were already organizing to nominate him for governor. He accepted immediately, only to find that Augustus Van Wyck, his Democratic opponent, seemed likely to win the election. TR responded with characteristic energy, orienting his campaign around battling the party machines and campaigning across the state. In a single day he traveled 212 miles by train, making seventeen stops and speaking at each. He turned forty only a few days before the election and won by just fewer than eighteen thousand votes, a triumph that even the party bosses whom he attacked acknowledged was entirely a product of his force of personality.[25]

As governor TR continued his war with the political bosses, focusing particularly on attacking the power of Mark Hanna. In a single session of the state legislature he secured the passage of bills that reformed the New York Civil Service, improved working conditions in sweatshops, limited women and children's working hours, mandated an eight-hour day for state employees, and strengthened unions. He also wrote his thirteenth book, a biography of Oliver Cromwell, in less than a month.[26]

In November 1899 McKinley's vice president Garret Hobart died, opening a slot on the Republican ticket. TR already had his eye on a presidential run in 1904. He didn't want to be vice president. Business and machine interests in New York, however, hated TR's reforms and became even more focused on removing him from his position of power when they saw his plans for his next annual message, which included calls to regulate utilities, inspect corporations, protect the environment, and remove corrupt officials. Once he began to implement these priorities, the New York Republican machine began drumming up support for his nomination for the vice presidency. Despite TR's best efforts, he was so unable to prevent this effort that it was said that "Roosevelt might as well stand under Niagara Falls and try to spit water back as to stop his nomination by this convention." Hanna was his major opposition. As TR's nomination became more certain he asked, "Don't any of you realize that there's only one life between this madman and the Presidency?" Hanna had lost much of his influence over McKinley, however. When the votes were counted, the only vote against TR was TR himself.[27]

The election was a rematch of the 1896 contest between McKinley and Bryan. McKinley once again ran a "front porch" campaign in which he did not travel, while TR crisscrossed the country lending his energy and oratory to the ticket. Buoyed by a booming economy and victory in the Spanish-American War, McKinley and Roosevelt won handily. On

September 5, only a few months into McKinley's second term, an anarchist named Leon Czolgosz shot him in Buffalo. Doctors initially believed that the wounds were so minor that TR left for vacation in the Adirondacks. A little over a week later, however, McKinley's condition deteriorated dramatically. TR frantically rushed back, and McKinley died early in the morning on September 14. TR was sworn in as president immediately thereafter.[28] This path to the presidency gives him a Filtration Score of 0.

THE IMPACT OF THE BIG STICK: THE PRESIDENCY OF THEODORE ROOSEVELT

Hanna's foreboding that TR would be dramatically different from the conservative McKinley was soon fulfilled. Of the five presidents highest-ranked by historians, only TR achieved this position without the benefit of some extraordinary crisis during his terms in office (Washington with the founding, Lincoln the Civil War, Franklin Roosevelt the Great Depression and World War II) or enormous unsought opportunity (Jefferson with the Louisiana Purchase).

TR did not replace a passive president. It is McKinley, not TR, whom the presidential scholar Lewis Gould credits with the invention of the modern presidency. TR's charisma, even at a remove of more than a century, is such that he tends to overshadow his predecessor.[29] In many ways, though, his choices represented less of a break with McKinley's than they did an expansion of ambition and an acceleration of execution far beyond what he might have attempted.

TR, partly through sheer force of personality, expanded the presidency and its powers. He initially proclaimed his intention to continue McKinley's policies in an "absolutely unbroken" fashion. In private, however, he soon showed his independence by stating, "I will be President." There was certainly some continuity, but he moved quickly to put his own mark on the government. Within three days after McKinley's death he had already changed how government appointments worked, and within a year he had replaced almost the entire cabinet with younger and more progressive appointees. He transformed the role of the presidency in American life by, for the first time, using his family to win popularity, while his own adventures, from rock-climbing with ambassadors to holding boxing matches in the White House, captivated the public.[30]

TR's foreign policy likely advanced the United States' involvement in global great-power politics by a decade.[31] He famously said that his policy was to "speak softly and carry a big stick." No one ever accused TR of speaking softly, but despite his assertiveness the United States avoided war during his presidency. TR ended up far less belligerent than Hanna had feared or might reasonably have been expected given both his pre-presidential attitudes and his frequent glorification of war.

TR nevertheless asserted American power more than any previous president, including issuing the "Roosevelt Corollary" to the Monroe Doctrine, which claimed that the United States had the right to intervene in Western Hemisphere nations, and fomenting a rebellion in Panama against Colombia to enable the construction of the Panama Canal. His signature achievement on the international scene was, ironically, his successful mediation of the Treaty of Portsmouth, which ended the Russo-Japanese War and won him the Nobel Peace Prize.[32]

In domestic policy too, Roosevelt moved much further than his predecessor. McKinley's administration had endorsed the Supreme Court's ruling that the federal government could only regulate trusts that had a monopoly over interstate commerce. TR took a far more aggressive stance. He used the Sherman Antitrust Act to regulate large businesses. He brought forty-four antitrust suits, more than twice as many as his three predecessors combined. He intervened in a strike by coal miners to help them win better working conditions. He removed corrupt officials from the government, worked with opposition Democrats to strengthen the government's ability to regulate railroads, strengthened regulations governing the purity of food and drugs, and put more than 230 million acres of public land under federal protection. He so vastly expanded the powers of the presidency that in his seven years in office he issued almost as many executive orders as all his predecessors combined.[33]

Perhaps more than anything else TR, partly through sheer force of personality, permanently shifted the relationship between the federal government, particularly the president, and other powerful actors in American society. Before TR the president was, in many ways, first among equals. Instead of accepting the Supreme Court's limits on federal power over monopolies, he decided to challenge them by suing to prevent the

J. P. Morgan–backed merger of two railroads. Morgan was, at the time, unquestionably the most powerful businessman in the world.[34]

Morgan and his allies came to the White House the next day, when Morgan told TR, "If we have done anything wrong, send your man [the attorney general] to my man and they can fix it up." Morgan's belief that the attorney general was simply a peer to his own counsel speaks for itself. TR's reply was simple: "That can't be done." Philander Knox, the attorney general, elaborated: "We don't want to fix it up. We want to stop it." Morgan asked, "Are you going to attack my other interests, the Steel Trust and others?" TR replied, "Certainly not—unless we find out that in any case they have done something we regard as wrong."[35]

The federal government's eventual victory in its lawsuit was a landmark expansion of its antitrust powers. It both paved the way for even more aggressive antitrust policies by TR's successors and demonstrated that business's domination of American economic life would be subject to "popular approval" via the president and Justice Department through the Sherman Antitrust Act and mediated by the court system.[36]

As with any president, TR's record is far from flawless. Even the most admiring biographer would concede that not all his innovations were successful or wise, perhaps most strikingly his abuse of executive power by threatening to use the Secret Service to investigate his political opponents in Congress. Nor was he progressive in all areas—despite his own self-image as Lincoln's heir on the issue, he did little to improve civil rights for African Americans while he was president. The overarching effect, however, was such that historians consistently rank TR only behind the unapproachable trinity of Washington, Lincoln, and his cousin Franklin when they assess presidential performance. When he stepped down in 1909, having declared that he would not run for a third term, he did so on a wave of popularity at home and esteem abroad that left him towering over American, and even world, politics.[37]

THE BULLY PULPIT: LEADER FILTRATION THEORY AND THEODORE ROOSEVELT

Describing TR as Unfiltered is almost redundant. He embodies the term. His meteoric rise was enabled by his family's wealth and influence. He was "a heartbeat away" from the presidency only because party elites specifically wanted to *remove* him from power. They had, essentially, identified TR as the person they most wanted to filter out, only for him to suddenly become president because of McKinley's assassination. Chester A. Arthur was also elevated to the presidency by an assassin, however, and he will never be suggested as an addition to Mount Rushmore.[38] So why did TR have such a huge impact, and why is it still viewed so positively?

Theodore Roosevelt's Intensifiers

If the first and most important intensifier for a presidential candidate is charisma, it's possible that no one in American history matches TR. It was so great, in fact, that it makes it difficult to write about him. A century after his death the sheer Brobdingnagian scale of his life and personality remains magnetic. If you've ever tucked a child into bed with a teddy bear, you're within the long shadow of Theodore Roosevelt. His contemporaries similarly found his charisma overwhelming. From his ability to draw media attention, to TR costumes eagerly purchased by ordinary New Yorkers, to his ability to win over hostile crowds with his presence, his charisma paved his path to the White House.

Almost as important, TR was also boosted by the enormous fame he sought and earned in Cuba. His book *The Rough Riders* was serialized in Scribner's magazine and so centered on his own exploits that the humorist Finley Peter Dunne said that it should have been titled "Alone in Cuba."[39] Similarly, the Roosevelts were one of the most prominent families in New York, and it's impossible to imagine TR's career following an even remotely similar path without his family's political and financial assistance. The presence of such intensifiers in such great strength means that the scale of TR's impact is less surprising than it first appears.

Theodore Roosevelt: Characteristics and Career

If the most important indicator of success is an absence of clear negative characteristics, TR scores well. TR had a healthy ego, to put it mildly. A true narcissist, however, would never have responded to Dunne's jest by writing back, "I regret to state that my family and friends are delighted with your review of my book" and making him a frequent guest at the White House.[40]

TR, with his boldness, charm, and almost suicidal courage, is the incarnation of Fearless Dominance. He has the highest score on that measure of any president.[41] While he was far more comfortable with violence than most of his contemporaries—in wartime TR had no hesitation about killing and seems to have had no mixed feelings afterward—none of his behavior in peacetime, particularly his strict personal morality, hints at Impulsive Antisociality.

TR's ideology shifted considerably over the course of his life but was mostly not out of the Progressive mainstream before and during his presidency. The exception is his unabashed and often racially loaded imperialism and enthusiasm for war, which were remarkable even for the era and the source of some elite Republican opposition to his rise in politics, but which, perhaps surprisingly, did not plunge the nation into war. That is, the strongest negative signal about him—Hanna's concerns that TR would plunge the United States into reckless wars—was not borne out, but was certainly entirely reasonable. It's easy to imagine a slightly less gifted version of TR allowing these worst instincts to lead him and the country into a disaster. Through some combination of luck, constraints, and perhaps maturation on the part of Roosevelt, he managed to avoid this dark path. His racial views would have been unacceptable in any modern setting, but they were—in sharp contrast to those of Andrew Johnson—well within the mainstream of the Republican politics of his era.

TR's Intellectual Brilliance is so clear and overwhelming it is almost intimidating. He wrote twelve books and one book of speeches and essays before he became vice president, with at least two acknowledged as classics. He spoke multiple languages and was "equally at home with experts in naval strategy, forestry, Greek drama, cowpunching, metaphysics, protective coloration, and football techniques."[42]

He was the youngest president, and his energy level was so high that simply reading about him can be tiring. While out west he was able to "ride a hundred miles a day, stay up all night on watch, and be back at work after a hastily gulped 3:00 A.M. breakfast." He had occasional depressive episodes, although the most pronounced was triggered by the simultaneous death of his wife and mother and may not say much about his temperament.[43]

TR did not have every possible positive signal or entirely lack negative ones, but the balance is so in his favor that his extraordinary success is less surprising than it might otherwise appear. He was the quintessential generalist, having succeeded as a soldier, author, police commissioner, and governor before becoming president. He was able to rally supporters so powerfully that he won over ranch hands and earned the adulation of the Rough Riders. He had negative signs. He was not self-made—few have ever had his family advantages. His imperialism was out of the mainstream, even by the standards of early-twentieth-century America.

That being said, TR seems as likely to succeed as an Unfiltered president as anyone could be, even without external circumstances that afforded him a singular opportunity like those offered to his peers at the top of the rankings.

"I Like Ike": Dwight David Eisenhower

Perhaps no president since Washington was more popular than Dwight Eisenhower, and none since Grant has served the country so well before becoming president. During his presidency Eisenhower was viewed as so passive that it was commonly joked that while it would be a national tragedy if he died and Nixon became president, the real catastrophe would be if his chief of staff Sherman Adams died, and Eisenhower were to take charge.

Research since then, aided by the declassification of the Eisenhower administration's internal discussions, has painted a completely different image of his eight years in office, where "an alert, politically astute Eisenhower . . . characteristically worked his will by indirection, concealing those of his maneuvers that belied his apolitical exterior." Eisenhower was simply so self-assured that he was happy to be perceived as a dunce if that helped him fulfill his goals.[44]

FROM ABILENE TO THE WHITE HOUSE VIA NORMANDY:
EISENHOWER'S RISE FROM OBSCURITY

Eisenhower was born in Texas on October 14, 1890, the third of seven sons in a lower-middle-class family. He had an undistinguished academic record and worked for two years before gaining his admission to West Point, where he graduated 61st in his class of 164 as a member of the legendary Class of 1915—"the class the stars fell on"—which produced two five-star generals, two four-star generals, seven lieutenant generals, twenty-four major generals, and twenty-five brigadier generals.[45]

Eisenhower missed combat in World War I but demonstrated an ability to acquire mentors by impressing some of the most important officers in the army. In 1926 he attended the army's competitive Command and General Staff College and, despite lacking many of the usual prerequisites, graduated first in his class. Afterwards he worked directly with Pershing, the general who had successfully led American soldiers in the First World War. He was famously reluctant to issue words of praise, yet described Eisenhower as possessing "unusual intelligence and constant devotion to duty."[46]

Eisenhower continued his army career, now boosted by Pershing's patronage. He was stationed in the Philippines as aide to Douglas MacArthur, then commanding American forces there. Despite Eisenhower's personal differences with the supremely egotistical MacArthur, his senior officer described Eisenhower in his final report as "a brilliant officer" who "in time of war . . . should be promoted to General rank immediately." Eisenhower returned to the United States and was made the chief of staff of the Third Infantry Division, then was brought to Washington to command the War Plans Division and report directly to the army's new chief of staff, George Marshall, who had once held the same post. Eisenhower was also promoted to brigadier general and, once the United States entered the Second World War, to major general. As head of the newly rechristened Operations Division, Eisenhower was functionally Marshall's deputy until he was given command of Operation Torch, the Allied invasion of North Africa.[47]

Torch was a clear field for the virtues that had won Eisenhower the respect of generals from Pershing to Marshall. No one has ever described Eisenhower as a tactical or operational genius, but even in the assessment of the British general Bernard Montgomery, usually quick to claim credit for himself and disparage any American rival, "he was a great Supreme Commander—a military statesman." After the success of Torch Eisenhower commanded the successful invasion of Sicily, then moved to London when FDR picked him over Marshall to command Operation Overlord, the planned invasion of France.[48]

It was Overlord and the eventual defeat of Nazi Germany that secured Eisenhower's place in history and the esteem of the American people.

Every Allied leader acknowledged that Eisenhower's management of the complexities of coalition warfare was masterful. Perhaps most revelatory of Eisenhower's underlying character, however, is the note that he wrote the evening before the D-Day landings in case they failed:

> Our landings in the Cherbourg-Havre area have failed to gain a satisfactory foothold and I have withdrawn the troops. My decision to attack at this time was based upon the best information available. The troops, the air, and the Navy did all that bravery and devotion to duty could do. If any blame or fault attaches to the attempt it is mine alone.[49]

As the war wound to a close, Eisenhower's potential political future became increasingly important. It is a testament to both his towering popularity and the esteem in which he was held by those who knew him best that when he and General Omar Bradley met with Truman during the Potsdam Conference, Bradley reported that Truman said to Eisenhower, "General, there is nothing that you may want that I won't try to help you get. That definitely and specifically includes the presidency in 1948." Eisenhower assured Truman that he had no plans to run in 1948, but no clearer acknowledgment of his extraordinary stature is imaginable.[50]

After the war Eisenhower served briefly as American military governor in Germany before returning to Washington to replace Marshall as army chief of staff. In June 1947 he retired from the army and was made president of Columbia University. There he wrote *Crusade in Europe,* a memoir of his experience in World War II that was heralded as a classic and has remained a vital resource for historians. It is not a literary masterpiece like Grant's *Personal Memoirs,* but it is one of the best books written by a president and made even more impressive by the speed with which it was produced. He worked with two editors, but Eisenhower was very much the book's author. One of them described watching him dictate five thousand words extemporaneously that required almost no editing to be published.[51]

Leading members of both parties tried to get him to run on their ticket. A Gallup poll found that he would be the most popular candidate for the nomination in *either* party. As primaries played only a relatively small role in nominations at the time, however, it is unlikely Eisenhower could have won the Republican nomination, as Governor Thomas Dewey, the eventual nominee, and Senator Robert Taft, the leader of the party's isolationist wing, had already captured the support of most state delegations.

Eisenhower was an effective administrator at Columbia but never understood academic life or gelled with the faculty there. He was also distracted for most of his brief tenure by Truman's request that he continue to serve the country, first as an adviser to the secretary of defense and then as the informal chairman of the Joint Chiefs (the position had not yet been statutorily established). In December 1950 he took a leave of absence to become the Supreme Commander of NATO, a position he held until May 1952, when he finally retired from the army once again. He returned to Columbia for a few months, technically, but was in practice largely running for the White House.[52]

Eisenhower was drawn to politics by his desire to ensure that the United States maintain its commitment to NATO. Powerful forces in the Republican Party, including Hoover, the last Republican president, and Taft, the likely next Republican nominee, opposed American participation in the alliance and were calling for American forces to withdraw from Europe. Early in 1951 Eisenhower, on his own initiative, asked Taft to visit him for a secret meeting. Eisenhower told Taft that if he committed to collective security, Eisenhower would announce that he was not interested in the Republican nomination. Such an announcement would make Taft the virtually certain nominee and the likely next president. Taft refused, so enraging the normally controlled Eisenhower that he described Taft to a reporter as "a very stupid man."[53]

While Eisenhower remained ambivalent about running, Dewey, the leader of the Republican internationalist wing that had been discredited by its candidates' defeats in 1940, 1944, and 1948, took the initiative in getting him to run. Dewey endorsed Eisenhower on *Meet the Press*, then Eisenhower's friend and fellow general Lucius Clay simply informed Sherman Adams, then governor of New Hampshire, that Eisenhower was a Republican and willing to appear on the ballot in that crucial primary state, forcing the issue. Isolationist Republicans rallied behind Taft to stop Eisenhower, boosted by the fact that Taft had already secured 450 of the 604 delegates necessary to win the nomination. By the time the primaries were over, Taft had 525 delegates and Eisenhower 500. Dewey's influence over the New York delegation was enough, however, to swing some of

Taft's delegates there to Eisenhower on the first ballot, setting off a stampede in Eisenhower's favor that allowed him to scrape to a victory.[54]

The general election was a one-sided affair with Eisenhower romping to victory with perhaps the most insipid, yet effective, slogan in American political history: "I like Ike." The major issue was American involvement in Korea, which naturally advantaged the conqueror of Nazi Germany over the seemingly bookish Democratic nominee, Adlai Stevenson. Any remaining drama was eliminated when Eisenhower promised to personally visit Korea. Eisenhower won 55 percent of the popular vote, 39 of the 48 states, and 442 of 531 Electoral College votes. Republicans rode his coattails to control of both the House and Senate.[55]

A NEW LOOK AT THE COLD WAR: THE IMPACT OF EISENHOWER'S PRESIDENCY

As president, Eisenhower's impact vastly exceeded anything contemporaneously understood by those outside his administration, although his administration was far from flawless. His interventions in Iran and Guatemala are black marks. He has also tends to be marked down for his seeming lack of public opposition to McCarthyism or support for civil rights, although recent research suggests that both may have been the continuation of Eisenhower's general strategy of working behind the scenes. Particularly on civil rights, he may have been far more effective in advancing the cause than had previously been believed.[56] Similarly, the Eisenhower-era economy, although rosy in retrospect, had two significant recessions during his eight years in office, although it is hard to know how much of the blame for that should be attributed to his policies.[57]

Balanced against these, however, is a record of extraordinary success, particularly in foreign policy, that stretches far beyond the interstate highway system for which his presidency is remembered today.[58] In terms of impact, Eisenhower's first and largest contribution was assuring the defeat of the Republican Party's isolationist wing, which rejected both American involvement in Western Europe and the social programs of the New Deal. That branch of the party was powerful enough that Taft came close to the nomination despite Eisenhower's popularity, and it is likely Taft would have won the 1952 election. (Democrats had won the last five presidential elections, and six consecutive victories by the same party, especially given the stalemate in Korea, would have been difficult even for FDR's coalition.)

A Republican like Taft, who was pledged to withdraw from NATO and minimize American commitments, would have set the Cold War on a very different course. This danger was so pressing that Truman only decided not to run for reelection after Eisenhower entered the race, assuring him that the postwar structure that he had created would be maintained. Eisenhower's positions were so far from those that dominated the Republican Party that his relations with Congress improved once Democrats regained control there. Late in his presidency a frustrated Eisenhower once told his secretary, "I don't know why anyone should be a member of the Republican Party."[59]

Second, Eisenhower was, in the words of John Lewis Gaddis, the dean of Cold War historians, "at once the most subtle and brutal strategist of the nuclear age." Unlike most of his predecessors and any of his successors, he was intimately familiar with the carnage of total war. This resulted in his adopting two seemingly contradictory, but in fact complementary, stances. Eisenhower insisted that American plans for war with the Soviet Union have no restrictions on the use of nuclear weapons, a strategy he termed "Massive Retaliation." He rejected the idea that any war with the Soviet Union would be as "nice [and] sweet" as World War II. Instead he assumed that both sides would freely use every weapon at their disposal. By doing so he sought to ensure that any war would be so terrible that it could never be fought.[60]

This strategic posture allowed Eisenhower to bluff far more effectively. Making credible threats is one of the most important, and most difficult, acts in international politics. A president's threat to use nuclear weapons might be ignored if the United States had nonnuclear options. By ensuring that American war plans required the use of nuclear weapons, Eisenhower made his nuclear threats credible, which allowed him to bluff that he was willing to use them and extract significant concessions in crises. This bluffing played a crucial role in his successful negotiations to end the Korean War.[61]

Because nuclear weapons are considerably less expensive than conventional forces, Massive Retaliation let Eisenhower slash the defense budget. He called this approach the "New Look." He viewed the Cold War as a long-term political, military, and economic struggle, and believed that maximizing American economic strength was crucial to eventual victory.[62]

Measured in constant dollars, from 1953 to 1956 Eisenhower shrank the defense budget by almost 30 percent despite vigorous opposition from both the military and his own party. His unique prestige on military matters, combined with his well-honed skill at managing large bureaucracies, allowed him to win political fights that no one else could have.[63]

Third, although Eisenhower was willing to make nuclear *threats,* he was extraordinarily unwilling to use nuclear weapons or, indeed, go to war at all. Eisenhower was the only American representative at the Potsdam Conference who opposed using nuclear bombs against Japan. When French soldiers were trapped at Dien Bien Phu in Vietnam, Eisenhower was the only member of the National Security Council who refused to intervene to rescue them, and when his national security assistant gave him the Joint Chiefs' plan, which required nuclear weapons, he responded, "I certainly do not think that the atomic bomb can be used by the United States unilaterally. You boys must be crazy. We can't use those awful things against Asians for the second time in less than ten years. My God." In fact, after the Korean War he inherited ended in July 1953, not one American soldier was killed in combat for the rest of his term. Eisenhower proudly and justly boasted that "the United States never lost a soldier or a foot of ground in my administration. We kept the peace. People ask how it happened—by God, it didn't just happen, I'll tell you that."[64] No other postwar president could say the same.

Eisenhower's aversion to both war and defense spending was deeply felt. Early in his presidency, against the advice of his cabinet, he gave his most eloquent speech:

> Every gun that is made, every warship launched, every rocket fired signifies, in the final sense, a theft from those who hunger and are not fed, those who are cold and are not clothed. This world in arms is not spending money alone. It is spending the sweat of its laborers, the genius of its scientists, the hopes of its children. The cost of one modern heavy bomber is this: a modern brick school in more than 30 cities. It is two electric power plants, each serving a town of 60,000 population. It is two fine, fully equipped hospitals. It is some fifty miles of concrete pavement. We pay for a single fighter plane with half a million bushels of wheat. We pay for a single destroyer with new homes that

could have housed more than 8,000 people. This is, I repeat, the best way of life to be found on the road the world has been taking. This is not a way of life at all, in any true sense. Under the cloud of threatening war, it is humanity hanging from a cross of iron ... Is there no other way the world may live?[65]

THE DEXTEROUS HIDDEN HAND: LFT AND
THE EISENHOWER PRESIDENCY

What can we learn about successful Unfiltered presidents from Eisenhower? His classification as Filtered or Unfiltered is the closest call of the presidents in this chapter. He spent six-and-a-half years as a general from late 1941 to early 1948, then slightly over a year back in service as Supreme Commander of NATO. In length of service this gives him just under eight years, normally making him a borderline case.[66]

What tips the scales is his extraordinary status as an American hero. Some Republican elites backed Eisenhower, but they were from the internationalist wing that had been discredited by repeated defeats and whose only chance of victory was Eisenhower's immense popularity. Eisenhower's political views were largely irrelevant to his rise to the presidency. They were probably, in fact, a hindrance, as his path to the Republican nomination would have been much smoother had he aped Taft's views. The combination makes him Unfiltered, with a Filtration Score of 3.5, which is lower than that of almost three-fourths of the presidents.

Eisenhower's Intensifiers

Eisenhower's most important intensifier was his overwhelming prestige. Only Grant and Washington can match or surpass his extraordinary position when he took office, and there's no question that this produced a halo effect of extraordinary power. Simonton does not rate Eisenhower as particularly charismatic, but this did not matter.[67] In the minds of many, perhaps even most, Americans, he was the man who defeated Nazi Germany. What charisma could match that?

Eisenhower: Characteristics and Career

In predicting whether he would have a negative or positive impact, Eisenhower's prepresidential career gives many reasons for optimism. He was clearly up to the job. Eisenhower may not have had the astonishing

Intellectual Brilliance of Jefferson or TR, but he had the horsepower to lead Overlord, one of the most complex endeavors in human history, and to write a book that has stood the test of time. Eisenhower was no intellectual, but anyone who doubts that he had the baseline intelligence to be a successful president is revealing far more about themselves than him. Similarly, no president, perhaps even no person, has ever faced a harder managerial challenge than Eisenhower did in World War II.

Eisenhower also seems to have entirely lacked façades. There is nothing in his background that even hints at the Dark Triad. No one with high levels of Impulsive Antisociality could ever have written the note Eisenhower did assuming personal responsibility for a possible failure on D-Day. Nothing about his career suggests any tendency to take unnecessary risks, and his whole motivation for running for the presidency was an ideology far more complex than Taft's isolationism. The major concern about Eisenhower is likely his age and health, and his presidency suffered from his health issues, particularly his heart attack in 1955. Even so, his prepresidential energy level was so high that at sixty-one he routinely worked more than eighty hours a week.[68]

Finally, Eisenhower's career also seems a strong indicator of success. Although he made his career almost entirely in the military, his experience in World War II was not that of a pure battlefield commander. Even his most favorable biographers have never suggested that Eisenhower was Patton's equal as a tactician, but no one could have handled the diplomatic and strategic tasks required of a supreme commander as well as Eisenhower did. At least on the foreign policy side of a president's job, it's hard to imagine a better test, and Eisenhower passed with flying colors. Absent a candidate with TR's unique capabilities, Eisenhower may be the best-case Unfiltered presidential candidate. The U.S. Army's normal bureaucratic filtration system, combined with George Marshall's extraordinary eye for talent, combined to find the very best person for the job, and the same qualities that served him so well during the war helped make his presidency a success.

Shadow Cases: "The Audacity of Hope": Barack Hussein Obama

It's not necessary to plunge into Barack Obama's path to the presidency, given how recent it was, but a quick survey helps show how we can use the theory to assess modern candidates. Obama was born on August 4, 1961, in Hawaii. He was the only child of Barack Obama Sr., a Kenyan, and Ann Dunham, a white woman studying at the University of Hawaii. Obama's parents divorced less than three years after he was born. His father returned to Kenya while his mother married a man from Indonesia and moved there with her son, where he lived until he was ten. He returned to Hawaii to live with his maternal grandparents and, with help from a scholarship, attended the elite Punahou private school. In 1979 he went to Occidental College, then transferred to Columbia in 1981. After graduating he worked for Business International Corporation for a year, then moved to Chicago to work as a community organizer.[69]

Obama entered Harvard Law in 1988. He became the first African American president of the *Law Review*. He graduated magna cum laude from law school and accepted a job teaching at the University of Chicago Law School, where he taught until 2004. While there he wrote a memoir, *Dreams from My Father*, which did not gain much attention when it was published but received rapturous reviews after Obama became a political star.[70]

In 1996 Obama made his first run for office when he ran for the Illinois State Senate. He displayed a knack for sharp political maneuvering when his campaign successfully challenged the legitimacy of the nominating petitions for his opponents in the Democratic primary, removing them from the race and leaving him unopposed for the nomination. He had a successful but not enormously distinguished career there, punctuated by an unsuccessful run for the House of Representatives. In 2004 he ran for the Senate when the incumbent Democrat, Carol Moseley Braun, decided not to run for reelection. Obama had stated his objection to the Iraq War before the campaign and used that to separate himself from his Democratic rivals.[71]

After Obama won the primary, he was picked to deliver a keynote at that year's Democratic National Convention. While walking the stage before his speech, the reporter David Mendell remarked that he was impressing the most powerful people in the party. His legendary reply perfectly expressed the supreme confidence that had brought him to the stage. "I'm LeBron, baby," he said, "I can play on this level. I got some game." His speech that night was instantly legendary, reducing many in the audience to tears and catapulting him into the national spotlight.[72] Even now, seventeen years later, I remember watching it with my parents on television and turning to them afterwards, thunderstruck, to say, "My God, that guy's going to be president one day." I had no idea it would happen so quickly.

Obama won his Senate race handily, aided greatly by his Republican opponent withdrawing from the race close to Election Day after revelations from his divorce filing. He stayed in the Senate until just after his election as president, serving on a variety of committees and voting with the Democratic Party but, unsurprisingly for a new senator, had no major legislative achievements.[73]

In February 2007 Obama began his run. The luck that paved his way to the Senate helped again. He won the Iowa caucuses while John Edwards barely beat Hillary Clinton for second. Edwards soon withdrew from the race because of a scandal over adultery and campaign finance. Had he dropped out before the caucuses, it is likely that Clinton would have won. Before his victory Obama was not polling very well with African American voters, who feared that he could never garner enough white support to vote. Once he proved he could win lily-white Iowa, the African American vote consolidated behind him.[74]

Had Edwards withdrawn earlier, and Obama lost to Clinton in Iowa, then again in New Hampshire, this might never have happened. The two ran an extremely close race, with Obama finally winning the nomination when Clinton withdrew four days *after* the last primary votes were cast. He won the general election in a landslide over Republican John McCain, with his campaign boosted by the same string of catastrophes described in chapter 4.[75]

OBAMA THROUGH THE LENS OF FILTRATION

This brief narrative suggests just how Unfiltered Obama was. He had spent barely three years in the Senate when he became the nominee. He had *never* won a federal or statewide election against a credible opponent. Had Edwards withdrawn even a few weeks earlier, he might never have won the nomination. Even the general election did little to filter him. Democrats' advantages were so vast that it is difficult to see how any

Democrat could have lost. This gives Obama a Filtration Score of 4, comfortably in the lower half of all presidents.

OBAMA'S IMPACT

In some ways it's difficult to assess Obama's impact when he still looms so large in our collective memory. I believe it was far larger than the one he's currently credited with, but that assessment is tentative at best and subject to historical reassessments, revelations from the archives, and the simple passage of time.[76] One example of his impact is likely to be the passage of the Affordable Care Act (ACA). The reason for that is simple. Whether or not the ACA was wise legislation, there is simply no question that when it was passed, and for years afterwards, it was hugely unpopular. In 2013, four years after it was drafted, the ACA had 40 percent approval and 50 percent disapproval, a number that had been roughly constant for the past four years.[77] That unpopularity helped drive the enormous Republican victories of the 2010 midterm elections.

Reforming the American health care system and expanding medical insurance coverage had been a central priority of the Democratic Party for generations. Any Democratic president would have attempted to do so, as Obama's Democratic predecessor, Bill Clinton, did. Clinton's health care reform effort foundered, however, on the simple fact that health care reform was incredibly unpopular.[78] This would have been enough to stop any normal politician. If you want to predict the position of almost anyone in politics, the popular one is a good first guess. But, rarely, Obamacare was passed despite absolute opposition from the Republican Party and deep skepticism from the public.

Although the idea of reform was always received positively, any specific reform met enormous opposition from an electorate where voters were far more likely to have health insurance than Americans in general did. Normal politicians simply do not pass incredibly unpopular bills. Clinton was as skilled a political operator as the White House has ever seen—one vastly more experienced than Obama—and his attempt failed completely and helped to produce the Republican Party's enormous victory in 1994. Obama, under similar political circumstances, nonetheless pushed his party to pass the bill and take the hit at the polls. That simply was not the act of a normal politician. It suggests that when a full analysis of his administration is possible, his individual impact is likely to be judged quite high.

Obama's Intensifiers

Obama clearly had a powerful charismatic impact on his followers. Surely no other modern American politician could have drawn a crowd of tens of thousands to a speech in Berlin even before he won the 2008 election, a crowd that the *Guardian* said was brought there by his "rock star charisma."[79] Obama's rhetorical skill and the charisma that came with it were a key component of his meteoric ascent, and it rallied adoring supporters who carried him through the primaries despite the support of the Democratic Party establishment for Hillary Clinton.

Obama: Characteristics and Career

Assessing Obama as a success or failure is beyond the scope of this book, and impossible with any degree of certainty this soon after his term in office. As with all the other presidents in this study, I'm using the historians' rankings to classify Obama as a success here. For what it's worth, their assessment accords with my own. The important question here, though, is if the theory would have picked Obama as a likely success.

Yes. Most importantly, there is nothing in his background that hints at major façades. The former president of *Harvard Law Review* and instructor in constitutional law at the University of Chicago who wrote a well-received memoir clearly had the Intellectual Brilliance to succeed as president.

Obama's background also has an array of positive signs. On top of his intellectual abilities, he was young enough and had high enough energy levels to leave little doubt that he could handle the physical strains of the office. He came from a much poorer family than most of his predecessors, and there can be no doubt that being Black made it considerably harder for him to rise in politics. Even his name, distinctively foreign-sounding to most American ears, and with the middle name Hussein inevitably associated with the country's greatest enemy of the two decades before his election, was a barrier. These are exactly the sort of handicaps that strongly indicate positive future performance. He had negative indicators, most strikingly a lack of managerial experience at any scale larger than a Senate office. Overall this record suggests, however, that he was a far better bet than most Unfiltered presidents.

THE PROMISE OF UNFILTERED PRESIDENTS

Unfiltered presidential candidates are a gamble. If the system is functioning well, that gamble will generally be a bad one. If you have a high degree of confidence that you could get a capable and moderately successful leader, then betting on a wild card would require either a truly dire situation or great confidence that you could somehow make sure your wild card came up a winner. Unfiltered presidents are, under normal circumstances, a bad bet.

From Washington and Lincoln to the Roosevelts and Eisenhower, however, the United States has sometimes won that bet to an extent that even the wealthiest lottery winner would envy. The result has been a government that has, on occasion, been led by remarkable Unfiltered presidents who left their mark on the nation and the world. There are few, if any, nations on earth that would not feel blessed if they had ended up with an Eisenhower or a Theodore Roosevelt.

The nature of the American political system means, furthermore, that the United States has taken this bet often and is likely to continue doing so. This makes the job of identifying which Unfiltered presidential candidates are likely to succeed extraordinarily important. If the task is performed successfully, however, it can remake, or even save, the country.

Most presidents should be Filtered precisely because they can address normal problems without Unfiltered presidents' risk of catastrophe. A long string of Trumans and H. W. Bushes would serve any country well. If they did not reach Lincoln's towering heights, they are also unlikely to follow in Andrew Johnson's footsteps. They can deliver good leadership, but rarely great leadership.

This chapter, however, presents us with an even more tempting prospect. Imagine how different American history would have been if we had replaced just one disastrous president like Pierce or Buchanan, or even a mediocrity like Coolidge or Carter, with an Eisenhower or (either) Roosevelt.

Filtered presidents handle the normal problems that are the normal business of government. Unfiltered presidents can, sometimes, do the nearly impossible. Abraham Lincoln saved the United States. Theodore Roosevelt changed our conception of the role of government and greatly accelerated the process of preserving the American natural environment. Eisenhower ended the Korean War, slashed defense budgets, and committed Republicans to an internationalist stance that lasted for two generations. None were perfect. But each left the country and the world in a far better place than anyone else could have.

If we evaluate Unfiltered candidates to eliminate those with inadequacies and façades, while picking brilliant ones who are healthy and high-energy, who have succeeded across a wide variety of fields, and who have overcome significant handicaps to their rise to the elite of American society, we might be able to do better than good. Greatness requires luck. But, as the scientist Louis Pasteur said, "Luck favors the prepared mind." Or, if you prefer baseball, Branch Rickey once said, "Luck is the residue of design."[80] This chapter gives us the tools, if we choose to use them, to maximize the United States' odds of picking truly great presidents. We have rarely needed one more.

6 Assessing Filtered and Unfiltered Candidates

Almost half of the presidents of the United States are Unfiltered, and American elections are frequently swayed by essentially random events—third-party candidates (1912 and 1992), terrorist attacks (1860), assassination attempts (1912), and the death of the member of a candidate's family (1892).[1] Just in the last few years we have seen one whose outcome may have been swung by ballot design in a single county of a single state (2000) and the various extraordinary events (an FBI investigation and foreign interference) of 2016, whose full impact it is still too early to assess.

The American political system, in other words, has long been dancing on the edge of a cliff. If the populist demagogue Huey Long had won the presidency during the Great Depression, the United States would likely look very different today. If anyone other than Lincoln had won in 1860, it might not exist. If the previous five chapters have convinced you of nothing else, I hope you left them believing that the identity of the president sometimes matters immensely, but that presidents have often been chosen for awful reasons, or sometimes even no reason at all. Some presidents have been so extraordinary that one can only look back and marvel at the combination of luck, skill, and perhaps divine intervention that put them in the White House, but the system has also struggled to block candidates who simply are not up to the job.

To see how the theory can help us do a better job today, let's use it to assess the forty-fifth and forty-sixth presidents of the United States, Donald J. Trump and Joseph Robinette Biden, when they were candidates. Before going further, two facts. First, I developed the theory in my doctoral dissertation, which I finished in 2010, and first published it in *Indispensable* in 2012. It was originally meant to examine leaders of all kinds of organizations, from CEOs to dictators. As my research developed, I examined presidents largely because historians' rankings of them made it possible to test my theory quantitatively, and because there is more data available about them than any other set of leaders. In the 2012 election, between an incumbent and an Unfiltered challenger who had many positive signs, assessing the options using Leader Filtration Theory was an interesting but largely theoretical exercise.

It is fair to say that the risks and rewards of Unfiltered leaders became much more salient in 2016—which leads to the second fact: in 2016 candidate Trump, as evaluated by the theory, and particularly by the more-developed version of the theory that I had been working on since writing *Indispensable,* which has been published for the first time in this book, set off alarm bells. Given the intense partisanship of American politics, I have written this section keeping two guidelines strictly in mind. The first is that, in the spirit of fairness and to show how to use the theory to evaluate candidates prospectively, it uses only information available prior to Trump's 2016 victory.

Second, I underscore again that the questions the theory asks of any candidate are (within broad bounds) *policy agnostic.* They don't care what party you're a member of. Charisma and Intellectual Brilliance, for example, aren't matters of party, and they are usually equally represented in both. Which means, regardless of whether you agree with a candidate's platform, arriving at the right answers to these questions should leave you comfortable (though maybe not happy) that a candidate gains the Oval Office. Correspondingly, if a candidate had your ideal set of policies in every way, but flunked these questions, you should still not want him or her to be president. To put it in the most extreme terms, policy differences don't matter in a nuclear wasteland.

Table 5   LFT's Questions for Candidates

Question 1: Filtered or unfiltered?	
UNFILTERED	**FILTERED**
Question 2: Inadequacies?	Question 2: Support or opposition from political elites?
Intellectual brilliance Managerial ability	
Question 3: Intensifiers?	Question 3: Representing a single concentrated interest?
Charisma Fame Unearned advantages	
Question 4: Façades?	Question 4: Warnings of decline?
Question 5: Positive Indicators?	

There are distinct questions for Filtered and Unfiltered presidents (table 5). Because we have more confidence in the basic capability of Filtered presidents, the questions about Filtered presidents are simpler. I'll start with them, then move on to analyzing Unfiltered candidates. With that said, let's go back in time and consider Biden and Trump. Are they Filtered or Unfiltered?

QUESTION 1: FILTERED OR UNFILTERED?

This one isn't a close call for either. Candidate Trump was the most Unfiltered candidate to ever earn a major party's nomination. He entered the race with no prior governmental or political service and garnered little support from party elites until his capture of the nomination was inevitable, with some, including his last remaining opponent in the primaries,

Texas senator Ted Cruz, refusing to endorse him even at the convention. Trump had a prolonged career in business working for his father's company, but Trump's Filtration Score of 0 makes him as entirely Unfiltered as it is possible for an elected president to be.

Candidate Biden, on the other hand, was as far on the Filtered end of the spectrum as Trump was on the Unfiltered. He spent thirty-six years in the Senate and eight years as the vice president before capturing the Democratic Party nomination as the clear choice of the party's establishment. This gives Biden a Filtration Score of 44—almost twice that of the previous record holders, Buchanan and Ford, both of whom are tied at 24. Biden and Trump, in other words, are paradigmatic examples of Filtered and Unfiltered candidates.

Assessing Filtered Candidates

Filtered candidates are, in a sense, preassessed. That's what filtration is, after all. So success is our baseline expectation of Filtered candidates for the presidency, and evaluating them is far less complex than it is for their Unfiltered counterparts. Given our baseline expectation of Filtered Success, we're looking for reasons particular to an individual candidate that explain why, in his or her case, the filtration system might have failed. Based on the research described in the previous chapters, we need to ask three relatively simple questions:

1. How do the candidate's peers in the political system respond to his or her candidacy? Are they enthusiastic or horrified? If they're enthusiastic, or at least accepting, then we should have confidence that the Filtered candidate meets the basic requirements of the presidency. If they're horrified, then we should guess there's a reason for that and think of it as a strong warning sign. In 2016, for example, Republican elites clearly strongly opposed the presidential campaign of Republican senator Ted Cruz, suggesting that their close experience with him had left them very hostile to the idea of him as president.

2. Is the candidate the representative of a single concentrated interest that has seized control of his or her party? That interest need not be as purely malign as slavery to have enormously negative effects as it distorts national policy more and more in its own favor. Every political

party has interest groups with power disproportionate to their size. But when one or a small coalition of those groups has become so powerful that they can sacrifice broader interests to their own welfare and choose a nominee to pursue that policy, the filtration system can fail, as it did with Buchanan. That judgment is, of course, inherently subjective. But we can make it less so by seeing if there are disjunctions between the policies pursued by a party's elected officials and the majority of its members. This would be strong evidence that a party's elite are catering to a powerful interest group instead of the broader party.

3. Does the candidate have characteristics that suggest that their abilities may decline while in office? Filtration is based on elites' close contact with the candidate in the past. If a candidate's past is not a likely reflection of their future, then, essentially, what they filtered won't be what they get.

So, how does candidate Biden score on these questions? On the first, Biden was clearly the choice of the party establishment. His position as Barack Obama's vice president, his unparalleled length of time in senior political office, and his apparent appeal to critical lower-middle-class white voters all combined to make him the overwhelming choice of Democratic Party elites. Once his campaign stabilized after his victory in South Carolina, he was able to rapidly assemble endorsements from many of his primary opponents, with even his last opponent, Bernie Sanders, conceding and endorsing him far more quickly than he had done with Hillary Clinton four years earlier. Biden might not have been the first choice of all Democratic elites, but virtually all of them were happy to support him for the presidency.[2]

Second, was Biden chosen for the nomination primarily by a single powerful interest group? Once again, the 2020 primaries provide an unambiguous answer to this question. Over the course of his long career, Biden maintained a position extremely close to that of the median Democrat. He built on this track record during the campaign by consciously positioning himself as the candidate of the center, even highlighting his long history of working with Republicans. His campaign, which initially stumbled badly, was rescued by strong support from the Black community in South Carolina.[3] Far from being forced on the party by a single interest group, Biden captured the nomination by being the most broadly acceptable of the candidates.

Biden's performance on the third question, however, is far less reassuring. His unprecedentedly long career at the senior levels of American politics means that his age is equally unprecedented—when elected, he was the oldest person ever elected president by seven years over the previous record holder (Trump). Biden has released his medical records and has not had a major health incident in thirty years. For a seventy-seven-year-old man, his health is exceptional.[4]

For a seventy-seven-year-old man is, however, a very important caveat. Aging has significant effects on leader performance, including a decrease in energy levels, an increase in vulnerability to illness, and shifts in personality, and these risks increase substantially with each year as someone gets into their late seventies. This risk is so pronounced, in fact, that a man of Biden's age and health history would probably not qualify for life insurance under any terms and, if it were issued, a simple ten-year term life policy that would pay out $400,000 would likely cost almost $4,000 per month—more than two hundred times what it would cost Pete Buttigieg, one of Biden's rivals in the primaries.[5]

An overall assessment of Biden, therefore, is that we should have a high expectation that he would succeed as a Filtered president (that is, good but not great performance and a high degree of skill at using the president's levers of power). The greatest risk he presents is that his performance in office will not reflect his track record due to the health risks of aging, a risk that will increase the longer he spends in office. At the time this was written, it was far too soon into Biden's presidency to judge the accuracy of this forecast.

Assessing Unfiltered Candidates: Donald J. Trump

Assessing a supremely Filtered candidate like Biden is relatively straightforward. The political system, after all, has already done it for you. That's what filtration is. With an Unfiltered presidential candidate, we need to do what the system couldn't. Even if you think the product of the system will be a disaster, you want to avoid an Andrew Johnson scenario. What, then, would the way of assessing Unfiltered candidates presented by this book have said about the most Unfiltered presidential candidate (and president) of all time, Donald J. Trump.

QUESTION 2: INADEQUACIES

Since Trump is Unfiltered, the next question is, does his background tell us that he has the basic capabilities to succeed as president? Answering that requires us to assess his Intellectual Brilliance and managerial abilities.

Intellectual Brilliance

As a candidate, Trump often claimed to have extraordinary intelligence. He frequently mentioned his status as a graduate of the Wharton School of Business and has claimed to have graduated first in his class, although the evidence available in 2016 suggested that he was in fact an undistinguished student who was admitted to Wharton's undergraduate program because of his father's influence. Trump's refusal to release his academic transcripts means they are not available to substantiate his claims of academic excellence.[6]

Trump claims credit for nineteen books, a total higher than any of his predecessors except Theodore Roosevelt. The 2016 evidence is overwhelming, however, that he had little to do with writing them. His first and most successful one, *The Art of the Deal,* was ghostwritten by Tony Schwartz, and Trump's total contributions, per Schwartz, "were a few red marks made with a fat-tipped Magic Marker, most of which deleted criticisms that Trump had made of powerful individuals he no longer wanted to offend." Otherwise, Schwartz told *The New Yorker* in 2016, "Trump changed almost nothing." The same appears to be true for his other books, rendering them unhelpful in establishing the candidate's Intellectual Brilliance.[7]

Candidate Trump frequently cited his wealth as evidence of his genius. Although success in business (or most other fields) is no guarantee of high intelligence, it is certainly a positive indicator. Trump claimed to be a "self-made" man whose only assistance from his father was a "small loan" of $1 million. At the time of the election, it was clear that he had received significantly more help from his father than that, although its true magnitude was unknown. Trump refused to publish tax returns or business records that would allow the amount of aid he received from his family to be judged.

Investigative reporting by the *New York Times* after the election revealed that he had actually inherited hundreds of millions of dollars from his father through a variety of tax evasion schemes, many of them likely entirely illegal, but that information was not available during the campaign. Similarly, other leaks of his taxes show that Trump's businesses routinely ran at a loss and were burdened by hundreds of millions of dollars in debt, suggesting that even receiving the enormous benefit of hundreds of millions of tax-free dollars from his father did not enable Trump to run a profitable company.[8] That information, however, was similarly not available before the election.

The other key signs of Intellectual Brilliance are curiosity, sophistication, and inventiveness. By his own testimony Trump does not read much if at all. When in May 2016, he was asked to name the last book he read, he replied, "I read passages, I read areas, chapters, I don't have the time." In his own description of his life before the presidency, "I live in the building where I work. I take an elevator from my bedroom to my office. The rest of the time, I'm either in my stretch limousine, my private jet, my helicopter, or my private club in Palm Beach, Florida." Despite having the resources to go anywhere in the world or eat anything he wished, he rarely traveled to any place that didn't have a Trump property or ate foods different from those he grew up with in the 1950s.[9]

On the other hand, Trump has launched businesses in industries ranging from airlines to steak. Whatever his track record, these efforts suggest interests that span a much broader range of industries than most businesspeople. Similarly, even the most hostile commentator would have to concede that he has demonstrated extraordinary mastery of branding and has used Twitter more effectively than any other politician. Both require an ability to adapt skills that he honed in New York real estate to twenty-first-century global media.

Beyond that, Trump's record displays a remarkable level of understanding of how far he could push laws and norms without facing prosecution. Highlights include being caught on tape saying of women he was attracted to that he liked to "Grab them by the pussy" and being accused of sexual assault by a number of women. He was accused of housing discrimination for refusing to rent to Black tenants and settled without admitting guilt. He has a variety of ties to the Mafia. He founded "Trump University," which promised to teach paying customers how to invest in real estate, and was sued for fraud, settling for $25 million. He used illegal Polish immigrants as labor in the construction of Trump Tower. He routinely refused to pay contractors for and workers at his company. He repeatedly broke the rules governing casino operations, including receiving an illegal $3.5 million bailout from his father when he was on the point of bankruptcy. And his eponymous foundation repeatedly broke rules on "self-dealing," including making illegal campaign donations.[10] Information on all of these was widely available before the election.

Overall, this record suggests that Trump's claims to extraordinary levels of Intellectual Brilliance were surely unjustified. His ability at managing his business and personal life at the very edge of illegality is clearly remarkable—but it further undercuts his claims to success in business, since despite this ability he was unable to run his company successfully. Despite Trump's prolonged time in the national spotlight, the Trump Organization's status as a privately held company meant that it released very little information about its performance under his stewardship and even less about the extent to which his father's fortune gave him a head start on his own wealth. By November of 2016 it was clear that Trump's level of Intellectual Brilliance would not be a strength during his presidency, but there simply wasn't enough information available to judge with certainty if it was so lacking as to be likely to cripple his presidency.

Managerial Ability

Trump had significantly more managerial experience than most presidential candidates. The Trump Organization was founded by his father in 1923 and by 2016 one estimate, based on information he supplied, was that it was the forty-eighth largest private company in the United States, with 22,450 employees and revenues of just under $10 billion. Journalists who had studied his company believed that it was much smaller.[11] By the standards of American corporations it is relatively small, but it is vastly larger than, say, a Senate office, which is the largest previous managerial challenge faced by many presidential candidates.

Experience, however, is not the same thing as capability. Remember that while experience can be a developmental process (that is, you learn things from experience and become more capable), it is also a revelatory one (experience allows other people to judge *you* and your capabilities). Trump had managerial experience. But what did that experience tell us about his managerial abilities?

The evidence on Trump's managerial acumen is mixed at best. There are several key episodes in his business career that seem like textbook examples of mismanagement. His misadventures in the casino industry were so costly that he was bailed out by his family at least twice, including an illegal loan that his father gave him by purchasing $3.5 million in chips from one of his son's casinos but never cashing them in. His businesses have filed for bankruptcy six times and many more have been closed or sold at a loss. Trump was nearly forced into personal bankruptcy by his decision to guarantee loans to the Trump Taj Mahal.[12]

One defense of Trump's record, made most prominently by Nassim Taleb, is that many entrepreneurs have many more failures than successes, but if the losses are limited to bearable amounts the eventual rewards from one success will swamp the losses from the failures.[13]

Trump's refusal to release his financial records made the validity of this counterargument impossible to assess in November 2016. Its power is weakened by the fact that Trump was saved from complete bankruptcy at least once only by the intervention of his family. It was, however, impossible to know with certainty before the election whether Trump made profits from relatively less conspicuous investments that made up for his visible failures. Here again we would have had to conclude that the evidence for Trump's managerial abilities was mixed at best, with no strong evidence that he had exceptionally good capabilities and several warning signs, but no indisputable evidence one way or the other.

QUESTION 3: INTENSIFIERS

Intensifiers play a crucial role in determining the magnitude of an Unfiltered candidate's potential impact. For the United States the risks of presidential impact are asymmetric. A great president cannot turn the United States into the world's wealthiest, most powerful nation. It already is. A catastrophic president, however, could tumble it from that perch. Intensifiers influence the height of the hurdle an Unfiltered candidate must leap. The stronger the intensifiers, the more certain we need to be that this candidate will succeed.

The most important intensifier is charisma. Trump has a strong charismatic hold on many supporters. In his own words, "I have the most loyal people . . . I could stand in the middle of Fifth Avenue and shoot somebody, okay, and I wouldn't lose any voters."[14] It's hard to imagine a better description of a leader's charismatic hold on followers than that.

Trump also had extraordinary fame before his candidacy. He had undoubtedly been one of the most famous businesspeople in the world since the 1980s. He courted celebrity his entire adult life, using tactics including pretending to own properties that were owned by his father in his first-ever *New York Times* profile. His rise was enabled by his starring role on *The Apprentice*, a television program that portrayed him (falsely) as the largest and most successful developer in New York. Polling suggests that in the primaries viewers of *The Apprentice* were more supportive of Trump than nonviewers.[15]

Finally, Trump was born with enormous advantages. His first significant real estate deal, for example, was the purchase of the Commodore Hotel on East Forty-Second Street, which he profitably converted into a Hyatt. Yet, absent his father guaranteeing the necessary loan and helping through his political connections, it is highly unlikely Trump would have been able to buy the property.[16]

QUESTION 4: FAÇADES

Identifying façades is the single most important task in evaluating Unfiltered candidates. They don't just make judging a candidate more difficult, the way intensifiers do. They make it more likely that the candidate will fail if those clouded evaluations allow him or her to slip through filtration and win the presidency. Think of façades as the real-life equivalent of the mythical hypnotic powers of the King Cobra. They grab your attention and let someone put themselves into a position to strike.

The Dark Triad

Perhaps the most dangerous set of façades is the Dark Triad of narcissism, Machiavellianism, and psychopathy. Together they can both elevate someone into a position of power and turn them into a catastrophe. If a filtration system does nothing more than block candidates with Dark Triad traits, then it has done a great service. Dark Triad traits are, it is important to emphasize, *subclinical* manifestations of narcissism, Machiavellianism, and psychopathy. Someone whose personality is characterized by the Dark Triad is more narcissistic than most people, but they do not have Narcissistic Personality Disorder.[17] I am not qualified to diagnose anyone, and it is irrelevant to the theory anyways. What is relevant, and entirely possible to judge from a distance, is whether a presidential candidate has an out-of-the-ordinary (even by the standards of politics) levels of narcissistic, Machiavellian, and psychopathic behaviors.

NARCISSISM

The clinical psychologist George Simon said of Trump, "I'm archiving video clips of him to use in workshops [on narcissism] because there's no better example of his characteristics . . . Otherwise, I would have had to hire actors and write vignettes. He's like a dream come true." Before the 2016 election Trump had described himself as among the world's foremost experts on many topics, including: drones, Osama bin Laden's plans to attack the United States, border security, campaign contributions, the court system, debt, Facebook, infrastructure, money, nuclear weapons, television ratings, politicians, renewable energy, taxes, technology, trade, and Wall Street. Narcissists also believe in their own physical attractiveness, and Trump often comments on how attractive he is.[18]

MACHIAVELLIANISM

Machiavellianism—the use of deception and manipulation—is hardly uncommon amongst politicians. Even by those standards, Trump remains exceptional. During the 1980s Trump adopted the pseudonym John Barron to plant favorable stories about himself. In *The Art of the Deal*, which he has falsely claimed is the best-selling business book of all time, he describes faking activity at a construction site to trick Holiday Inn, a potential business partner, into buying a stake in a casino he was building in Atlantic City. The pantomime worked, although the casino itself went bankrupt and he was sued by Holiday Inn.[19]

Among his documented deceptions in politics, Trump repeatedly claimed without evidence that Barack Obama was not born in the United States; implied that the father of Texas senator Ted Cruz, his last primary opponent, was involved in the assassination of John F. Kennedy; claimed that 81 percent of murdered whites were killed by African Americans (the correct number is 15 percent); and lied that the Obama administration sent Syrian refugees only to states with Republican governors. In 2015 his political campaign was chosen as the "Lie of the Year" by PolitiFact, which assessed a staggering 76 percent of his statements as "mostly false" or worse, a substantially higher proportion than any other politician.[20]

PSYCHOPATHY

Psychopathy is nothing like the Hollywood stereotype. Its hallmark is a lack of conscience, and its most dangerous form in leaders is when it manifests as Impulsive Antisociality, which adds poor impulse control, self-centeredness, and a tendency to blame others. A panel of psychologists trained to assess personality found that their ratings of Trump matched with those of "people scoring high on psychopathy and narcissism," including scoring him below the first percentile on "Honesty-Humility."[21]

Trump has imitated a disabled reporter, publicly attacked the parents of an American soldier who was killed in Iraq, stated that U.S. senator John McCain was not a war hero because he was captured, reacted to the September 11 attacks on the day they occurred by boasting that one of his properties was now the tallest building in downtown Manhattan, and urged his supporters to "knock the crap" out of protesters at his rallies.[22]

In one striking case, Trump took a seat reserved for major donors at the opening of a new nursery school for children with AIDS, displacing the real donor, then left without giving a penny to the charity whose ceremony he usurped. He has proudly described using his ownership of the Miss Universe pageant to walk into the dressing room of naked teenage pageant contestants, which multiple contestants have confirmed.[23]

Risk-Taking

Trump has had significant business successes. The most striking were his construction of Trump Tower and his first major real estate deal, the conversion of the decrepit Commodore Hotel in Manhattan into a Grand Hyatt.[24]

He has also had failures. These were severe enough that they include, but are not limited to, six bankruptcies (the Trump Taj Mahal in 1990 and again in 1991, two other Trump casinos in Atlantic City in 1992, the Plaza Hotel in New York also in 1992, Trump Hotels and Casinos Resorts in 2004, and Trump Entertainment Resorts in 2009).[25]

Trump's proclivity for business collapses that left his creditors holding the bag was so pronounced, in fact, that bankers coined the term "Donald risk" to shorthand why they would not lend to him. By the 1990s these had become so costly that his company was $3.4 billion in debt, with $900 million of that personally guaranteed. Trump acknowledges telling his second wife, Marla Maples, that a homeless man sleeping on the street was $900 million dollars wealthier than he was.[26]

In 1989 Trump announced the launch of Trump Shuttle, a rebranded Eastern Airlines Shuttle that he had bought for $365 million, even though his own team argued that creating a new airline from scratch would have cost no more than $300 million. At the launch ceremony Trump made unfounded claims that his shuttle was much safer than Pam Am's, its major competitor. He spent more than $1 million on each plane to refurbish it and paint the name Trump on the planes as large as possible and gave up on installing real marble fixtures in the plane's bathrooms only after being convinced that this would make the planes too heavy. He owned the airline for eighteen months and lost $128 million over that span before relinquishing the airline to his creditors in exchange for debt relief.[27]

Trump made a similar foray into football by purchasing the New Jersey Generals of the United States Football League (USFL), a now-defunct rival to the National Football League (NFL). The league's major source of differentiation from the NFL (other than inferior quality of play) was that its teams played in the spring, when NFL teams have their offseason. Trump purchased a team for $9 million and immediately persuaded the other owners to challenge the NFL directly by shifting their season to the fall. He spent millions on bringing high-priced players to his team, boosting his public profile. The USFL and its teams began to suffer devastating losses, which Trump attempted to recoup through an antitrust lawsuit against the NFL. He won but received only $1 in damages, because almost all the harm had been self-inflicted. An appeals court upheld this ruling, memorably declaring that "courts do not exclude evidence of a victim's suicide in a murder trial."[28]

Trump's purchase of the Plaza Hotel followed the same pattern. He purchased the hotel for more than $400 million in 1988, at the time by far the highest price ever paid for a hotel. Trump declared in a full-page ad in *New York* magazine, "I can never justify the price I paid, no matter how successful the Plaza becomes." He was right. Simply to service its debt, the hotel would have needed to generate more than $40 million in operating profit annually. Trump put his first wife in charge, but it never approached that number, even losing $74 million in one year. As the New York real estate market decayed and his businesses declined, Trump forfeited the Plaza to his lenders in exchange for relief from personal debts. The hotel was eventually sold by his bankers for $325 million in 1995. Despite Trump's claims that he still owned it, he did not receive a penny from the sale.[29]

Again, without any detailed credible information about the overall performance of the Trump Organization, it was difficult in 2016 to be certain whether these failures were typical or atypical of Trump's normal managerial approach. Even so, these failures and others seem to be part of a pattern of desiring prestige and publicity so much that it motivated Trump to make deals that would have been rejected by any competent executive even when that threatened the survival of his company. Taken together with Trump's lack of experience in the government and the differences between management in government and in business, particularly a privately held business like the Trump Organization, and this left great room for concern about Trump's ability to manage the White House and the government.

Ideology

Trump's ideology was most commonly described as "populism" based on its rhetorical focus on attacking American elites. Its ideological content was largely provided by Steve Bannon, the campaign's chief executive, and Stephen Miller, who became its chief speechwriter.[30] Populism can be defined as "a thin-centered ideology that considers society to be ultimately separated into two homogenous and antagonistic camps, 'the pure people' versus 'the corrupt elite,' and which argues that politics should be an expression of the *volonté genèrale* (general will) of the people."[31] The thinness of that ideology, however, means that populism rarely if ever provides a coherent set of policies. It is simply about purging the government of the malign influences of elites, which often results in populist governments replicating the behaviors they claimed to despise.[32]

Trumpian populism is intensely bound up in the individual figure of Trump himself. When Trump announced his run for the presidency, he used some variant of the word *I* 256 times, and he accepted the Republican nomination by proclaiming that "I am your voice" and "I alone can fix it."[33] Trump's populism based its claims to future success on his claimed unique brilliance in a way without precedent for an American major party candidate.

Trumpian populism is also deeply racially inflected. Trump had a long history of racist comments and actions that continued through his campaign, including, but not limited to: refusing to rent to African Americans in the 1970s; calling for the death penalty for four African American teenagers and one Latino teenager who were convicted of rape even after DNA evidence proved their innocence; and objecting to an African American accountant by saying, "Black guys counting my money! I hate it."[34]

This racist posture provided Trump a significant advantage in the Republican primaries. The more hostility Republican primary voters had towards minorities, the higher the likelihood that they would vote for Trump. If a Republican primary voter thought of their identity as white as "extremely important," they were more than 30 percent more likely to support Trump. If they thought it was "extremely likely" that "many whites are unable to find a job because employers are hiring minorities instead," they were more than 50 percent more likely to support him.[35]

These views certainly were not held by all, or even most, Republican voters. The fractured state of the Republican field in 2016, however, meant that voters who did share them coalesced behind Trump and helped put him in the lead for the nomination and, as his opponents dropped out, to win it, as well as proving an asset in the general election.[36]

Health

Trump's age is one of the few facts about him that are completely undisputed. Trump was 70 years and 220 days old on the day he was inaugurated, making him the oldest president (over Ronald Reagan) by almost a year. Although medical technology has increased life spans, it remains true that advancing age vastly increases people's vulnerability to all forms of medical disorder, including cognitive decline. Furthermore, there has been essentially no progress on treatments for Alzheimer's disease, probably both the most threatening age-related condition for presidents and one that may have affected the latter parts of the Reagan administration. Trump's age and family history—his father had Alzheimer's disease for the last six years of his very long life—are thus warning signs.[37]

Trump released no credible information about his health during the campaign. He published a letter supposedly written by his doctor Harold Bornstein that stated, without evidence, that Trump's "laboratory test results were astonishingly excellent" and that "Mr. Trump, I can state unequivocally, will be the healthiest individual ever elected to the presidency." Given its tone and the lack of information supporting it, however, there was little reason to take its claims seriously, and few were surprised when Bornstein revealed in 2018 that Trump had written the letter himself.[38]

Finally, there is a possibility that Trump may have been suffering cognitive decline. His verbal fluency has significantly decreased since the 1980s and 1990s, with his vocabulary contracting and the grammar of his sentences often collapsing into virtual gibberish.[39] This is not dispositive. It may simply be a product of stress or repetition. It is simply another warning sign.

QUESTION 5: POSITIVE INDICATORS

Does Trump have significant positive indicators? He had very high energy levels when he was younger and is able to deliver multihour speeches well into his seventies, a feat that would strain most far-younger politicians.[40]

On the other hand, Trump did not have any handicaps that made his rise more difficult. His refusal to release information on his business career made it difficult or impossible to judge his success in business, his primary field. His political team is not an all-star one by any measure. It has few significant highly capable long-term loyalists, instead being largely made up of people who joined when they saw that he could capture the Republican nomination.[41]

Trump: An Overall Assessment

It is, admittedly, difficult to make a neutral assessment of Trump, surely the most polarizing figure in modern American history. The one here relies solely on information that was publicly available about his background before his election.

Overall, my judgment is that the theory would find Trump to have more warning signs than any other major party nominee in American history. Most of his claims to strengths and positive traits are obscured by his refusal to release any verifiable information on his financial status or business history. His Dark Triad traits, particularly narcissism, on the other hand, are so clear-cut as to be unmistakable, as are his predilection for poorly calculated risks, his racially inflected populism, and his advanced age. All these warning signs are made even more concerning by his charismatic hold on his supporters, which acts as an intensifier of any underlying tendencies, positive or negative. Overall, it is difficult to imagine a plausible major party nominee whom the theory would consider more likely to do poorly as president.

I believe that Trump's record as president provides overwhelming verification of the theory's preelection concerns. While it is too soon for a definitive assessment, when this was written in August of 2021 there seemed little doubt that LFT's predictions about Trump were entirely borne out.

A complete discussion of the Trump administration's scandals and failures would require a book considerably longer than this one. Even the briefest summary is, however, telling. On the critical issue of using the power of the presidency to attack democracy—the most profound possible violation of the president's oath of office to "preserve, protect, and defend the Constitution of the United States"—Trump was impeached twice, once for attempting to coerce the government of Ukraine into helping his presidential campaign and once for fomenting a violent assault by his followers on the Capitol in order to disrupt the certification of the electoral vote by Congress.

Further revelations of events within the administration in the wake of Trump's defeat in the 2020 elections make the threat to American institutions seem even larger than they did at the time, as they include the revelation that the president pressured the Justice Department to falsely declare the election results corrupt and said that if they did so, they could "leave the rest to me."[42] It is impossible to interpret this as anything other than a declaration of his intent to overturn the election and remain in power if a Justice Department run by his own appointees gave him the excuse to do so.

Stretching beyond the stability of American democracy, however, were the administration's failures of governance. By far the most important was its response to the COVID-19 pandemic, which killed more than four hundred thousand Americans while he was in office—a higher per capita number than that of almost any other industrialized nation, despite the fact that a 2019 Johns Hopkins study ranked the United States first in the world in pandemic preparedness.[43]

America's response to the pandemic was crippled by Trump's failures, ranging from his refusal to act when the virus first began to spread, to his unwillingness to prioritize testing, to his obsession with the useless drug hydroxchloroquine, to the incompetence that characterized the efforts to acquire critical personal protective equipment. The disastrous response to COVID perfectly distilled every earlier failure of the Trump administration, only with the highest possible stakes. With American deaths from the disease having crossed eight hundred thousand by the end of 2021, it may well be remembered as the single greatest failure of governance in American history.[44]

Trump failed, in other words, as the theory predicted he would. Just as importantly, he failed *in the ways* that the theory predicted he would. He was not even slightly bound by the normative constraints felt by most people in his shoes, even going so far as to refer to a group that included neo-Nazis as "very fine people" and inciting his supporters to use violence to overturn his electoral defeat. His narcissism was so extreme that when visiting the CDC, he dismissed the advice of medical experts there and proclaimed, "I like this stuff, I really get it," and "maybe I have a natural ability" to understand medicine. Barely a month later he suggested to his scientific advisors during a press conference that household disinfectants and ultraviolet light could be useful to treat COVID-19 in an infected patient. Such statements would be surprising from most people, but not from someone with such extraordinary Dark Triad characteristics.[45]

In the face of the worst public health crisis in more than a century, Trump gambled on the success of an unproven drug, hydroxychloroquine, instead of committing to the difficult political and logistical tasks that might have more successfully managed the pandemic. This too is unsurprising from someone with his history of risk-taking and managerial failures. Even his health issues became politically significant when, at least in part because of his refusal to follow expert advice on how to protect yourself from COVID, he came down with an extremely severe case of the disease, even coming very close to being placed on a ventilator.[46]

The Trump administration was a four-year case study in the perils of electing an Unfiltered president. It took a leader with an extraordinary charismatic hold on his followers but no meaningful ethical constraints or ability to manage the federal bureaucracy and then put the vast powers of the presidency in his hands. Bad luck played a role in the scale of the disaster. Without the COVID-19 pandemic the damage might have been far smaller. But it could also have been much worse. Trump did not face any international crises on the same scale as many of his predecessors, for example, and it is easy to imagine how the same failures that crippled his performance in dealing with a disease could have been even more dangerous during a war. Hard as it is to believe, it's my belief that future historians' assessment of the forty-fifth president of the United States will be that the country got off lucky.

Conclusion

I hope this book has convinced you that the modern presidency contains the seeds of disaster. The way the United States selects presidents allows far too high a chance of electing someone whom no rational person would allow to have the power to suspend large portions of the Constitution or even, in the final extremis, destroy the world. This suggests two potential avenues for reform. The first is improving the way in which presidential candidates are currently nominated, subject to the constraints of political realism. The second is to imagine plausible ways to limit the presidency to reduce the possible damage under the worst-case scenario. Improving presidential quality, and particularly ensuring that we will not get disastrous presidents, might be the most important task facing the American political system.

HOW DANGEROUS CAN A PRESIDENT BE?

The Trump administration might seem the worst-case scenario. But it was just a warning of what a truly catastrophic presidency could be. Forget about differences in policy. Those are the topics of ordinary politics. Just imagine how the president might threaten the United States' status as a stable democratic republic or even the existence of human civilization. Let's start with the ultimate catastrophe—nuclear war. The president of the United States is one of only two people on earth who control a nuclear arsenal large enough to end human civilization. That control is, for all practical purposes, absolute. The command and control system for American nuclear weapons was designed with fear of a "bolt from the blue" in mind—a Pearl Harbor–style surprise attack that destroyed American missiles in their silos and bombers at their bases, eliminating the ability to strike back and leaving the United States at the mercy of its enemies. Because of this fear, American nuclear forces can be deployed quickly and used preemptively. Quickly here means that five minutes after a president gives the order, a salvo of four hundred American Minuteman missiles are irrevocably on their way to their targets. Ten minutes later, two hundred missiles launched from American submarines would follow. Each missile has a warhead many times more powerful than the bombs that devastated Hiroshima and Nagasaki.[1]

The chain of command for nuclear weapons goes from the president to the head of Strategic Command (STRATCOM), and then to missile crews in their bunkers and submarine crews under the ocean. No civilian—not even the secretary of defense—has any right to intervene once the president has decided. The president has no legal obligation to consult with advisers before initiating a strike, or to follow their advice if it is given, and the commander of STRATCOM is legally required to obey the president. The commander can refuse to follow orders if deeming them illegal, but the president can also bypass the commander. The only restraint on the president launching a nuclear strike, in other words, is the willingness of the thousands of men and women who would fire the missiles to obey the order to launch. These men and women have spent their careers being taught to obey that order immediately and without question.[2]

Nuclear war might be the worst possible outcome of a catastrophic president, but it's not the only nightmare. We saw in Andrew Johnson just how bad a real, not hypothetical, Unfiltered president can be. It could get worse. Could a president turn him or herself into a dictator? Most Americans would be very surprised to learn just how far the president's powers can be made to stretch. The president has an almost unrestricted ability to declare a national emergency and access to extraordinary powers once that declaration is made (on the day I wrote this paragraph, by coincidence President Trump chose to make just such a declaration to expedite construction of a border wall). This power, in the words of Supreme Court Justice Robert Jackson's dissent in *Korematsu v. United States,* the case that sanctioned the internment of Japanese Americans during the Second World War, "lies about like a loaded weapon, ready for the hand of any authority that can bring forward a plausible claim of an urgent need."[3]

The Constitution provides no specifics on the declaration of a state of emergency, and most of the special emergency powers it does mention are accorded to the Congress, not the president. But, starting with Lincoln, presidents, with and without the consent of Congress, have steadily expanded the scope of their emergency powers. Under the National Emergencies Act of 1976, presidents can declare a state of emergency at their discretion. Although it was meant to limit the declaration of emergencies, in 2019 thirty-one of them remained in effect.[4]

States of emergency give presidents powers that seem entirely foreign to the American government, including: suspending the law that bans testing of biological and chemical weapons on nonconsenting people; shutting down all forms of electronic communication (including the Internet); levying sanctions against other countries without the consent of Congress; designating any person, including an American citizen, as a supporter of terrorism, which makes any form of financial transaction with him or her illegal; and even suspending the posse comitatus act, which normally forbids the use of the military for domestic law enforcement. Although the boundaries of these powers have not yet been tested in the courts, they remain available to any president willing to use them.[5]

Even less dramatic, less clearly egregious uses of power by the president could be perverted to threaten the American democratic system. Under J. Edgar Hoover, the FBI demonstrated just how much it could threaten American civil liberties. Hoover had his own political goals and was often in conflict with the presidents he was serving under. Had he been a willing tool in the hands of his supposed master, the damage to American democracy could have been far greater.[6]

After Hoover the FBI was reformed to limit its ability to go rogue and to improve its adherence to the law, but the president retains the ability to fire the FBI director and appoint a new one.[7] Furthermore, the FBI is part of the Justice Department, which is led by the attorney general, who is also a presidential appointee. A sufficiently aggressive president could use these powers to suppress his or her political opposition, even if the court system eventually acted to limit these actions.

Imagine, for example, a president who ordered the attorney general to commence—and announce—FBI investigations into, and even criminal prosecutions of, his or her political opposition. Even if the charges were baseless, being investigated would make it very difficult to function effectively, and the financial costs of a legal defense would themselves be a significant deterrent to becoming politically active against the president.

Even the simple measure of the attorney general announcing an investigation or prosecution in the closing days of a campaign would likely have a significant impact on the race, as it would probably take weeks or months for it to become clear that the investigation had no real basis. The federal government's enormous investigative and prosecutorial powers, for example, could effectively hinder political opposition through harassment even if they could not conduct successful prosecutions. The preceding sentences were written in 2018, but they became a far less hypothetical concern when President Trump openly pressured his attorney general to investigate Hunter Biden, the son of his rival for the presidency.[8]

Every president has powers so great they could threaten the stability of the American system. So far, presidents have more often chosen to use those powers to strengthen the system than to attack it. But that was a choice.

REFORMING THE NOMINATING PROCESS

Using Leader Filtration Theory to improve the nominating process means increasing the quantity and quality of information available about candidates and improving the ability to take that information into account when choosing the nominee. The rules of the nominating process crucially influence the identity of the winner.[9]

There have been many proposals to reform the nominating process. Some changes usually happen after every election cycle. Proposed reforms include cutting the length of the primaries to make fundraising less important, changing the order of state primaries, and even moving the conventions to before the primaries to nominate two candidates who have the party's seal of approval and then allowing the voters to choose between those two.[10]

The nomination process seeks to maximize four, sometimes competing, goals: candidate quality, voter information, participation, and equality across states.[11] LFT demonstrates that the first two of those are intrinsically linked, and this book has shown that the nomination process, both as it has existed historically and as it does now, fails to achieve both.

Among the responses to these failures of the nomination process are proposals to strengthen the role of party elites. Although that may seem to be a logical response to the 2016 election, the Democratic Party took the opposite approach. After that race, the rules were changed to decrease the role of "superdelegates" (party leaders who were not chosen to support a candidate at the state level) in response to pressure from supporters of Bernie Sanders. Under the new rules, the number of superdelegates was reduced by almost 60 percent from the numbers in 2016 and those delegates were denied the right to vote on the first ballot at the convention.[12] This change makes it clear that at least on the Democratic side, and likely on the Republican one as well, for the foreseeable future any proposed reform to the delegate selection process that involves giving more power to party elites to select a nominee is dead on arrival.

The theory suggests other approaches to improving the quality of nominees, and particularly blocking potentially catastrophic ones. This depends, crucially, on maximizing the available information about candidates. Information takes time to discover, so reforms aimed at shortening the primary process are misguided, because they will deprive the media and rival candidates of the time necessary to fully investigate nominees. On the other hand, changes to the primary calendar to backload the primaries—so the most important ones happen last, when more information is available—may be helpful.

LFT's focus on the importance of removing candidates, instead of selecting them, also suggests the possibility of an entirely new reform to the process that could simultaneously improve the ability of party elites to block disastrous candidates while further limiting their power. The parties could change their voting rules to restore the number of superdelegates from the

2016 election but eliminate their right to vote *for* any candidate. Instead, they should only be able to vote *against* a candidate. To win the nomination, a candidate should still have to win the votes of a majority of pledged (that is, elected) delegates. But the votes of superdelegates could, if they chose, be subtracted from the total of one candidate. Superdelegates would thus be unable to select a winner but could block a potential disaster.

A candidate would still have to get votes equal to or greater than the majority of pledged delegates, and the superdelegates could not contribute to that total. They would, however, be able to block a candidate from capturing the nomination, thus transforming the convention into a brokered one where the delegates would have to negotiate amongst themselves to pick a nominee. In a brokered convention the elected delegates would be released from the candidates they were pledged to after the first ballot and could conceivably vote for anyone. Party elites would have to scramble for their support, trading favors and working their personal connections behind the scenes, just as they did in the nineteenth century, but without the advantage of familiarity. It would be a spectacle to warm the hearts of political junkies across the world, but it would be unlikely to result in the selection of anyone who was not already a prominent figure in the party. This would maintain the role of the popular vote in selecting the party nominee while significantly improving filtering.

A second set of reforms to the process would increase the information about presidential candidates available to both party elites and ordinary voters. Many of these reforms could be implemented at the state level, where legislators could potentially forbid candidates from appearing on the ballot unless they met transparency requirements. At a minimum this would include requirements that candidates release their tax returns and medical histories. A better standard would be to require candidates to submit to an independent examination by a board of medical professionals that covers physical and psychological health as well as cognitive acuity. This would certainly mean a significant sacrifice of privacy by candidates. But the only fair answer to that is—so what? If you want to be the most powerful person on earth, giving the rest of us confidence that you don't have any medical issues that could come into play is the least voters should expect. The creation of such an independent group of experts was suggested by former president Carter in 1994.[13]

SHRINKING THE PRESIDENCY

The American presidency is, because of the veto, difficult to limit legislatively once a dangerous president has taken the office. The next Congress, however, should make restricting the powers of the presidency its highest priority. The three most important are: (1) eliminating the president's ability to initiate the use of nuclear weapons without the consent of Congress; (2) decreasing and time-limiting the president's currently expansive emergency powers; and (3) minimizing the president's ability to use the federal government's investigative and prosecutorial powers against political opponents.

The simplest, but perhaps most important, reform of the powers of the presidency is eliminating the president's power to initiate the use of nuclear weapons without the consent of Congress, other than in response to an attack on the United States, American forces, or American allies using weapons of mass destruction. Massachusetts senator Ed Markey and California representative Ted Lieu have introduced a bill holding that since the use of nuclear weapons is functionally a declaration of war, which is a power of Congress, not the presidency, the president cannot order a first use of America's nuclear arsenal without a congressional declaration of war.[14]

The counterargument to such laws is that they limit the president's ability to use the threat of nuclear weapons to deter America's enemies or to protect American forces in danger of being overwhelmed. This is not persuasive given just how easily an unreliable president can slip through the filtration system and take power. This is not a pledge that the United States would never use nuclear weapons first. It simply says that the president should not be able to initiate their use, and potentially threaten the existence of human civilization, on a whim.

The power of the American military is so great that a strike by purely conventional forces could inflict devastating damage on most countries, providing significant deterrence by itself. That also means that, while Russian and Chinese forces may be able to achieve superiority in their home regions, the prospect of a sizable American military force being overwhelmed so quickly that it could only be saved by a unilateral presidential decision to use nuclear weapons is remote. Given the vanishingly small odds that such a constraint on the president could ever harm American security, it is a critically needed and long-overdue precaution.[15]

Second, the vast emergency powers available to the president are not justifiable in any democracy that wishes to remain one. Inherent in the idea of emergencies is that they may come quickly and require rapid responses backed by the full force of the federal government. Giving the national government that sort of energy and decisiveness is precisely why the Founders created the office of the presidency in the first place. Once a president has invoked a state of emergency, however, it can only be repealed by an act of Congress, which is itself subject to a presidential veto.

An authoritarian-inclined president could conceivably seize extraordinary powers and keep them with the support of only one-third of one house of Congress. This is not enough to justify giving the presidency powers so far beyond those accorded it in the American constitutional structure. Congress should take a close look at the powers that it has chosen to give the president during an emergency. Even more important, the National Emergencies Act should be amended to make any declared emergency expire within a short time—perhaps sixty days –with majority support from both houses of Congress required to extend it. Any litigation relating to the emergency should be fast-tracked to the Supreme Court and, if possible, justices appointed by the president who declared the emergency should be recused from ruling on it.

Third, the president's power over the federal investigative apparatus might also be limited in some ways. Investigations of public officials are the area where politically ordered investigations seem likely to be most dangerous. Given the danger, it might be possible to move public integrity investigations and prosecutions to a separate institutional structure, one modeled on the independent counsel statute or the Federal Reserve, which would have authority over all investigations that involve political figures. A permanent institutional structure would remove the pressure to make a case against a single subject that caused previous independent counsels to expand their mandate and, eventually, led Congress to allow the statute authorizing them to expire. Instead, investigations and prosecutions of public officials could be handled by a well-funded and permanently established independent office whose head was chosen for extended terms (perhaps five years) unanimously by a panel of judges nominated by presidents of both parties.

Finally, the increasing age of American political leaders makes it important to reform both the process for removing the president and to change the line of succession. Section 4 of the 25th Amendment to the Constitution specifies that "whenever the Vice President and a majority of either the principal officers of the executive departments or of such other body as Congress may by law provide, transmit to the President pro tempore of the Senate and the Speaker of the House of Representatives their written declaration that the President is unable to discharge the powers and duties of his office, the Vice President shall immediately assume the powers and duties of the Acting President."

Although discussions of using the 25th Amendment to remove an erratic or incapacitated president usually involve only the cabinet and the vice president (unless the President objects, in which case Congress has twenty-one days to vote on whether to uphold that objection, with two-thirds of Congress needed to support his or her removal from office), the amendment clearly allows Congress to specify another body that could fill that role. Congressman Jamie Raskin of Maryland has introduced a bill that would create a Commission on Presidential Capacity, which could be empowered by a concurring resolution of Congress (which would not be vulnerable to a presidential veto) to assess the president's physical and psychological fitness, report its findings to Congress and, if necessary, transfer the powers of the presidency to the vice president. Although this bill has not passed, it or one like it should be enacted as soon as possible.[16]

In a similar vein, the presidential order of succession currently runs from the vice president, to the Speaker of the House, to the president pro tempore of the Senate. By custom, since 1949 the president pro tempore is the seniormost member of the Senate's majority party—as such, he or she is virtually guaranteed to be of advanced age. Any situation in which the presidency has passed into his or her hands would be a moment of supreme national crisis requiring extraordinary energy from the president. Recent presidents pro tempore of the Senate have been in their 80s or even, in the case of South Carolina senator Strom Thurmond, their late 90s. Thurmond's diminished health and capacity was an open secret in

Washington at the time, and he was certainly unable to handle the presidency under any circumstances.[17] To avoid such a possibility, the Presidential Succession Act should be amended to keep the line of succession within the executive branch, moving from the vice president to the secretary of state and other members of the cabinet.

FUTURE CAPTAINS OF THE AMERICAN SHIP OF STATE

In the Federalist Papers, Madison argued that large republics have two crucial advantages over small ones. He believed that large republics would be far more difficult for demagogues to sway, and, because there can be only one leader no matter how large a country becomes and larger countries have a larger population from which to draw talent, that large countries would tend to have better leadership.[18] The United States has now grown to a size that Madison could never have imagined and today, with access to the talents of the entire population instead of just the white and male portions of it, it should be able to do better still. Yet few would argue that the quality of presidential leadership today is significantly higher than it was in the past, and there are at least a few recent examples which suggest that it might be lower.

There are many possible reasons for why modern presidents have struggled so much that serious observers have argued that the job is itself impossible.[19] I hope that this book has persuaded you that perhaps the most important of those reasons is that we simply are not doing a very good job of picking presidents. Forty-five men have served as president of the United States. Some have been so transcendently great that even now, with centuries of perspective, we can struggle to understand how achievements of such extraordinary scale were possible. Others were such catastrophic failures that we can only imagine how much better off America and the world would be if they had never set foot in the White House. Each was, in his own way, a product of the United States' leadership filtration process. But the process can clearly be improved. Imagine how different—how much better—American history would have been if Andrew Johnson had never become president, if Pierce and Buchanan had never been elected, or if George W. Bush had avoided the Iraq War or prevented the 2008 financial crisis.

American elites have clearly failed at the job of properly screening presidential candidates, partly because reforms to the nominating process have weakened their ability to do so. Fundamentally, however, the responsibility for picking presidents lies in the hands of every American citizen. American voters played little or no role in the selection of Andrew Johnson or, for that matter, Theodore Roosevelt. They did choose Buchanan and Pierce, and a combination of a large fraction of the voters and the vagaries of the Electoral College elected George W. Bush and, of course, Donald Trump. The United States' system for electing presidents has evolved greatly over time. Through some combination of luck and skill it has produced extraordinary men at extraordinary moments. If it can no longer do so—if, in fact, it begins picking the worst instead of the best, then the success of the American experiment is at risk as it has not been since at least the Great Depression, and perhaps even the Civil War.

The unprecedented power of the United States means that this failure would stretch far beyond America's shores. Even the strongest empire can fall. When they do the consequences can be disastrous. The Roman Empire was maintained by ruthless militarism amounting in some cases to genocide, but when it fell it took between six and eight hundred years for the population of the territories it governed to return to its imperial peak.[20] A modern fall, with all the incomprehensible destructive power of today's weapons, could be unimaginably worse. Avoiding that catastrophe is among the foremost responsibilities of every American citizen. It is a small price to pay for the extraordinary luck of being a citizen of this uniquely blessed nation. Yet I fear that we, as a collective whole, are not doing nearly a good enough job.

Yet the future of the presidency is far more about hope than fear. The story of the presidency has more greatness than anyone could reasonably have hoped for when that office was created. Despite all the pitfalls inherent in its two-century-old system of government, the United States has, time and again, produced leadership of the highest caliber when it was needed. The nation and the world are better off because of it.

Disaster is and always will be a possibility. LFT and this book both show, however, that inherent in the possibility of great disaster is the chance of great triumph. Any country that produced Washington and Lincoln should count itself extraordinarily fortunate. In living memory, the United States was governed for twenty-eight years by the sequence of Franklin Roosevelt, Harry Truman, and Dwight Eisenhower, a triumvirate who created the modern world and show that the American system, old though it may be, retains the potential for sustained excellence. We have done better. We must do better. We can do better again. No matter who you are, this book is meant to help you understand what it takes to be a great president of the United States and play your part in helping ensure that we get more of them.

Statistical Analysis, Case
Selection, and Theoretical
Concerns

Leader Filtration Theory is ideally suited to a mixed-methods research design. Its first main prediction, that Unfiltered leaders will have a higher variance in performance than Filtered ones, is best tested quantitatively. Its second, that Unfiltered leaders will have a higher unique impact (measured counterfactually) than Filtered ones, can only be tested qualitatively. The quantitative tests were conducted using historians' and political scientists' rankings of presidential performance, while the qualitative ones were done via five case studies in the preceding chapters.

RANKING THE PRESIDENTS

The three most recent significant survey-based rankings of presidents were conducted by C-SPAN, the American Political Science Association, and the Siena Institute. I modified these rankings when necessary to eliminate William Henry Harrison and James Garfield because both spent so little time in office (Harrison only thirty-one days and Garfield only six months and fifteen days) that their rankings are not meaningful, and Trump because his term was completed so recently.[1]

To check these three rankings for various forms of bias, I also analyzed eighteen other earlier rankings of presidents. Two of these rankings were surveys of conservative historians conducted by the *Wall Street Journal* conducted specifically to counteract potential liberal bias among the historians who are usually included in the survey pool. Finally, I averaged all twenty-one rankings and tested this meta-rank as well.[2] As most of these sets of rankings did not include one or more recent presidents, I converted the rankings into percentile scores and averaged each president's score, then ranked all the presidents by the average percentile score.

These twenty-one surveys captured a wide array of different approaches and methodologies to ranking the presidents. Twenty of the twenty-one rankings are surveys of many historians, while one is a ranking conducted by a single individual with significant historical training and experience as a practitioner. Some asked historians and political scientists to simply rank presidents; others broke down their performance on specific facets of the presidency.

I did not include several rankings that were focused only on economic performance or methodologically suspect. Of the two rankings looking solely at economics, one, by the economists Alan Blinder and Mark Watson, covers only post–World War II presidents.[3] The second, by the Georgia Tech political scientist Mark Zachary Taylor, uses a variety of economic data to rank every president from 1789 through 2009. Taylor's paper tests Leader Filtration Theory and finds, unsurprisingly, that it does not predict short-term economic performance. As Taylor notes, his data on short-term economic performance have little correlation with overall rankings of presidential performance. It scores Lincoln, for example, as the twenty-sixth best president but does not account for either the short- or long-term effects of the Civil War.[4]

Presidents' control over the economic policy agenda is limited at best,[5] and presidential influence on short-term economic performance is limited, mostly indirect, and the cumulation of many decisions, not a small number of high-impact ones.[6] The combination makes short-run economic performance perhaps the best example of a policy area where Leader Filtration Theory is unlikely to provide much, if any, insight.

I did not analyze two other rankings. The first, done by the Mises Institute, assesses presidents solely on the extent to which the growth of the federal government was limited during their term. As this criterion has no apparent match with the preferences of any significant portion of the American public, I did not include it.[7] The second, by two baseball writers, assessed presidents using data sources of such questionable validity it did not meet the same standards as better-known surveys.[8]

The historians' and political scientists' rankings of presidents have substantial weaknesses and have been the subject of considerable research and debate. First, they mostly do not account for circumstances, including the political context when a president was elected and whether the president led the nation during a war. The strongest predictor of a president's rank is just the time when they served as president.[9]

Statistical analyses show that serving at the beginning of a party system (supporting Skowronek's hypothesis about political time, as presidents at the beginning of a system seem to closely parallel his "Reconstructive" type of great presidents who create new strong political institutions) and during wartime both improve position in the rankings,[10] with larger wars seeming to elevate presidents in the rankings.[11]

On the other hand, other statistical research has found that winning wars does not elevate presidents in the rankings when economic performance is accounted for[12], that presidents who fought wars of choice are generally not helped by doing so, and that those who led in wartime but performed poorly as war leaders are likely hurt in the rankings.[13] If a president does well in wartime, it seems logical to give him credit for it in the rankings.

Political context undoubtedly has a significant impact on presidential performance, but not an absolute one. Presidents can maneuver within a context, even an unfavorable one.[14] Furthermore, the most Unfiltered presidents are vice presidents who became president through the death of their predecessor, an event unlinked to the political context. The same political context—weak institutions—also creates the potential in Skowronek's model for both the best and worst presidents, but it's unclear that this has any relationship to how Filtered or Unfiltered presidents will be.

The prominence of vice presidents who become Unfiltered presidents also obviates concerns that the rankings are likely to give extreme rankings to Unfiltered presidents because they are generally inexperienced and therefore expectations for them are low. Elected Unfiltered presidents are usually inexperienced, but vice presidents who arrive at the presidency through a president's death need not be, so ratings of them would not be influenced by any such expectations.

In some ways, context clearly biases the rankings against Leader Filtration Theory. The rankings do not differentiate between impact and successes accrued during a president's time in office but not because of him. Jefferson, for example, ranks highly primarily because of the Louisiana Purchase, which doubled the size of the United States. The purchase, however, was an opportunity that fell into his lap when Napoleon offered to sell it to the United States to finance his wars. Jefferson's presidency is rated as very successful given this enormous triumph, but it did not occur because of anything special about Jefferson himself or the choices that he made. If one of the likely counterfactual presidents—John Adams or James Madison—had been president instead, the outcome would likely have been the same.[15]

Presidents with high impact will be disproportionately at the top and bottom of the rankings because impact leads to extreme performance, but the rankings are a noisy and imperfect proxy for impact, not a direct measure of it. The fact that the rankings may be biased against Leader Filtration Theory, however, increases their usefulness as a test of the theory if it passes, because passing a hard test is strong evidence in favor of a theory.[16]

The second weakness of the rankings is that they inevitably reflect the biases of present-day historians. The first of these biases is presentism. Modern historians who abhor slavery will, naturally, rate the Great Emancipator much more highly than his predecessor who supported slavery at every turn. The rankings therefore conflate presidents who effectively pursued goals that modern historians find mistaken or even repugnant and presidents who were simply ineffective at pursuing unobjectionable ones.

To a large extent this is simply an unavoidable issue for any attempt to judge the performance of presidents. We do not simply want competent presidents; we want presidents who direct that competence in productive directions. For the rankings themselves, there is no way to mitigate this presentist bias. In the case studies, however, historians' assessments are also matched with the views of presidents' contemporaries. For example, historians' condemnation of Andrew Johnson's time in office is driven by the goals he pursued—but that condemnation was shared by the dominant political forces of his era and led to his impeachment. Johnson may have succeeded in many of his goals in the White House, but both his contemporaries and today's historians viewed that success as a national catastrophe.

There are two other reasons to believe that the ratings retain their power despite presentism. First, American historians have been surveyed many times over several decades since Arthur Schlesinger Sr. polled a group of fifty-five of them in 1948. "Present" views clearly change over the course of seventy-one years, yet the rankings have agreed with one another and remained extremely stable over time, with the only major changes being the modern ascent of Eisenhower and Grant. Second, here we are most interested in the extreme performers—the very best and very worst presidents—and there is little disagreement about which presidents belong in those slots.[17]

Another form of bias that may affect the usefulness of the rankings is the political bias—presumably liberal—of historians and social scientists. Political views affect how people award credit and blame to politicians.[18] The raters for most of the surveys are academics, who are disproportionately liberal and Democratic, which may bias the rankings in favor of liberal and Democratic presidents and against conservative and Republican ones, particularly modern ones.[19]

Political bias is a very real problem in political science research, one sufficiently severe that it calls into question many of the most important findings in the field of political psychology, for example.[20] Lending strength to this concern is the fact that the rankings assembled by surveying academics rank Democratic presidents approximately ten places higher than Republican ones, while rankings assembled by surveying members of the public do not.[21]

To counteract this bias, the *Wall Street Journal* conducted two rankings of presidents by conservative historians and political figures, and the theory was tested independently against both of those rankings. Analysis of these rankings, however, shows that "regardless of the number of participants or their ideologies, the rankings are quite consistent in identifying presidents at both ends of the spectrum."[22]

These political concerns may also be somewhat obviated by the passage of time. The partisan passions aroused by FDR and Eisenhower, for example, however powerful they were then, seem likely to have cooled at least a little eighty-nine and sixty-nine years, respectively, after they were first elected. If both rankings deliberately assembled by conservatives to remove conservative bias and rankings conducted more than seven decades apart yield roughly the same results, this strongly suggests that political bias does not explain it.

Finally, we can broadly question whether experts have the political judgment required to meaningfully assess presidential performance. Tetlock's groundbreaking work on expert political judgment has shown that even highly credentialed experts on politics often perform little or no better than random chance when asked to make predictions about the future of the subject of their study.[23]

Tetlock's findings are among the most important foundations of Leader Filtration Theory. If experts *were* able to consistently foresee the future, then they would be able to accurately forecast the outcome of picking different leaders and would, when they are able to select their preferred candidate, always pick the best-performing one. Filtered candidates, in that circumstance, would nearly always outperform Unfiltered ones. It is the essential unpredictability of the future that makes the key prediction for Unfiltered leaders' higher *variance* in performance, not simply lower performance. Although it is possible to create systems and structures that improve the quality of expert judgment, these structures are certainly not in place for the rankings.[24] Additionally, just given the press of time and events, it's unclear how much effort all the respondents to the surveys put into their responses.

Concerns about expert judgment are very real but mitigated by several factors. First, Tetlock's work concentrates on *prediction,* not retrospective assessment. As Yogi Berra supposedly once said, "It's tough to make predictions, especially about the future." Here experts are asked not to guess what will happen in the future, but to assess what already has happened. This is still a difficult task, but a more manageable one.

Second, concerns about the level of attention paid and effort put into the assessments are obviated by the fact that all the rankings (save Felzenberg's) used here are surveys. Ample research shows that under a wide variety of circumstances, aggregations of opinions can outperform any single person, even when that person has considerable expertise.[25] In this case, a respondent to the survey who fills it out at random is introducing noise into the results, but that noise is likely to be canceled out by equally noisy answers from other respondents, allowing a better picture to emerge by synthesizing their answers into a single result.

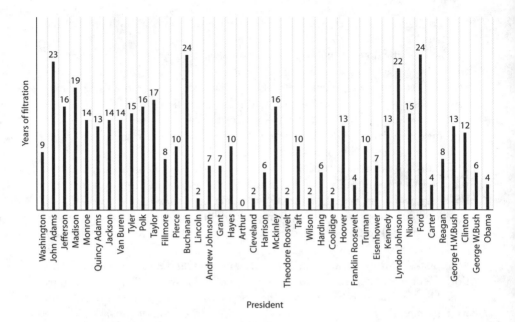

Figure A.1:   Presidents' Length of Filtration

Taken all in all, this assessment suggests that the rankings, despite their limitations, are an extremely useful tool to use to test Leader Filtration Theory, particularly its application to presidents of the United States. The long history of both research on the rankings and using them to guide research and draw conclusions about presidents and other leaders is, by itself, a validation of their value. The concerns that have been raised about them, while significant, are all limited by research that shows the rankings have at least face validity and by the diversity of different rankings tested here. The concerns are material enough that validation of the theory by the presidential rankings is suggestive, not dispositive, but they remain an enormously useful way to test Leader Filtration Theory.

ASSESSING PRESIDENTS' LEVELS OF FILTRATION

Presidents vary widely in their prepresidential experience and in the extent to which they have been filtered by the electoral system. If we count years of filtration as time in senior offices (vice president, member of the cabinet or equivalent executive position, general or admiral, senator, member of Congress, governor, or membership in the national or state supreme courts), then presidents vary from 0 to 44 years of filtration (figure A.1).

Table A.1 Presidents' Filtration Rank and Distance from Mean Survey Rank

President	Consolidated Rank	Filtration Score	Filtration Rank
Biden	n/a	44	1
Buchanan	41	24	2
Ford	26	24	2
John Adams	13	23	4
Lyndon Johnson	15	22	5
Madison	16	19	6
Jefferson	5	16	7
McKinley	18	16	7
Nixon	35	15	9
Monroe	17	14	10
Van Buren	24	14	10
Quincy Adams	21	13	12
Hoover	33	13	12
Kennedy	10	13	12
George H. W. Bush	22	13	12
Clinton	19	12	16
Hayes	25	10	17
Taft	23	10	17
Truman	6	10	17
Taylor	32	8.5	20
Reagan	14	8	21
Jackson	9	7	22
Benjamin Harrison	29	6	23
George W. Bush	31	6	23
Washington	3	4.5	25
Polk	11	4	26
Franklin Roosevelt	2	4	26
Carter	27	4	26
Obama	12	4	26
Grant	34	3.5	30
Eisenhower	8	3.5	30
Pierce	38	2.5	32
Cleveland	20	2	33
Harding	40	1.5	34
Lincoln	1	0.5	35
Wilson	7	0.5	35
Tyler	36	0	37

Table A.1   Continued

President	Consolidated Rank	Filtration Score	Filtration Rank
Fillmore	37	0	37
A. Johnson	39	0	37
Arthur	28	0	37
T. Roosevelt	4	0	37
Coolidge	30	0	37
Trump	n/a	0	37

NOTE: Shading indicates unfiltered

Length of filtration, however, does not map directly to a candidate's level of filtration. Vice-presidential candidates, for example, are often picked with no attention paid to how they might perform as president, but they must move up if the president resigns or dies. On the other hand, some vice presidents were chosen to unify the party precisely because they came very close to capturing the nomination. We should thus weight a vice president who is elevated to the presidency's years of filtration at 0 unless they were chosen as vice president in the expectation that they would soon become president (Truman and Ford) or they came close to capturing the nomination from the president who selected them (Lyndon Johnson). Similarly, we should weight years of filtration to account for dark horse candidates, who were nominated not because the party thought they were presidential material but simply because major candidates deadlocked or were otherwise unable to capture the nomination. I assigned a 0.25 weight to years of filtration for such candidates.

Similarly, the data collected during the filtration process is less meaningful if a candidate has a status as a national hero (Washington, Jackson, Taylor, Grant, and Eisenhower), but since not all national heroes with presidential ambitions become president (e.g., MacArthur) some filtration clearly still occurs, so I assigned a weight of 0.5. In all three cases weights were assigned only once with no adjustments to eliminate the possibility of curve-fitting to the data. Once these weights are considered, every president can be assigned a filtration score (table A.1).

Note that the twenty presidents with the lowest filtration score are, except for Barack Obama, who was not assessed in that book, the same presidents coded as Unfiltered in *Indispensable*.

Table A.2 Variance Significance Tests for Filtration as a Dichotomous Variable

Survey	RMS Ratio	Significance Level
C-SPAN-2017	1.39856535	99.01%
APSA-2018	1.369572253	98.56%
Siena-2019	1.458465554	99.55%
Felzenberg	1.160060097	84.74%
APSA-2015	1.31273387	97.09%
USPC-2011	1.478920966	99.64%
Siena-2010	1.437476676	99.41%
C-SPAN-2009	1.426959255	99.28%
WSJ-2005	1.438776741	99.39%
Siena-2002	1.532773019	99.83%
WSJ-2000	1.463029701	99.53%
C-SPAN-2000	1.551967187	99.87%
Schlesinger-1996	1.409967072	99.06%
R-M-1996	1.618646818	99.95%
Siena-1994	1.610231744	99.94%
Siena-1990	1.483523091	99.59%
Siena-1982	1.574179891	99.85%
C-T-1982	1.475039028	99.37%
M-B-1982	1.444648173	99.10%
Schlesinger-1962	1.636963309	99.73%
Schlesing-1948	1.570533523	99.31%
Meta-Ranking	1.477036015	99.65%

TESTING FILTRATION AS A DICHOTOMOUS VARIABLE

Filtered and Unfiltered presidents are "fuzzy sets"—two sets that are clearly distinct, but that also have ambiguous and even potentially overlapping boundaries.[26] This makes it appropriate to test differences between them using filtration as both a dichotomous and a continuous variable. Using a dichotomous coding scheme, we can see if Unfiltered presidents have more variance in their rankings than Filtered ones. If the theory passes this test, we can then subject it to the much harder one of seeing if there is a statistically significant relationship between filtration score and presidential rankings.

The root-mean-square of the distance between the rankings of Unfiltered and Filtered presidents from the median rank of all the individual surveys and the meta-rank was calculated, along with the ratio between the RMS difference and the mean for Unfiltered and Filtered presidents. If that ratio is higher than 1, Unfiltered presidents have a larger distance from the mean than Filtered ones. This is true for all twenty-one sets of rankings and the meta-ranking (table A.2).

A Monte Carlo using ten million runs was employed to test these results for statistical significance. For each run every president was randomly classed as Filtered or Unfiltered with the probability initially determined by the ratio of Filtered to all presidents, then adjusting based on the previous assignment to ensure that every run maintained the correct number of Filtered and Unfiltered presidents in that survey. After each run, the ratio of the RMS difference to the mean for Unfiltered and Filtered presidents was calculated. Table A.2 shows the percent chance that this ratio would result from random chance for every survey and for the meta-rank. Except for the Felzenberg survey—the only ranking compiled by a single individual, instead of surveying many historians—every survey shows a higher variance for Unfiltered presidents that is statistically significant at the 95 percent level. Even Felzenberg is almost 85 percent. For eighteen of the twenty-one rankings, the higher variance for Unfiltered presidents is significant at the 99 percent level, as it is in the meta-ranking. Both *Wall Street Journal* surveys, which are meant to correct for political bias, show higher variance that is significant at the 99 percent level. This is exceptionally strong support for the theory.

TESTING FILTRATION AS A CONTINUOUS VARIABLE

Filtration scores create the possibility of assessing filtration as a continuous variable instead of a dichotomous one. We can assess presidents as "more or less filtered," in other words, not just as Filtered or Unfiltered (table A.1). Such an assessment is made more difficult, however, by several factors. First, historians' rankings of presidents are a proxy for impact, not a measure of impact. Some presidents (e.g., Jefferson, Buchanan, Truman) can have extreme positions in the rankings but still have a low impact. This introduces noise into the dependent variable, which is complicated by the small number of observations ($n = 41$).

Second, a lower level of filtration creates the possibility for individual impact, but the magnitude of that impact is likely driven by circumstances. Lincoln would have had impact whenever he was elected, in other words, but the scale of his impact was only possible in the unique situation of Civil War America. This means that the functional form predicted by the theory is clearly not linear, although it may be monotonic. The less Filtered a leader is, the more likely it is that he or she will have an impact. It does not follow, however, that a leader who is entirely Unfiltered (like a vice president who comes into office because of assassination) must have a higher impact than a more Filtered leader, because circumstances will play a large role (table A.1).

Both sources of error mean that standard statistical tests will be biased against the theory, likely very strongly so, because of noise in the dependent variable and the lack of a linear functional form relating the independent and dependent variables. Because the direction of the relationship between filtration and impact does mean there should be a correlation between filtration score and ranking, however, a sufficiently strong relationship would overcome this bias and still be detectable using standard statistical methods.

We need to transform both independent and dependent variables here to account for the fact that the dependent variable is a rank. First, we should transform the Filtration Scores into a ranking, and second transform the historians' rankings into a ranking by the magnitude of the distance from the median rank to account for the theory's prediction of greater variance, not a change in mean.

The nonlinear relationship between Filtration Score and difference from median rank means that we should use Spearman's rank-order correlation, which measures the strength and direction of the monotonic relationship between two ranked variables (table A.3). The data show a r_s of 0.35 for the C-SPAN survey and 0.30 for the APSA survey, which means that Filtration Score accounts for about one-third of the distance from mean rankings in all the rankings except Felzenberg. This is a strikingly strong result given the amount of noise in the data. It is statistically significant at the 97 percent level for the C-SPAN survey and the 95 percent level for APSA. Especially given the constraints of the available data, this result is strongly supportive of the application of LFT to presidents of the United States.

CASE SELECTION

Case selection methodology in this book was driven by its central purpose—further developing Leader Filtration Theory, a theory whose fundamental purpose of identifying the circumstances in which the rare, high-impact event of a leader utilizing their discretion to generate a large unique impact occur. This makes the purpose of the cases a combination of theory development and testing, both meant to develop Leader Filtration Theory as a causal explanation for the success and failure of presidents of the United States. Cases were chosen using the typology proposed by Gerring and Cojocaru.[27]

Case study analyses of rare events, especially those used in theory development, are primarily exploratory. The effect explored here is nonlinear, because a candidate's level of filtration affects the likelihood that they will be willing to use their discretion in ways that are very different from those of a Filtered Modal president. The use of discretion in such a way is a requirement for unique impact.

Table A.3 Spearman Rank Correlation Results

	C-SPAN	*APSA*	*Felzenberg*	*Siena 2019*	*APSA 2015*	*USPC 2011*	*Siena 2010*	*C-SPAN 2009*	*WSJ 2005*	*Siena 2002*	*WSJ 2000*	*C-SPAN 2000*	*Schles 1996*	*R-M 1996*	*Siena 1994*	*Siena 1990*	*Siena 1982*	*C-T 1982*	*M-B 1982*	*Schles 1962*	*Schles 1948*	*Meta-Rank*
rs	0.345	0.304	0.195	0.330	0.323	0.409	0.309	0.370	0.364	0.391	0.407	0.456	0.345	0.444	0.399	0.390	0.377	0.440	0.375	0.461	0.392	0.413
n	41	41	40	41	41	40	41	40	40	40	39	39	39	39	39	38	37	36	36	31	29	41
df	39	39	38	39	39	38	39	38	38	38	37	37	37	37	37	36	35	34	34	29	27	39
t	2.296	1.994	1.223	2.182	2.135	2.766	2.030	2.456	2.410	2.621	2.710	3.117	2.236	3.010	2.649	2.540	2.412	2.854	2.359	2.799	2.216	2.835
p-value	0.027	0.053	0.229	0.035	0.039	0.009	0.049	0.019	0.021	0.013	0.010	0.004	0.031	0.005	0.012	0.016	0.021	0.007	0.024	0.009	0.035	0.007

The magnitude of unique impact, however, is determined by the situation in which that discretion is used and is therefore unrelated to the president's level of filtration. Large unique impact is, essentially, a leader-driven "black swan" event, and Leader Filtration Theory is meant to identify the circumstances in which this can occur.

Case studies of black swan events are critical because they can establish that the possibility of such events exists, the circumstances in which they can occur, and the mechanisms that lead to them, but they are necessarily nonrepresentative. A representative case study of financial risk management systems, for example, would show them working well, which they do most of the time—except in a crisis, which is when their performance is most important. Understanding the causes of a financial crisis requires selecting on the dependent variable, as does understanding any other rare but high-impact event. This requirement for case selection creates two limitations. First, the cases cannot be used to estimate the magnitude of the effect. Estimating the magnitude of such black swan events is in any case exceptionally difficult given the extent to which this can vary based on subtle or previously regarded as unimportant features of the context.[28]

Second, rare and extreme events necessarily involve a large amount of uncertainty, complicating the link between independent and dependent variables. Just as in financial crises, where the underlying circumstances that enable a crisis can exist for years before a seemingly minor event triggers a bank run or stock market crash, the election of an Unfiltered president substantially increases the chances of a president using their discretion to have a large unique impact and therefore perform either very well or very poorly, but if this will actually happen depends on everything from the broader context to their particular, and very human, preferences and decisions.[29]

The cases here are meant for theory development and causal inference. This makes them primarily exploratory—we are trying to establish the existence of the effect, not measure its size. This means they should be selected to maximize variation in outcome—Truman, Theodore Roosevelt, and Eisenhower for success, and Buchanan and Andrew Johnson for failure. The shadow cases, combined with the quantitative analysis, indicate that the theory plausibly has out-of-sample power, but do not definitively demonstrate this.

The book's secondary purpose is to describe how Leader Filtration Theory works to help readers evaluate contemporary presidential candidates, so where possible, cases were chosen to be typical as well. Here Truman was a vice president selected to be the next president, Buchanan a normally elected president, Theodore Roosevelt and Andrew Johnson vice presidents who became president because of an assassination, and Eisenhower a national hero who swept to the presidency on a wave of popularity. These cases thus give a sweep of the different possible ways a candidate can become president, ranging from sheer chance to overwhelming national stature.

The two sets of Truman and Buchanan and Johnson, Roosevelt, and Eisenhower maximize variation on the most important independent variable, level of filtration. Truman and Buchanan maximize variation on presidential performance within the high-filtration set, while Johnson, Roosevelt, and Eisenhower maximize it within the low-filtration set. This book also has several shadow cases, but these are indicative and meant to show how the theory might apply to presidents outside of the five ones that are the major focus of the analysis here.

Finally, a note on Warren G. Harding. Harding is classified as Unfiltered because of his relatively short career in the Senate and status as a dark horse candidate, and as a failure by the historians' and political scientists' rankings. The traditional view of Harding is that he was a corrupt womanizer who was simply not up to the job of the presidency.[30] This view is supported by Simonton's objective assessments of his Intellectual Brilliance, where he is scored last by a considerable margin out of all forty-three presidents up through George W. Bush, a full two standard deviations below the mean.[31]

On the other hand, this evaluation of Harding and his presidency is under a full-fledged assault by both historians[32] and popular authors.[33] Harding's untimely death denied him the opportunity to defend himself from the corruption charges and various posthumous attacks on his reputation. Given the historical debate over his capabilities and performance, his abbreviated time in office (at barely more than two years, he had the third-shortest presidency in American history), and the fact that his administration was, to my mind, relatively inconsequential compared to the ones profiled here, I have decided to wait on the emergence of a more stable historical consensus on him before exploring how his presidency fits with Leader Filtration Theory.

WEAKNESSES AND LIMITATIONS OF APPLYING
LEADER FILTRATION THEORY TO PRESIDENTS

The most critical weakness of Leader Filtration Theory when using it as a guide to the success and failure of individual presidents is that it is a probabilistic theory about rare and extreme events. It describes general tendencies. Individual leaders have free will. They can surprise you. At most, the theory can tell you which leaders are most likely to do that—it cannot tell you, with certainty, which will. Just in looking at modern presidents, for example, the theory almost certainly struggles to predict Lyndon Johnson's sudden turn to supporting civil rights legislation after a long career as a racial conservative,[34] and would not have predicted that the highly filtered Nixon would engage in the wide-ranging criminal behavior that came to be known as Watergate.[35]

Second, the rare events describe not just presidents themselves but the particular moments or decisions in which even the most Unfiltered president might have a large unique impact. Leaders, even presidents, are always constrained by circumstances, and in most cases, circumstances are the dominant factor. I believe that Lincoln would have been a successful president in any era, but even he would likely only have been a transcendently great president given the unique circumstances of the Civil War.

A generation later, Chester A. Arthur became president following the assassination of James Garfield. Arthur had been chosen for the vice presidency as a sop to the corrupt New York Tammany Hall machine, but once in office he surprisingly supported civil service reform, a crucial anticorruption measure.[36] This seems exactly like the sort of behavior you would expect from an Unfiltered president, but despite this surprising choice Arthur's presidency remained otherwise unmemorable. Perhaps that was because Arthur was a normal president, or perhaps it was because a sufficiently weighty occasion for him to use his discretion in a way another president would not simply did not arise.

All of this means, however, that most presidential behavior is driven by the nature of the presidency, not the president. We should draw on structural and institutionally driven models to explain most political behavior, including that of the president. Even if a president chooses to exercise that discretion in a unique way, it might be on a matter so trivial that it has no significant impact. Unfiltered presidents may be willing to use their discretion to generate a unique impact, but they do not have to, and they will likely do so on only a handful of key decisions at most. This means that as a president's level of filtration decreases, the *likelihood* that they will have a large impact will increase (because the odds that they are different enough to act in a unique fashion increase), but the predicted *magnitude* of that impact will not (because magnitude will be driven by circumstances and the moments when they choose to use that discretion).

Third, Leader Filtration Theory is an organizational theory. Applying it to an institution as idiosyncratic as the American presidency requires some compromises. No company, and few other countries, would allow their leader to be chosen through a process as baroque and rickety as the one the United States uses today. I can think of no company not controlled by a family, for example, that has an institution even vaguely comparable to the vice presidency, where someone who is usually chosen with little or no regard for their governing ability may, at any moment, suddenly be elevated to power no matter what even the most powerful other members of the system might desire.

Fourth, extending Leader Filtration Theory from unique impact to predicting performance necessarily injects uncertainty and subjectivity into the analysis. Only forty-five people, after all, have ever been president. That is not a very large sample. I have tried to mitigate this concern by basing my assessments on the historical consensus and drawing on research in political science, management, psychology, and other fields.

The question of whether a president succeeded is, of course, inherently a judgment call that goes beyond the boundaries of pure science. There are, surely, a small number of people in the United States today who condemn instead of praise Lincoln for issuing the Emancipation Proclamation and who think that Buchanan's radically different stance towards slavery and secession was the right one. While I have attempted to minimize this problem by relying on the collective judgments of political scientists and historians (in all cases I have classified presidents as a success or failure based on their position in the rankings, not my own views), it remains intrinsic to the project. I am sure that, particularly when looking at more modern Presidents, some readers will vigorously disagree with those assessments. Even if you do, I believe that you will still be able to draw much from this approach.

Notes

CHAPTER 1

1. Carl J. Richard, *The Founders and the Classics: Greece, Rome, and the American Enlightenment* (Cambridge, MA: Harvard University Press, 1994).

2. Morris P. Fiorina, "The Political Parties Have Sorted," Hoover Institution Essay on Contemporary American Politics, Series 3, September 21, 2016, www .hoover.org/sites/default/files/research/docs/fiorina_3_finalfile.pdf.

3. Jennifer A. Chatman, "Improving Interactional Organizational Research: A Model of Person-Organization Fit," *Academy of Management Review* 14, no. 3 (1989); Benjamin Schneider, "The People Make the Place," *Personnel Psychology* 40, no. 3 (September 1987); Benjamin Schneider, Harold W. Goldstein, and D. Brent Smith, "The ASA Framework: An Update," *Personnel Psychology* 48, no. 4 (1995); Rakesh Khurana, *Searching for a Corporate Savior: The Irrational Quest for Charismatic CEOs* (Princeton, NJ: Princeton University Press, 2002); James G. March, "How We Talk and How We Act: Administrative Theory and Administrative Life," in *Leadership and Organizational Culture*, ed. Thomas J. Sergiovanni and John E. Corbally (Urbana: University of Illinois Press, 1984), 21; Jeffrey Pfeffer, "The Ambiguity of Leadership," *Academy of Management Review* 2, no. 1 (January 1977): 106.

4. James D. Fearon, "Counterfactuals and Hypothesis Testing in Political Science," *World Politics* 43, no. 2 (January 1991); Fred I. Greenstein, "The Impact of Personality on the End of the Cold War: A Counterfactual Analysis," *Political*

Psychology 19, no. 1 (1998); Philip Tetlock and Aaron Belkin, *Counterfactual Thought Experiments in World Politics: Logical, Methodological, and Psychological Perspectives* (Princeton, NJ: Princeton University Press, 1996); Joseph S. Nye, *Presidential Leadership and the Creation of the American Era* (Princeton, NJ: Princeton University Press, 2013); Jeffrey M. Chwieroth, "Counterfactuals and the Study of the American Presidency," *Presidential Studies Quarterly* 32, no. 2 (April 2004).

5. Gautam Mukunda, *Indispensable: When Leaders Really Matter* (Boston: Harvard Business Review Press, 2012).

A related concept to WAR—Wins Above Expectation—was applied to presidential legislative success rates in Manuel P. Teodoro and Jon R. Bond, "Presidents, Baseball, and Wins above Expectations: What Can Sabermetrics Tell Us about Presidential Success?," *PS: Political Science & Politics* 50, no. 2 (April 2017).

6. These three forces were first explicitly identified in Stanley Lieberson and James F. O'Connor, "Leadership and Organizational Performance: A Study of Large Corporations," *American Sociological Review* 37, no. 2 (1972).

For organizational behavior in general, see: David Braybrooke and Charles E. Lindblom, *A Strategy of Decision* (London: The Free Press of Glencoe, 1963); Anthony Downs, *Inside Bureaucracy* (Boston: Little, Brown, 1991); James G. March and Herbert A. Simon, *Organizations* (New York: John Wiley and Sons, 1959); Herbert A. Simon, *Administrative Behavior* (New York: The Free Press, 1968); John D. Steinbruner, *The Cybernetic Theory of Decision* (Princeton, NJ: Princeton University Press, 1974); James D. Thompson, *Organizations in Action* (New York: McGraw-Hill, 1967).

In business, see: Michael T. Hannan and John H. Freeman, *Organizational Ecology* (Cambridge, MA: Harvard University Press, 1989); Lieberson and O'Connor, "Leadership and Organizational Performance"; Jeffrey Pfeffer and Gerald R. Salancik, *The External Control of Organizations: A Resource Dependence Perspective* (Stanford, CA: Stanford Business Classics, 2003).

Theories of international relations usually hold that leaders are unimportant by omission, with some of the most influential works simply ignoring leaders entirely. See, for the single most influential modern work of international relations theory: Kenneth N. Waltz, *Theory of International Politics* (Boston: McGraw Hill, 1979). Also the highly influential: Robert Gilpin, *War and Change in World Politics* (New York: Cambridge University Press, 1981).

Some, however, explicitly argue that leaders are unimportant. See: Stephen M. Walt, *Revolution and War* (Ithaca, NY: Cornell University Press, 1996); Kenneth N. Waltz, *Man, The State, and War*, revised ed. (New York: Columbia University Press, 2001); Graham T. Allison and Philip Zelikow, *Essence of Decision: Explaining the Cuban Missile Crisis*, 2nd ed. (New York: Longman, 1999).

7. Donald C. Hambrick, "Upper Echelons Theory: An Update," *Academy of Management Review* 32, no. 2 (April 2007); Donald C. Hambrick and Eric Abra-

hamson, "Assessing Managerial Discretion across Industries: A Multimethod Approach," *Academy of Management Journal* 38, no. 5 (October 1995); Donald C. Hambrick and Phyllis A. Mason, "Upper Echelons: The Organization as a Reflection of Its Top Managers," *Academy of Management Review* 9, no. 2 (1984); Noam Wasserman, Bharat Anand, and Nitin Nohria, "When Does Leadership Matter? A Contingent Opportunities View of CEO Leadership," in *Handbook of Leadership Theory and Practice*, ed. Nitin Nohria and Rakesh Khurana (Boston: Harvard Business Press, 2010); Benjamin F. Jones and Benjamin A. Olken, "Do Leaders Matter? National Leadership and Growth since World War II," *Quarterly Journal of Economics* 120, no. 3 (August 2005); Benjamin F. Jones and Benjamin A. Olken, "Hit or Miss? The Effect of Assassinations on Institutions and War," *American Economic Journal: Macroeconomics* 1, no. 2 (July 2009); Glenn D. Paige, *The Scientific Study of Political Leadership* (New York: The Free Press, 1977); Richard J. Samuels, *Machiavelli's Children: Leaders and Their Legacies in Italy and Japan* (Ithaca, NY: Cornell University Press, 2003); "Roundtable Discussion of Richard J. Samuels's *Machiavelli's Children: Leaders and Their Legacies in Italy and Japan*," *Journal of East Asian Studies* 6, no. 1 (January–April 2006); Ole R. Holsti, "Foreign Policy Decision Makers Viewed Psychologically: 'Cognitive Process' Approaches," in *In Search of Global Patterns*, ed. James N. Rosenau (New York: The Free Press, 1976).

8. Matthew Eshbaugh-Soha and Jeffrey S. Peake, "Presidents and the Economic Agenda," *Political Research Quarterly* 58, no. 1 (2005); Terry M. Moe, "The Revolution in Presidential Studies," *Presidential Studies Quarterly* 39, no. 4 (2009); G. L. Hager and T. Sullivan, "President-Centered and Presidency-Centered Explanations of Presidential Public Activity," *American Journal of Political Science* 38, no. 4 (1994); Bert A. Rockman, "Does the Revolution in Presidential Studies Mean 'Off with the President's Head'?," *Presidential Studies Quarterly* 39, no. 4 (2009).

9. Brian Newman and Adrian Davis, "Polls and Elections: Character and Political Time as Sources of Presidential Greatness," *Presidential Studies Quarterly* 46, no. 2 (2016); Curt Nichols, "The Presidential Ranking Game: Critical Review and Some New Discoveries," *Presidential Studies Quarterly* 42, no. 2 (2012); Stephen Skowronek, *The Politics Presidents Make: Leadership from John Adams to Bill Clinton* (Cambridge, MA: The Belknap Press of Harvard University Press, 1997); Stephen Skowronek, "Theory and History, Structure and Agency," *Presidential Studies Quarterly* 29, no. 3 (1999); Lee Ross, "The Intuitive Psychologist and His Shortcomings: Distortions in the Attribution Process," in *Advances in Experimental Social Psychology*, ed. L. Berkowitz (New York: Academic Press, 1977); Randolph P. Beatty and Edward J. Zajac, "CEO Change and Firm Performance in Large Corporations: Succession Effects and Manager Effects," *Strategic Management Journal* 8, no. 4 (1987); Morten Bennedsen, Francisco Pérez-González, and Daniel Wolfenzon, "Do CEOs Matter?" (Online

paper at Columbia University, 2006), www0.gsb.columbia.edu/mygsb/faculty /research/pubfiles/3177/valueceos.pdf.

10. John Balz, "Ready to Lead on Day One: Predicting Presidential Greatness from Experience," *PS: Political Science and Politics* 43 (July 2010); Mark Zachary Taylor, "An Economic Ranking of the US Presidents, 1789–2009: A Data-Based Approach," *PS: Political Science & Politics* 45, no. 4 (2012); Theresa Marchant-Shapiro, *Professional Pathways to the Presidency* (New York: Palgrave Macmillan, 2015); Charles O. Jones, "The Legitimacy of Inexperience: Leadership from Outside," *The Forum: A Journal of Applied Research in Contemporary Politics* 7, no. 1 (2009); Robert K. Murray and Tim H. Blessing, *Greatness in the White House: Rating the Presidents, Washington through Carter; Final Report, the Presidential Performance Study* (University Park: Pennsylvania State University Press, 1988); Jack E. Holmes and Robert E. Elder Jr., "Our Best and Worst Presidents: Some Possible Reasons for Perceived Performance," *Presidential Studies Quarterly* 19, no. 3 (1989); Arthur M. Simon and Joseph E. Uscinski, "Prior Experience Predicts Presidential Performance," *Presidential Studies Quarterly* 42, no. 3 (2012).

11. Maryann E. Gallagher and Susan H. Allen, "Presidential Personality: Not Just a Nuisance," *Foreign Policy Analysis* 10, no. 1 (2014); Maryann E. Gallagher and Bethany Blackstone, "Taking Matters into Their Own Hands: Presidents' Personality Traits and the Use of Executive Orders," *Presidential Studies Quarterly* 45, no. 2 (2015); Douglas J. Hoekstra, "The Politics of *Politics:* Skowronek and Presidential Research," *Presidential Studies Quarterly* 29, no. 3 (1999); Simon and Uscinski, "Prior Experience," 8; Dean Keith Simonton, "Presidential IQ, Openness, Intellectual Brilliance, and Leadership: Estimates and Correlations for 42 U.S. Chief Executives," *Political Psychology* 27, no. 4 (2006); Dean Keith Simonton, *Why Presidents Succeed: A Political Psychology of Leadership* (New Haven, CT: Yale University Press, 1987); Dean Keith Simonton, "Presidential Style: Personality, Biography, and Performance," *Journal of Personality and Social Psychology* 55, no. 6 (1988); Dean Keith Simonton, "Putting the Best Leaders in the White House: Personality, Policy, and Performance," *Political Psychology* 14, no. 3 (1993); Dean Keith Simonton, "Presidential Greatness and Performance: Can We Predict Leadership in the White House?," *Journal of Personality* 49, no. 3 (September 1981); Dean Keith Simonton, "Intellectual Brilliance and Presidential Performance: Why Pure Intelligence (or Openness) Doesn't Suffice," *Journal of Intelligence* 6, no. 2 (2018); Stephen J. Wayne, "Presidential Character and Judgment: Obama's Afghanistan and Health Care Decisions," *Presidential Studies Quarterly* 41, no. 2 (2011).

12. James W. Ceaser, *Presidential Selection: Theory and Development* (Princeton, NJ: Princeton University Press, 1979), 10.

13. Michael Burlingame, *Abraham Lincoln: A Life* (Baltimore: Johns Hopkins University Press, 2008), 4116 of 61039, Kindle; David Herbert Donald, *Lincoln*

(New York: Touchstone, 1996); Don E. Fehrenbacher, ed., *Abraham Lincoln: Speeches and Writings 1832-1858* (New York: Penguin Books, 1989).

14. James Madison, "Federalist No. 57," in *The Federalist Papers* (Seattle: AmazonClassics, 2017), 5518.

15. Alexander Hamilton, "Federalist No. 68," in *The Federalist Papers* (Seattle: AmazonClassics, 2017), 6543-85.

16. James Madison, "Federalist No. 10," in *The Federalist Papers* (Seattle: AmazonClassics, 2017), 63-72.

17. Richard Ben Cramer, *What It Takes: The Way to the White House* (New York: Random House, 1992); Samuel Popkin, *The Candidate: What It Takes to Win—and Hold—the White House* (New York: Oxford University Press, 2012); Martin P. Wattenberg, "Elections: Reliability Trumps Competence: Personal Attributes in the 2004 Presidential Election," *Presidential Studies Quarterly* 36, no. 4 (2006); Martin P. Wattenberg, "The Declining Relevance of Candidate Personal Attributes in Presidential Elections," *Presidential Studies Quarterly* 46, no. 1 (2016); Theodore H. White, *The Making of the President, 1960* (New York: Pocket Books, 1962); Theodore H. White, *The Making of the President, 1964* (New York: Atheneum, 1965); Theodore H. White, *The Making of the President, 1968* (New York: Atheneum, 1969); Theodore H. White, *The Making of the President, 1972* (New York: Atheneum, 1973).

18. Steven E. Finkel, "Reexamining the 'Minimal Effects' Model in Recent Presidential Campaigns," *Journal of Politics* 55, no. 1 (1993); Barbara G. Salmore and Stephen A. Salmore, *Candidates, Parties, and Campaigns: Electoral Politics in America*, 2nd ed. (Washington, DC: CQ Press, 1989); Bernard Berelson, *Voting: A Study of Opinion Formation in a Presidential Campaign* (Chicago: University of Chicago Press, 1954); D. Sunshine Hillygus and Simon Jackman, "Voter Decision Making in Election 2000: Campaign Effects, Partisan Activation, and the Clinton Legacy," *American Journal of Political Science* 47, no. 4 (2003); Stephen Ansolabehere, "The Paradox of Minimal Effects," in *Do Campaigns Matter?*, ed. Brady Henry and Johnson Richard (Ann Arbor: University of Michigan Press, 2001); Daron R. Shaw, "A Study of Presidential Campaign Event Effects from 1952 to 1992," *Journal of Politics* 61, no. 2 (1999); Samuel Popkin, *The Reasoning Voter: Communication and Persuasion in Presidential Campaigns*, 2nd ed. (Chicago: University of Chicago Press, 1994); W. Lance Bennett and Shanto Iyengar, "A New Era of Minimal Effects? The Changing Foundations of Political Communication," *Journal of Communication* 58, no. 4 (2008); Adam Shehata and Jesper Strömbäck, "Not (Yet) a New Era of Minimal Effects: A Study of Agenda Setting at the Aggregate and Individual Levels," *International Journal of Press/Politics* 18, no. 2 (2013).

19. Mukunda, *Indispensable*.

20. Malcolm Gladwell, *Blink: The Power of Thinking without Thinking* (New York: Little, Brown, 2005), 1050 of 3902, Kindle; Khurana, *Searching for a Corporate Savior*.

21. Robert Hogan and Robert B. Kaiser, "What We Know about Leadership," *Review of General Psychology* 9, no. 2 (June 2005).

22. Nathanael J. Fast et al., "Illusory Control: A Generative Force behind Power's Far-Reaching Effects," *Psychological Science* 20, no. 4 (2009); Adam D. Galinsky et al., "Power and Perspectives Not Taken," *Psychological Science* 17, no. 12 (2006); Dacher Keltner, Deborah H. Gruenfeld, and Cameron Anderson, "Power, Approach, and Inhibition,"*Psychological Review* 110, no. 2 (2003); Dacher Keltner, "Don't Let Power Corrupt You," *Harvard Business Review* 94, no. 10 (October 2016): 112; Ian H. Robertson, "How Power Affects the Brain," *The Psychologist* 26, no. 3 (March 2013); Jerry Useem, "Power Causes Brain Damage," *The Atlantic,* July/August 2017, www.theatlantic.com/magazine/archive/2017/07/power-causes-brain-damage/528711/; Vivek K. Wadhera, "Losing Touch," *Kellogg Insight,* November 1, 2009, https://insight.kellogg.northwestern.edu/article/losing_touch.

23. S. Chen, A. Y. Lee-Chai, and J. A. Bargh, "Relationship Orientation as a Moderator of the Effects of Social Power," *Journal of Personality and Social Psychology* 80, no. 2 (February 2001); Katherine A. DeCelles et al., "Does Power Corrupt or Enable? When and Why Power Facilitates Self-Interested Behavior," *Journal of Applied Psychology* 97, no. 3 (2012).

24. Khurana, *Searching for a Corporate Savior,* 3237 of 5794, Kindle.

25. Monica C. Higgins, *Career Imprints: Creating Leaders across an Industry* (San Francisco: Jossey-Bass, 2005); Daniel M. Cable and Charles K. Parsons, "Socialization Tactics and Person-Organization Fit," *Personnel Psychology* 54, no. 1 (2001); William Ocasio, "Towards an Attention-Based View of the Firm," *Strategic Management Journal* 18 (1997).

26. Boris Groysberg, *Chasing Stars: The Myth of Talent and the Portability of Performance* (Princeton, NJ: Princeton University Press, 2010); Boris Groysberg, Andrew N. McLean, and Nitin Nohria, "Are Leaders Portable?," *Harvard Business Review* 84, no. 5 (2006); Boris Groysberg, Ashish Nanda, and Nitin Nohria, "The Risky Business of Hiring Stars," *Harvard Business Review* 82 (2004); Robert S. Huckman and Gary P. Pisano, "The Firm Specificity of Individual Performance: Evidence from Cardiac Surgery," *Management Science* 52, no. 4 (April 2006).

27. Ronald S. Burt, *Brokerage and Closure: An Introduction to Social Capital* (New York: Oxford University Press, 2005), 1612–815.

28. Kathleen Dalton, *Theodore Roosevelt: A Strenuous Life* (New York: Alfred A. Knopf, 2002); Edmund Morris, *The Rise of Theodore Roosevelt* (New York: Ballantine Books, 1980); Edmund Morris, *Theodore Rex* (New York: Random House, 2001).

29. Marty Cohen et al., *The Party Decides: Presidential Nominations before and after Reform* (Chicago: University of Chicago Press, 2008).

30. Byron E. Shafer, *Bifurcated Politics: Evolution and Reform in the National Party Convention*, A Russell Sage Foundation Study (Cambridge, MA: Harvard University Press, 1988), 11.

31. "How Selecting U.S. Presidential Candidates Became the People's Choice," Reuters, March 29, 2016, www.reuters.com/article/us-usa-election-selection-process-factbox/how-selecting-u-s-presidential-candidates-became-the-peoples-choice-idUSKCN0WW001; James S. Chase, *Emergence of the Presidential Nominating Convention, 1789–1832* (Urbana: University of Illinois Press, 1973).

32. Tevi Troy, "The Evolution of Party Conventions," *National Affairs*, Summer 2016; "How Selecting U.S. Presidential Candidates Became the People's Choice"; Chase, *Emergence of the Presidential Nominating Convention*, 42–63.

33. Chase, *Emergence of the Presidential Nominating Convention*, 121–275.

34. Austin Ranney, *Curing the Mischiefs of Faction: Party Reform in America* (Berkeley: University of California Press, 1976), 121; Cohen et al., *The Party Decides;* Elaine Ciulla Kamarck, *Primary Politics: Everything You Need to Know about How America Nominates Its Presidential Candidates*, 2nd ed. (Washington, DC: Brookings Institution Press, 2015).

35. Kamarck, *Primary Politics*, 7, 10 of 5714, Kindle; Nelson W. Polsby, *Consequences of Party Reform* (Oxford: Oxford University Press, 1983), 13–15.

36. Cohen et al., *The Party Decides*, 691 of 5625, Kindle.

37. Polsby, *Consequences of Party Reform*, 55–64.

38. Cohen et al., *The Party Decides*, 82 of 5625, Kindle.

39. Cohen et al., *The Party Decides*, 181, 238, 322, 583, 665, 91, 2276 of 5625, Kindle.

40. Cohen et al., *The Party Decides*, 2448–2524, 4590, 849 of 5625, Kindle.

41. When sorting candidates into binary categories of Filtered and Unfiltered, I chose eight years as a cutoff, although choosing seven or six would not have affected the results.

42. Nichols, "Presidential Ranking Game"; Simonton, "Presidential Greatness and Performance"; Mukunda, *Indispensable*.

43. "Presidential Historians Survey 2017," C-SPAN, 2017, accessed April 2, 2018, www.c-span.org/presidentsurvey2017/?page=overall; Brandon Rottinghaus and Justin S. Vaughn, "Official Results of the 2018 Presidents & Executive Politics Presidential Greatness Survey" (online paper at Boise State University, 2018), www.boisestate.edu/sps-politicalscience/files/2018/02/Greatness.pdf; "Siena's 6th Presidential Expert Poll 1982–2018," Siena College Research Institute, February 13, 2019, https://scri.siena.edu/2019/02/13/sienas-6th-presidential-expert-poll-1982–2018/.

44. Nichols, "Presidential Ranking Game."

45. John Gerring, "Case-Selection for Case Study Analysis: Qualitative and Quantitative Techniques," in *Oxford Handbook on Political Methodology*, ed.

Janet M. Box-Steffensmeier, Henry E. Brady, and David Collier (Oxford: Oxford University Press, 2006); John Gerring, *Case Study Research: Principles and Practices* (New York: Cambridge University Press, 2007); John Gerring and Lee Cojocaru, "Selecting Cases for Intensive Analysis: A Diversity of Goals and Methods," *Sociological Methods & Research* 45, no. 3 (2016).

46. Daniel L. Byman and Kenneth M. Pollack, "Let Us Now Praise Great Men: Bringing the Statesman Back In," *International Security* 25, no. 4 (Spring 2001); Alexander L. George, *Presidential Decisionmaking in Foreign Policy: The Effective Use of Information and Advice* (Boulder, CO: Westview Press, 1980).

47. William C. Wohlforth, "The Stability of a Unipolar World," International Security 24, no. 1 (1999).

48. John Dickerson, "The Hardest Job in the World," *The Atlantic*, May 2018, www.theatlantic.com/magazine/archive/2018/05/a-broken-office/556883/.

49. Juan Linz, "The Perils of Presidentialism," *Journal of Democracy* 1, no. 1 (Winter 1990); Alfred Stepan and Cindy Skach, "Constitutional Frameworks and Democratic Consolidation: Parliamentarianism versus Presidentialism," *World Politics* 46, no. 1 (2011); Matthew Yglesias, "American Democracy Is Doomed," *Vox*, October 8, 2015, www.vox.com/2015/3/2/8120063/american-democracy-doomed.

50. Walter Russell Mead, *Special Providence: American Foreign Policy and How It Changed the World* (New York: Alfred A. Knopf, 2001); Mukunda, *Indispensable;* Gary L. Ecelbarger, *The Great Comeback: How Abraham Lincoln Beat the Odds to Win the 1860 Republican Nomination* (New York: Thomas Dunne Books, 2008); Otto von Bismarck, Wikiquote, accessed May 13, 2018, https://en.wikiquote.org/wiki/Otto_von_Bismarck; John C. Waugh, *One Man Great Enough: Abraham Lincoln's Road to Civil War* (Orlando, FL: Harcourt, 2007).

CHAPTER 2

1. Mukunda, *Indispensable;* Kenneth N. Waltz, *Foreign Policy and Democratic Politics: The American and British Experience* (Boston: Little, Brown, 1967).

2. Robert H. Ferrell, *Harry S. Truman: A Life* (Columbia: University of Missouri Press, 1994), 177 of 13400, Kindle; Alonzo L. Hamby, *Man of the People: A Life of Harry S. Truman,* (New York: Oxford University Press, 1995), 290; David G. McCullough, *Truman* (New York: Simon & Schuster, 1992), 6439 of 22565, Kindle; Robert Dallek, *Harry S. Truman* (New York: Times Books, 2008).

3. A. J. Baime, *The Accidental President: Harry S. Truman and the Four Months That Changed the World* (Boston: Houghton Mifflin Harcourt, 2017), 77 of 8943, Kindle.

4. Dallek, *Harry S. Truman*, 45–55 of 3039, Kindle; Ferrell, *Harry S. Truman*, 1–23; Hamby, *Man of the People*, 7–17; McCullough, *Truman*, 536–976 of 22565, Kindle.

5. Ferrell, *Harry S. Truman*, 22–35; Hamby, *Man of the People*, 18–23.

6. Ferrell, *Harry S. Truman*, 56; Hamby, *Man of the People*, 57–58; McCullough, *Truman*, 1761 of 22565, Kindle.

7. Ferrell, *Harry S. Truman*, 57–70; Hamby, *Man of the People*, 58–78; McCullough, *Truman*, 2042–161 of 22565, Kindle.

8. Ferrell, *Harry S. Truman*, 59–60, 72; Hamby, *Man of the People*, 94–100.

9. Ferrell, *Harry S. Truman*, 91–92; Hamby, *Man of the People*, 101–8; McCullough, *Truman*, 2773–868 of 22565, Kindle.

10. Dallek, *Harry S. Truman*, 124 of 3039, Kindle; Ferrell, *Harry S. Truman*, 92–115; Hamby, *Man of the People*, 109–85; McCullough, *Truman*, 2806–3447 of 22565, Kindle.

11. Ferrell, *Harry S. Truman*, 124–33; Hamby, *Man of the People: A Life of Harry S. Truman*, 186–208; McCullough, *Truman*, 3728–4322 of 22565, Kindle.

12. Ferrell, *Harry S. Truman*, 134–40; Hamby, *Man of the People*, 213–34; McCullough, *Truman*, 3728–4322 of 22565, Kindle.

13. Ferrell, *Harry S. Truman*, 140–51; Hamby, *Man of the People*, 234–46; McCullough, *Truman*, 4437–711 of 22565, Kindle.

14. Dallek, *Harry S. Truman*, 207–23 of 3039, Kindle; Ferrell, *Harry S. Truman*, 153–61; Hamby, *Man of the People*, 248–73; McCullough, *Truman*, 4737–5484 of 22565, Kindle.

15. James MacGregor Burns, *Roosevelt: The Soldier of Freedom* (New York: Open Road Media, 2012), 503 of 17122, Kindle.

16. Dallek, *Harry S. Truman*, 239–58 of of 3039, Kindle; Robert H. Ferrell, *Choosing Truman: The Democratic Convention of 1944* (Columbia: University of Missouri Press, 1944), 149–224 of 2973, Kindle; McCullough, *Truman*, 5492–534 of 22565, Kindle; Robert L. Messer, *The End of an Alliance: James F. Byrnes, Roosevelt, Truman, and the Origins of the Cold War* (Chapel Hill: University of North Carolina Press, 1982), 260 of 6447, Kindle.

17. Dallek, *Harry S. Truman*, 239 of 3039, Kindle; Ferrell, *Choosing Truman*, 50 of 2973, Kindle; McCullough, *Truman*, 5546–60 of 22565, Kindle; Messer, *End of an Alliance*, 311–12 of 6447, Kindle.

18. John C. Culver and John Hyde, *American Dreamer: The Life and Times of Henry A. Wallace* (New York: W. W. Norton, 2001), 7519 of 15699, Kindle; Ferrell, *Choosing Truman*, 396 of 2973, Kindle.

19. Ferrell, *Choosing Truman*, 212–24 of 2973, Kindle.

20. Ferrell, *Choosing Truman*, 321–74 of 2973, Kindle; Messer, *End of an Alliance*, 354 of 6447, Kindle.

21. McCullough, *Truman*, 5534–39 of 22565, Kindle.

22. Culver and Hyde, *American Dreamer*, 7315 of 15699, Kindle; Ferrell, *Choosing Truman*, 17–23 of 2973, Kindle.

23. Culver and Hyde, *American Dreamer*, 7696 of 15699, Kindle; Ferrell, *Choosing Truman*, 10–13; McCullough, *Truman*, 5577–661 of 22565, Kindle; Messer, *End of an Alliance*, 427–45 of 6447, Kindle.

24. Ferrell, *Choosing Truman*, 563–722 of 2973, Kindle; McCullough, *Truman*, 5716 of 22565, Kindle.

25. Ferrell, *Choosing Truman*, 760–857 of 2973, Kindle; McCullough, *Truman*, 5748 of 22565, Kindle.

26. Ferrell, *Choosing Truman*, 857–916 of 2973, Kindle; McCullough, *Truman*, 5748–93 of 22565, Kindle.

27. McCullough, *Truman*, 5819 of 22565, Kindle.

28. Ferrell, *Choosing Truman*, 938–1046 of 2973, Kindle; McCullough, *Truman*, 5853 of 22565, Kindle; Messer, *End of an Alliance*, 524 of 6447, Kindle.

29. Ferrell, *Choosing Truman*, 1046–102 of 2973, Kindle.

30. Ferrell, *Choosing Truman*, 1251 of 2973, Kindle; McCullough, *Truman*, 314 of 22565, Kindle; Culver and Hyde, *American Dreamer*, 7930 of 15699, Kindle.

31. Ferrell, *Choosing Truman*, 23 of 2973, Kindle.

32. Ferrell, *Choosing Truman*, 1608–20 of 2973, Kindle.

33. Culver and Hyde, *American Dreamer*, 7968 of 15699, Kindle; Ferrell, *Choosing Truman*, 77 of 2973, Kindle; McCullough, *Truman*.

34. Culver and Hyde, *American Dreamer*, 8005–37 of 15699, Kindle; Ferrell, *Choosing Truman*, 1572–83 of 2973, Kindle; McCullough, *Truman*, 5936–44 of 22565, Kindle.

35. Culver and Hyde, *American Dreamer*, 8005–37 of 15699, Kindle; Ferrell, *Choosing Truman*, 1588–600 of 2973, Kindle; McCullough, *Truman*, 5936 of 22565, Kindle.

36. Culver and Hyde, *American Dreamer*; Ferrell, *Choosing Truman*; McCullough, *Truman*.

37. Culver and Hyde, *American Dreamer*, 8005–37 of 15699, Kindle; Ferrell, *Choosing Truman*, 1555–72 of 2973, Kindle; McCullough, *Truman*, 5944–58 of 22565, Kindle.

38. Culver and Hyde, *American Dreamer*, 8005–37 of 15699, Kindle; Ferrell, *Choosing Truman*, 1575–608 of 2973, Kindle; McCullough, *Truman*, 5944–58 of 22565, Kindle.

39. Culver and Hyde, *American Dreamer*, 8005–37 of 15699, Kindle; Ferrell, *Choosing Truman*, 1575–608 of 2973, Kindle; McCullough, *Truman*, 5944–58 of 22565, Kindle.

40. Culver and Hyde, *American Dreamer*, 8037–61 of 15699, Kindle; Ferrell, *Choosing Truman*, 1608–96 of 2973, Kindle; McCullough, *Truman*, 5958–84 of 22565, Kindle.

41. Culver and Hyde, *American Dreamer*, 8037–61 of 15699, Kindle; Ferrell, *Choosing Truman*, 1608–727 of 2973, Kindle; McCullough, *Truman*, 5958–98 of 22565, Kindle.

42. Culver and Hyde, *American Dreamer*, 8037–61 of 15699, Kindle; Ferrell, *Choosing Truman*, 1696–727 of 2973, Kindle; McCullough, *Truman*, 5984–98 of 22565, Kindle.

43. Ferrell, *Choosing Truman*, 1727–44 of 2973, Kindle.

44. Culver and Hyde, *American Dreamer*, 8070–100 of 15699, Kindle.

45. Culver and Hyde, *American Dreamer*, 8070–100 of 15699, Kindle.

46. Dallek, *Harry S. Truman*, 260–70 of 3039, Kindle.

47. Harry S Truman, "The President's Farewell Address to the American People," January 15, 1953, The American Presidency Project, University of California, Santa Barbara, www.presidency.ucsb.edu/ws/index.php?pid=14392.

48. Glenn D. Paige, *The Korean Decision, June 24–30, 1950* (New York: Free Press, 1968), 189, 256; William Whitney Stueck, *Rethinking the Korean War: A New Diplomatic and Strategic History* (Princeton, NJ: Princeton University Press, 2002), 1.

49. John Lewis Gaddis, *The Cold War: A New History* (New York: Penguin Press, 2005), 15–27.

50. Gaddis, *Cold War*, 25–29.

51. Gaddis, *Cold War*, 31–32.

52. Andrei Cherny, *The Candy Bombers: The Untold Story of the Berlin Airlift and America's Finest Hour* (New York: G. P. Putnam's Sons, 2008); Gaddis, *Cold War*, 30–40.

53. John Lewis Gaddis and Paul Nitze, "NSC 68 and the Soviet Threat Reconsidered," *International Security* 4, no. 4 (Spring 1980); Samuel F. Wells Jr., "Sounding the Tocsin: NSC 68 and the Soviet Threat," *International Security* 4, no. 2 (Autumn 1979); NSC 68 (1950).

54. Stueck, *Rethinking the Korean War*.

55. Gary R. Hess, *Presidential Decisions for War: Korea, Vietnam, the Persian Gulf, and Iraq*, 2nd ed. (Baltimore: Johns Hopkins University Press, 2009), 210–25 of 4458, Kindle; Alexander L. George, "American Policy-Making and the North Korean Aggression," *World Politics* 7, no. 2 (January 1955).

56. Harry S. Truman, *Memoirs*, vol. 2, *Years of Trial and Hope* (Garden City, NY: Doubleday, 1956), 331–34; Hess, *Presidential Decisions for War*, 282–96 of 4458, Kindle; McCullough, *Truman*, 14606–99 of 22565, Kindle.

57. Hess, *Presidential Decisions for War*, 332–36 of 4458, Kindle; McCullough, *Truman*, 14704–7 of 22565, Kindle; Truman, *Memoirs*, 2:337–38.

58. Hess, *Presidential Decisions for War*, 366–79 of 4458, Kindle; Truman, *Memoirs*, 2:338–39.

59. Hess, *Presidential Decisions for War*, 411–85 of 4458, Kindle.

60. Randall L. Schweller, "Bandwagoning for Profit: Bringing the Revisionist State Back In," *International Security* 19, no. 1 (1994): 73, 96.

61. NSC 68, in *Foreign Relations of the United States, 1950, National Security Affairs; Foreign Economic Policy*, v. 1. https://history.state.gov/historicaldocuments /frus1950v01/d85.

62. NSC 68.

63. Estimates Group Office of Intelligence Research, Department of State, "Intelligence Estimate," *Foreign Relations of the United States* 7, no. Korea (1950).

64. Paige, *Korean Decision*, 115; Stueck, *Rethinking the Korean War*, 81.

65. Nye, *Presidential Leadership*, 68.

66. John Earl Haynes and Harvey Klehr, *Venona: Decoding Soviet Espionage in America*, (New Haven, CT: Yale University Press, 1999).

67. Culver and Hyde, *American Dreamer*, 11310–21 of 11699, Kindle.

68. Bradford DeLong, "Henry A. Wallace (1952) on the Ruthless Nature and Utter Evil of Soviet Communism: Cold-War Era God-That-Failed Weblogging," *Grasping Reality* (blog), July 24, 2013, http://delong.typepad.com/sdj/2013/02 /henry-a-wallace-1952-on-the-ruthless-nature-of-communism-cold-war-era-god-that-failed-weblogging.html.

69. Paul Campos, "The Truman Show," *New York Magazine*, July 24, 2021, https://nymag.com/intelligencer/2021/07/the-truman-show.html.

70. Robert Dallek, *An Unfinished Life: John F. Kennedy* (New York: Little, Brown, 2004).

71. Allison and Zelikow, *Essence of Decision*.

72. Jon Meacham, *Destiny and Power: The American Odyssey of George Herbert Walker Bush* (New York: Random House, 2015); Timothy J. Naftali, *George H. W. Bush* (New York: Times Books, 2007).

73. Nye, *Presidential Leadership*, 54; George Bush and Brent Scowcroft, *A World Transformed* (New York: Knopf, 1998).

74. Meacham, *Destiny and Power*, 8307–9494 of 23244, Kindle; William K. Black, *The Best Way to Rob a Bank Is to Own One: How Corporate Executives and Politicians Looted the S&L Industry* (Austin: University of Texas Press, 2005); Ailsa Chang, "Critics of President George H. W. Bush Reflect on His Handling of the AIDS Crisis," *All Things Considered*, National Public Radio, December 4, 2018, www.npr.org/2018/12/04/673398013/critics-of-president-george-h-w-bush-reflect-on-his-handling-of-the-aids-crisis.

75. David Maraniss, *First in His Class: A Biography of Bill Clinton* (New York: Simon & Schuster, 1995).

76. Catherine Baker, *The Yugoslav Wars of the 1990s* (New York: Palgrave, 2015); Paul Blustein, *The Chastening: Inside The Crisis That Rocked the Global Financial System and Humbled the IMF* (New York: PublicAffairs, 2001).

77. David Remnick, "The Wanderer," *The New Yorker,* September 18, 2006, www.newyorker.com/magazine/2006/09/18/the-wanderer-3; Gautam Mukunda, "The Price of Wall Street's Power," *Harvard Business Review* 92, no. 6 (June 2014).

CHAPTER 3

1. Tanisha M. Fazal, *State Death: The Politics and Geography of Conquest, Occupation, and Annexation* (Princeton, NJ: Princeton University Press, 2007); Waltz, *Theory of International Politics;* Kenneth N. Waltz, "Neorealism—Confusions and Criticisms," guest essay, *Journal of Politics and Society* 15 (2004); Adam Smith, *Inquiry into the Nature and Causes of the Wealth of Nations,* Penguin Classics (New York: Penguin, 1999); Charles Darwin, *Origin of Species:150th Anniversary Edition* (Alachua, FL: Bridge-Logos, 2009).

2. Philip E. Tetlock, *Expert Political Judgment: How Good Is It? How Can We Know?* (Princeton, NJ: Princeton University Press, 2006); Nassim Nicholas Taleb, *Fooled by Randomness: The Hidden Role of Chance in Life and in the Markets* (New York: Random House, 2005); Nassim Nicholas Taleb, *The Black Swan: The Impact of the Highly Improbable* (New York: Random House, 2007).

3. Skowronek, *Politics Presidents Make,* 39; Matthew Laing and Brendan McCaffrie, "The Impossible Leadership Situation? Analyzing Success for Disjunctive Presidents," *Presidential Studies Quarterly* 47, no. 2 (June 2017).

4. Cohen et al., *The Party Decides,* 665 of 5625, Kindle.

5. Jean H. Baker, *James Buchanan* (New York: Times Books, 2004), 1; Robert Strauss, *Worst. President. Ever.: James Buchanan, the POTUS Rating Game, and the Legacy of the Least of the Lesser Presidents* (Guilford, CT: Lyons Press, an imprint of Rowman & Littlefield, 2016); John W. Quist and Michael J. Birkner, "Introduction: Bum Rap or Bad Leadership?," in *James Buchanan and the Coming of the Civil War,* ed. John W. Quist and Michael J. Birkner (Gainesville: University of Florida Press, 2013); William E. Gienapp, "'No Bed of Roses': James Buchanan, Abraham Lincoln, and Presidential Leadership in the Civil War Era," in *James Buchanan and the Political Crisis of the 1850s,* ed. Michael J. Birkner (Cransbury, NJ: Associated University Presses, 1996).

6. Baker, *James Buchanan;* Garry Boulard, *The Worst President—The Story of James Buchanan* (Bloomington, IN: iUniverse, 2015); Philip Shriver Klein, *President James Buchanan, A Biography* (University Park: Pennsylvania State University Press, 1962), 1–27; Strauss, *Worst. President. Ever.*

7. Baker, *James Buchanan;* Boulard, *Worst President;* Klein, *President James Buchanan,* 13–43; Strauss, *Worst. President. Ever.*

8. Klein, 44–77.

9. Baker, *James Buchanan;* Boulard, *Worst President,* 508–47; Strauss, *Worst. President. Ever.*

10. Baker, *James Buchanan;* Boulard, *Worst President;* Strauss, *Worst. President. Ever.*

11. Baker, *James Buchanan,* 33–34; Strauss, *Worst. President. Ever.,* 1513 of 4082, Kindle.

12. Baker, *James Buchanan,* 33–36; Strauss, *Worst. President. Ever.,* 1585–679 of 4082, Kindle.

13. Baker, *James Buchanan,* 37–38; Strauss, *Worst. President. Ever.,* 1679–713 of 4082, Kindle.

14. Baker, *James Buchanan,* 38–42; Strauss, *Worst. President. Ever.,* 1733–808 of 4082, Kindle.

15. Boulard, *Worst President,* 624; Strauss, *Worst. President. Ever.,* 1808–21 of 4082, Kindle.

16. Baker, *James Buchanan,* 51–53; Strauss, *Worst. President. Ever.,* 1857–93 of 4082, Kindle.

17. Michael F. Holt, *Franklin Pierce* (New York: Times Books, 2010), 640–95 of 2887, Kindle.

18. Baker, *James Buchanan,* 60; Klein, *President James Buchanan,* 228–29.

19. Baker, *James Buchanan,* 64–67; Boulard, *Worst President,* 624–62.

20. Baker, *James Buchanan,* 67–68; Holt, *Franklin Pierce,* 1091–417 of 2887, Kindle; Klein, *President James Buchanan,* 234–41.

21. Baker, *James Buchanan,* 67–68; Holt, *Franklin Pierce,* 1091–417 of 2887, Kindle; Klein, *President James Buchanan,* 234–41.

22. Baker, *James Buchanan,* 69; Stephen B. Oates, *To Purge This Land with Blood: A Biography of John Brown* (Amherst: The University of Massachusetts Press, 1984).

23. Baker, *James Buchanan,* 69.

24. Baker, *James Buchanan;* Holt, *Franklin Pierce,* 1527 of 2887, Kindle; Klein, *President James Buchanan,* 255.

25. Michael F. Holt, "Another Look at the Election of 1856," in *James Buchanan and the Political Crisis of the 1850s,* ed. Michael J. Birkner (Cransbury, NJ: Associated University Presses, 1996).

26. Baker, *James Buchanan,* 79; Gienapp, "'No Bed of Roses,'" 101.

27. Paul Finkelman, "James Buchanan, Dred Scott, and the Whisper of Conspiracy," in *James Buchanan and the Coming of the Civil War,* ed. John W. Quist and Michael J. Birkner (Gainesville: University Press of Florida, 2013), 20–27; Kenneth M. Stampp, *America in 1857: A Nation on the Brink* (New York: Oxford University Press, 1992), 62–63 of 10471, Kindle.

28. Finkelman, "James Buchanan, Dred Scott, and the Whisper of Conspiracy," 33–35.

29. Baker, *James Buchanan*, 84–86; Finkelman, "James Buchanan, Dred Scott, and the Whisper of Conspiracy," 33–40; Stampp, *America in 1857*, 91–105 of 10471, Kindle; Strauss, *Worst. President. Ever.*, 2520–60 of 4082, Kindle.

30. Stampp, *America in 1857*, 124–70 of 10471, Kindle.

31. Nicole Etcheson, "General Jackson Is Dead: James Buchanan, Stephen A. Douglas, and Kansas Policy," in *James Buchanan and the Coming of the Civil War*, ed. John W. Quist and Michael J. Birkner (Gainesville: University Press of Florida, 2013), 98; Stampp, *America in 1857*, 278–85 of 10471, Kindle.

32. Etcheson, "General Jackson Is Dead," 98–99; Klein, *President James Buchanan*, 298–99; Stampp, *America in 1857*, 285–87 of 10471, Kindle.

33. Klein, *President James Buchanan*, 302–3; Stampp, *America in 1857*, 293–94 of 10471, Kindle.

34. Etcheson, "General Jackson Is Dead," 99.

35. Etcheson, "General Jackson Is Dead," 86; Stampp, *America in 1857*, 307 of 10471, Kindle.

36. James Buchanan, "First Annual Message to Congress on the State of the Union," December 8, 1857, The American Presidency Project, University of California, Santa Barbara, www.presidency.ucsb.edu/documents/first-annual-message-congress-the-state-the-union.

37. Doris Kearns Goodwin, *Team of Rivals: The Political Genius of Abraham Lincoln* (New York: Simon & Schuster, 2005), 163; Stampp, *America in 1857*, 315 of 10471, Kindle.

38. Stephen Arnold Douglas, "Kansas-Lecompton Convention: Speech of Senator Douglas, of Illinois, on the President's Message: Delivered in the Senate of the United States, December 9, 1857," Oberlin College Library Anti-Slavery Collection, https://archive.org/details/ASPC0005211000.

39. Baker, *James Buchanan*, 103, 14; Stampp, *America in 1857*, 317 of 10471, Kindle.

40. Baker, *James Buchanan*, 100.

41. Baker, *James Buchanan*, 102.

42. "The Most Infamous Brawl in the History of the U.S. House of Representatives," Historical Highlights, History, Art, & Archives of the United States House of Representatives, accessed August 11, 2018, https://history.house.gov/Historical-Highlights/1851–1900/The-most-infamous-floor-brawl-in-the-history-of-the-U-S--House-of-Representatives/; Matthew Wasniewski, "I've Scalped Him?," *History, Art & Archives of the United States House of Representatives*, February 6, 2014, http://history.house.gov/Blog/2014/February/2–06-I-ve-Scalped-Him/; Stampp, *America in 1857*, 341 of 10471, Kindle.

43. Baker, *James Buchanan*, 104–5; Klein, *President James Buchanan*, 308–12; Stampp, *America in 1857*, 341–43 of 10471, Kindle.

44. Baker, *James Buchanan*, 104–5; Klein, *President James Buchanan*, 308–12; Stampp, *America in 1857*, 341–43 of 10471, Kindle.

45. Baker, *James Buchanan*, 104–5; Klein, *President James Buchanan*, 308–12; Stampp, *America in 1857*, 341–43 of 10471, Kindle.

46. Baker, *James Buchanan*, 149.

47. Glen Jeansonne, *Herbert Hoover: A Life* (New York: New American Library, 2016); William Edward Leuchtenburg, *Herbert Hoover* (New York: Times Books, 2009), 162; Kenneth Whyte, *Hoover: An Extraordinary Life in Extraordinary Times* (New York: Alfred A. Knopf, 2017).

48. Leuchtenburg, *Herbert Hoover*, 1–41; Whyte, *Hoover*, 1–227 of 14395, Kindle.

49. Leuchtenburg, *Herbert Hoover*, 41–76; Whyte, *Hoover*, 229–360 of 14395, Kindle.

50. Leuchtenburg, *Herbert Hoover*, 131–33; Whyte, *Hoover*, 404–523 of 14395, Kindle.

51. Leuchtenburg, *Herbert Hoover*.

52. Leuchtenburg, *Herbert Hoover*, 148.

53. Ben S. Bernanke and Harold James, "The Gold Standard, Deflation, and Financial Crisis in the Great Depression: An International Comparison," in *Financial Markets and Financial Crises*, ed. R. Glenn Hubbard (Chicago: University of Chicago Press, 1990); Barry Eichengreen and Peter Temin, "The Gold Standard and the Great Depression," *Contemporary European History* 9, no. 2 (2000).

54. Ben S. Bernanke, "Economic Policy: Lessons from History," Board of Governors of the Federal Reserve System, April 6, 2010, www.federalreserve.gov/newsevents/speech/bernanke20100408a.htm.

55. Charles Rappleye, *Herbert Hoover in the White House: The Ordeal of the Presidency* (New York: Simon & Schuster, 2016).

56. Neil Weinberg, "Schapiro's Promontory Move Latest Sign of Too Much Coziness," *American Banker*, April 2, 2013, www.americanbanker.com/opinion/schapiros-promontory-move-latest-sign-of-too-much-coziness; Mukunda, "Price of Wall Street's Power."

57. Lou Cannon, *President Reagan: The Role of a Lifetime* (New York: Public Affairs, 2000).

58. Matthew Sherman, *A Short History of Financial Deregulation in the United States* (Washington, DC: Center for Economic and Policy Research, July 2009), http://cepr.net/documents/publications/dereg-timeline-2009-07.pdf.

59. Alan S. Blinder and Mark Zandi, *How the Great Recession Was Brought to an End* (New York: Moody's Analytics, 2010); J. W. Mason, *What Recovery? The Case for Continued Expansionary Policy at the Fed* (New York: Roosevelt Institute, July 25, 2017), https://rooseveltinstitute.org/wp-content/uploads/2020/07/RI-What-Recovery-report-201707.pdf; Regis Barnichon, Christian Matthes,

and Alexander Ziegenbein, "The Financial Crisis at 10: Will We Ever Recover?" Federal Reserve Bank of San Francisco Economic Letter, August 13, 2018, www .frbsf.org/economic-research/publications/economic-letter/2018/august/financial-crisis-at-10-years-will-we-ever-recover/.

60. Gerald A. Epstein, *Financialization and the World Economy* (Cheltenham: Edward Elgar, 2005); Richard B. Freeman, "It's Financialization!," *International Labour Review* 149, no. 2 (2010); Greta R Krippner, "The Financialization of the American Economy," *Socio-Economic Review* 3, no. 2 (2005); Mukunda, "Price of Wall Street's Power"; Özgür Orhangazi, *Financialization and the US Economy* (Cheltenham: Edward Elgar, 2008); Thomas Palley, *Financialization: What It Is and Why It Matters*, Working Paper no. 525 (Annendale-on-Hudson, NY: Levy Economics Institute of Bard College, 2007); Donald Tomaskovic-Devey and Ken-Hou Lin, "Income Dynamics, Economic Rents, and the Financialization of the U.S. Economy," *American Sociological Review* 76, no. 4 (2011); Natascha van der Zwan, "Making Sense of Financialization," *Socio-Economic Review* 12, no. 1 (2014).

61. Donald Tomaskovic-Devey and Ken-Hou Lin, "Financialization: Causes, Inequality Consequences, and Policy Implications," *North Carolina Banking Institute* 18, no. 1 (2013), http://scholarship.law.unc.edu/cgi/viewcontent .cgi?article=1365&context=ncbi.

CHAPTER 4

1. Mukunda, *Indispensable;* Waltz, *Foreign Policy and Democratic Politics.*

2. Dickerson, "Hardest Job in the World"; Aaron Antonovsky, "Social Class, Life Expectancy and Overall Mortality," *Milbank Memorial Fund Quarterly* 45, no. 2 (1967); Matthew D. Rablen and Arnold J. Oswald, "Mortality and Immortality: The Nobel Prize as an Experiment into the Effect of Status upon Longevity," *Journal of Health Economics* 27, no. 6 (December 2008).

3. Andrew R. Olenski, Matthew V. Abola, and Anupam B. Jena, "Do Heads of Government Age More Quickly? Observational Study Comparing Mortality between Elected Leaders and Runners-Up in National Elections of 17 Countries," *BMJ* 351 (2015).

4. Dean Keith Simonton, "Personality and Politics," in *Handbook of Personality Theory and Research,* ed. L. A. Pervin (New York: Guilford, 1990); Dean Keith Simonton, "Intergenerational Transfer of Individual Differences in Hereditary Monarchs: Genetic, Role-Modeling, Cohort, or Sociocultural Effects?," *Journal of Personality and Social Psychology* 44, no. 2 (1983); Keith Simonton Dean, "Leaders as Eponyms: Individual and Situational Determinants of Ruler Eminence," *Journal of Personality* 52, no. 1 (1984); Frank L Schmidt and John E Hunter, "The Validity and Utility of Selection Methods in Personnel Psychology:

Practical and Theoretical Implications of 85 Years of Research Findings," *Psychological Bulletin* 124, no. 2 (1998); Robert J. House and Ram N. Aditya, "The Social Scientific Study of Leadership: Quo Vadis?," *Journal of Management* 23, no. 3 (1997); Timothy A. Judge, Remus Ilies, and Amy E. Colbert, "Intelligence and Leadership: A Quantitative Review and Test of Theoretical Propositions," *Journal of Applied Psychology* 89, no. 3 (2004); Dean Keith Simonton, "Personality and Intellectual Predictors of Leadership," in *International Handbook of Personality and Intelligence*, ed. D. H. Saklofske and M. Zeidner (New York: Plenum, 1995).

5. Simonton, "Presidential Style"; Simonton, "Presidential IQ, Openness, Intellectual Brilliance, and Leadership"; Dean Keith Simonton, "Presidential Personality: Biographical Use of the Gough Adjective Check List," *Journal of Personality and Social Psychology* 51, no. 1 (1986) ; Dean Keith Simonton, "Predicting Presidential Performance in the United States: Equation Replication on Recent Survey Results," *Journal of Social Psychology* 141, no. 3 (2001)

6. Eugene Bardach, *The Implementation Game: What Happens After a Bill Becomes a Law* (Cambridge, MA: MIT Press, 1977); Jeffrey L. Pressman and Aaron Wildavsky, *Implementation: How Great Expectations in Washington Are Dashed in Oakland: or, Why It's Amazing That Federal Programs Work at All, This Being the Saga of the Economic Development Administration as Told by Two Sympathetic Observers Who Seek to Build Morals on a Foundation of Ruined Hopes* (Berkeley: University of California Press, 1973); James C. Scott, *Seeing like a State: How Certain Schemes to Improve the Human Condition Have Failed* (New Haven, CT: Yale University Press, 1998); Elaine Ciulla Kamarck, *Why Presidents Fail: And How They Can Succeed Again* (Washington, DC: Brookings Institution Press, 2016).

7. William Shakespeare, *Macbeth*, Act IV, Scene 3, in *The Norton Shakespeare*, ed. Stephen Greenblatt et al. (New York: W. W. Norton, 1997).

8. Phil Rosenzweig, *The Halo Effect . . . and the Eight Other Business Delusions That Deceive Managers* (New York: Free Press, 2007); Daniel Kahneman, *Thinking, Fast and Slow* (New York: Farrar, Straus and Giroux, 2011).

9. Nancy L. Etcoff, *Survival of the Prettiest: The Science of Beauty* (New York: Anchor, 1999); Daniel S. Hamermesh, *Beauty Pays: Why Attractive People Are More Successful* (Princeton, NJ: Princeton University Press, 2011); Daniel S. Hamermesh and Jeff E. Biddle, "Beauty and the Labor Market," *American Economic Review* 84, no. 5 (1994); Daniel Hamermesh and Amy M. Parker, "Beauty in the Classroom: Professors' Pulchritude and Putative Pedagogical Productivity," *Economics of Education Review* 24 (2005); John Potts, *A History of Charisma* (London: Palgrave Macmillan, 2009); Khurana, *Searching for a Corporate Savior;* Robert Hogan, Gordon J. Curphy, and Joyce Hogan, "What We Know about Leadership: Effectiveness and Personality," *American Psychologist* 49, no. 6 (June 1994); Olivia Fox Cabane, *The Charisma Myth: How Anyone Can*

Master the Art and Science of Personal Magnetism (New York, 2012); Timothy A. Judge, Ronald F. Piccolo, and Tomek Kosalka, "The Bright and Dark Sides of Leader Traits: A Review and Theoretical Extension of the Leader Trait Paradigm," *The Leadership Quarterly* 20, no. 6 (2009).

10. Popkin, *Candidate*, 97.

11. Huckman and Pisano, "Firm Specificity of Individual Performance"; Groysberg, *Chasing Stars;* Groysberg, McLean, and Nohria, "Are Leaders Portable?"; Groysberg, Nanda, and Nohria, "Risky Business of Hiring Stars."

12. Adrian Furnham, Steven C. Richards, and Delroy L. Paulhus, "The Dark Triad of Personality: A 10 Year Review," *Social and Personality Psychology Compass* 7, no. 3; Robert Hogan, *Personality and the Fate of Organizations* (Mahwah, NJ: Psychology Press, 2007); Delroy L. Paulhus and Kevin M. Williams, "The Dark Triad of Personality: Narcissism, Machiavellianism, and Psychopathy," *Journal of Research in Personality* 36, no. 6 (2002); Adrian Furnham, *The Elephant in the Boardroom: The Causes of Leadership Derailment* (London: Palgrave Macmillan, 2010).

13. Daniel Landau, "One Man's Wickedness: Malignant Narcissism and Major Blunders in International Relations" (MS thesis, Massachusetts Institute of Technology, 2004).

14. Jerrold M. Post, "Current Concepts of the Narcissistic Personality: Implications for Political Psychology," *Political Psychology* 14, no. 1 (March 1993): 99; Ashley L. Watts et al., "The Double-Edged Sword of Grandiose Narcissism: Implications for Successful and Unsuccessful Leadership among U.S. Presidents," *Psychological Science* 24, no. 12 (2013).

15. Michael Maccoby, *The Productive Narcissist: The Promise and Peril of Visionary Leadership* (New York: Broadway Books, 2003); Arijit Chatterjee and Donald C. Hambrick, "It's All about Me: Narcissistic Chief Executive Officers and Their Effects on Company Strategy and Performance," *Administrative Science Quarterly* 52, no. 3 (2007); Delroy L. Paulhus, "Interpersonal and Intrapsychic Adaptiveness of Trait Self-Enhancement: A Mixed Blessing?," *Journal of Personality and Social Psychology* 74, no. 5 (1998); Sampo V. Paunonen et al., "Narcissism and Emergent Leadership in Military Cadets," *The Leadership Quarterly* 17, no. 5 (2006); Judge, Piccolo, and Kosalka, "Bright and Dark Sides of Leader Traits"; Richard W. Robins and Jennifer S. Beer, "Positive Illusions about the Self: Short-Term Benefits and Long-Term Costs," *Journal of Personality and Social Psychology* 80, no. 2 (2001).

16. Ernest H. O'Boyle Jr. et al., "A Meta-Analysis of the Dark Triad and Work Behavior: A Social Exchange Perspective," *Journal of Applied Psychology* 97, no. 3 (2012); Judge, Piccolo, and Kosalka, "Bright and Dark Sides of Leader Traits," 867; Ronald J. Deluga, "American Presidential Machiavellianism: Implications for Charismatic Leadership and Rated Performance," *The Leadership Quarterly* 12, no. 3 (2001); Simonton, "Presidential Personality."

17. O'Boyle et al., "Meta-Analysis of the Dark Triad"; Paul Babiak and Robert D. Hare, *Snakes in Suits: When Psychopaths Go to Work* (New York: HarperCollins Publishers, 2006); Kevin Dutton, *The Wisdom of Psychopaths: Lessons in Life from Saints, Spies and Serial Killers* (London: William Heinemann, 2012); Jon Ronson, *The Psychopath Test: A Journey through the Madness Industry* (New York: Riverhead Books, 2012).

18. Martin Sellbom et al., "Development and Construct Validation of MMPI-2-RF Indices of Global Psychopathy, Fearless-Dominance, and Impulsive-Antisociality," *Personality Disorders* 3, no. 1 (January 2012); Edward A. Witt et al., "Assessment of Fearless Dominance and Impulsive Antisociality via Normal Personality Measures: Convergent Validity, Criterion Validity, and Developmental Change," *Journal of Personality Assessment* 91, no. 3 (May 2009); Tasha R. Phillips et al., "Further Development and Construct Validation of MMPI-2-RF Indices of Global Psychopathy, Fearless-Dominance, and Impulsive-Antisociality in a Sample of Incarcerated Women," *Law and Human Behavior* 38, no. 1 (February 2014); Daniel M. Blonigen et al., "Psychopathic Personality Traits: Heritability and Genetic Overlap with Internalizing and Externalizing Psychopathology," *Psychological Medicine* 35, no. 5 (May 2005).

19. Scott O. Lilienfeld et al., "Fearless Dominance and the US Presidency: Implications of Psychopathic Personality Traits for Successful and Unsuccessful Political Leadership," *Journal of Personality and Social Psychology* 103, no. 3 (2012).

20. Yehezkel Dror, "Statecraft as Prudent Risk-Taking: The Case of the Middle East Peace Process," *Journal of Contingencies and Crisis Management* 2, no. 3 (September 1994).

21. George W. Downs and David M. Rocke, "Conflict, Agency, and Gambling for Resurrection: The Principal-Agent Problem Goes to War," *American Journal of Political Science* 38, no. 2 (May 1994).

22. Michael J. Mauboussin, *The Success Equation: Untangling Skill and Luck in Business, Sports, and Investing* (Boston: Harvard Business Review Press, 2012).

23. Elizabeth Nathan Saunders, "Wars of Choice: Leadership, Threat Perception, and Military Interventions" (PhD diss., Yale University, 2007); Elizabeth N. Saunders, "Transformative Choices," *International Security* 34, no. 2 (Fall 2009); Elizabeth N. Saunders, *Leaders at War—How Presidents Shape Military Interventions* (Ithaca, NY: Cornell University Press, 2011).

24. Simonton, *Why Presidents Succeed*, 231; Dean Keith Simonton, "Land Battles, Generals, and Armies: Individual and Situational Determinants of Victory and Casualties," *Journal of Personality and Social Psychology* 38, no. 1 (1980); H. L. Mencken, Wikiquote, accessed April 24, 2018, https://en.wikiquote.org/wiki/H._L._Mencken.

25. Ian G. Anson, "Partisanship, Political Knowledge, and the Dunning-Kruger Effect," *Political Psychology* 39, no. 5 (2018); Michael Rozansky,

"Americans Know Surprisingly Little about Their Government, Survey Finds," news release, Annenberg Public Policy Center, September 17, 2014, www.annen-bergpublicpolicycenter.org/wp-content/uploads/Civics-survey-press-release-09-17-2014-for-PR-Newswire.pdf; "Just 37% of Americans Can Name Their Representative," Haven Insights, 2017, accessed March 27, 2018, www.haveninsights.com/just-37-percent-name-representative/; Nick Rossoll, "More Than 40 Percent of Americans Cannot Name VP Candidates," ABC News, October 2, 2016, http://abcnews.go.com/Politics/40-percent-americans-vp-candidates/story?id=42497013; Ilya Somin, *Democracy and Political Ignorance: Why Smaller Government Is Smarter,* 2nd ed. (Stanford, CA: Stanford University Press, 2016); David Dunning, "The Dunning-Kruger Effect: On Being Ignorant of One's Own Ignorance," in *Advances in Experimental Social Psychology,* ed. James M. Olson and Mark P. Zanna (Waltham, MA: Academic Press, 2011); Justin Kruger and David Dunning, "Unskilled and Unaware of It: How Difficulties in Recognizing One's Own Incompetence Lead to Inflated Self-Assessments," *Journal of Personality and Social Psychology* 77, no. 6 (1999).

26. Gautam Mukunda, "Don't Trust Anyone over 70," *Foreign Policy,* February 27, 2013, https://foreignpolicy.com/2013/02/27/dont-trust-anyone-over-70/.

27. Rose McDermott, *Presidential Leadership, Illness, and Decision Making* (New York: Cambridge University Press, 2008); Bert Edward Park, *The Impact of Illness on World Leaders* (Philadelphia: University of Pennsylvania Press, 1986); Jerrold M. Post and Robert S. Robins, "The Captive King and His Captive Court: The Psychopolitical Dynamics of the Disabled Leader and His Inner Circle," *Political Psychology* 11, no. 2 (June 1990); Jerrold M. Post and Robert S. Robins, *When Illness Strikes the Leader: The Dilemma of the Captive King* (New Haven, CT: Yale University Press, 1993); Dean Keith Simonton, "Mad King George: The Impact of Personal and Political Stress on Mental and Physical Health," *Journal of Personality* 66, no. 3 (June 1998); Bert E. Park, "Presidential Disability: Past Experiences and Future Implications," *Politics and the Life Sciences* 7, no. 1 (August 1988); Jerrold M. Post, *Leaders and Their Followers in a Dangerous World* (Ithaca, NY: Cornell University Press, 2004); Sumit Agarwal et al., "What Is the Age of Reason?," *Center for Retirement Research at Boston College,* no. 10–12 (July 2010), https://scholar.harvard.edu/files/laibson/files/ageofreason_supplement.pdf.

28. Norman Ohler, *Blitzed: Drugs in Nazi Germany,* trans. Shaun Whiteside (London: Allen Lane, 2016); McDermott, *Presidential Leadership, Illness, and Decision Making;* Arnold M. Ludwig, *King of the Mountain* (Lexington: University Press of Kentucky, 2002).

29. Roy F. Baumeister and Steven J. Scher, "Self-Defeating Behavior Patterns among Normal Individuals: Review and Analysis of Common Self-Destructive Tendencies," *Psychological Bulletin* 104, no. 1 (1988).

30. Holt, *Franklin Pierce,* 1–335; Peter A. Wallner, *Franklin Pierce: New Hampshire's Favorite Son* (Concord, NH: Plaidswede, 2004), 1–44.

31. Holt, *Franklin Pierce*, 352–458; Wallner, *Franklin Pierce: New Hampshire's Favorite Son*, 44–156.

32. Wallner, *Franklin Pierce: New Hampshire's Favorite Son*, 181–203.

33. Larry Gara, *The Presidency of Franklin Pierce* (Lawrence: University Press of Kansas, 1991), 17–41; Holt, *Franklin Pierce*, 635–742; David M. Potter, *The Impending Crisis: 1848–1861*, ed. Don E. Fehrenbacher (New York: Harper-Collins, 1976), 142–43; Thomas J. Rowland, *Franklin B. Pierce: The Twilight of Jacksonian Democracy* (Hauppauge, NY: Nova Science Publishers, 2011), 63–79; Wallner, *Franklin Pierce: New Hampshire's Favorite Son*, 205–31.

34. Holt, *Franklin Pierce*, 798; Rowland, *Franklin B. Pierce*, 81–82; Wallner, *Franklin Pierce: New Hampshire's Favorite Son*, 241.

35. Gara, *Presidency of Franklin Pierce*, 101–26; Holt, *Franklin Pierce*, 1106–676; Rowland, *Franklin B. Pierce*, 149–52; Peter A. Wallner, *Franklin Pierce: Martyr for the Union* (Concord, NH: Plaidswede Publishing, 2007), 90–123.

36. Wallner, *Franklin Pierce: Martyr for the Union*, 307.

37. Holt, *Franklin Pierce*; Wallner, *Franklin Pierce: Martyr for the Union*, 371–72.

38. Merrill D. Peterson, *Lincoln in American Memory* (New York: Oxford University Press, 1994).

39. Hans Louis Trefousse, *Andrew Johnson: A Biography* (New York: Norton, 1989), 17–40; Annette Gordon-Reed, *Andrew Johnson* (New York: Times Books, Henry Holt, 2011), 400–646 of 2892, Kindle.

40. Trefousse, *Andrew Johnson*, 42–83; Gordon-Reed, *Andrew Johnson*.

41. Trefousse, *Andrew Johnson*, 84–127; Gordon-Reed, *Andrew Johnson;* William C. Harris, *Lincoln's Rise to the Presidency* (Lawrence: University Press of Kansas, 2007); Waugh, *One Man Great Enough*.

42. Trefousse, *Andrew Johnson*, 128–75; Gordon-Reed, *Andrew Johnson*.

43. Don E. Fehrenbacher, ed., *Abraham Lincoln: Speeches and Writings, 1859–1865* (New York: Penguin Books, 1989).

44. Burlingame, *Abraham Lincoln*, 40117; Gordon-Reed, *Andrew Johnson*, 1132–97 of 2892, Kindle; Trefousse, *Andrew Johnson*, 176–79.

45. John C. Waugh, *Reelecting Lincoln: The Battle for the 1864 Presidency* (New York: Crown Publishers, 1997).

46. Gordon-Reed, *Andrew Johnson*, 1250–1691 of 2892, Kindle; Trefousse, *Andrew Johnson*, 236.

47. Gordon-Reed, *Andrew Johnson;* David O. Stewart, *Impeached: The Trial of President Andrew Johnson and the Fight for Lincoln's Legacy* (New York: Simon & Schuster, 2009), 18–19 of 7371, Kindle; Trefousse, *Andrew Johnson*, 197–227.

48. Stewart, *Impeached*, 19–20 of 7371, Kindle.

49. Gordon-Reed, *Andrew Johnson*, 1521–727 of 2892, Kindle; Stewart, *Impeached*, 42–49 of 7371, Kindle.

50. Stewart, *Impeached,* 48–69 of 7371, Kindle.

51. Stewart, *Impeached,* 71–97 of 7371, Kindle.

52. Stewart, *Impeached;* Trefousse, *Andrew Johnson;* Gordon-Reed, *Andrew Johnson.*

53. Trefousse, *Andrew Johnson,* 232–33.

54. Stewart, *Impeached;* Gordon-Reed, *Andrew Johnson.*

55. Trefousse, *Andrew Johnson,* 236–42; John Stauffer, *Giants: The Parallel Lives of Frederick Douglass and Abraham Lincoln* (New York: Twelve, 2009).

56. Gordon-Reed, *Andrew Johnson,* 1790 of 2892, Kindle.

57. Peter G. Bourne, *Jimmy Carter: A Comprehensive Biography from Plains to Post-Presidency* (New York: Scribner, 1997); Julian E. Zelizer, *Jimmy Carter* (New York: Times Books, 2010); Jean Edward Smith, *Bush* (New York: Simon & Schuster, 2016).

58. Zelizer, *Jimmy Carter;* Bourne, *Jimmy Carter;* Smith, *Bush.*

59. Thomas E. Ricks, *Fiasco: The American Military Adventure in Iraq* (New York: Penguin Press, 2006); Michael R. Gordon and Bernard E. Trainor, *Cobra II: The Inside Story of the Invasion and Occupation of Iraq* (New York: Pantheon Books, 2006); Rajiv Chandrasekaran, *Imperial Life in the Emerald City: Inside Iraq's Green Zone* (New York: Alfred A. Knopf, 2006); George Packer, *The Assassins' Gate: America in Iraq* (New York: Farrar, Strauss, and Giroux, 2005).

CHAPTER 5

1. Simonton, "Presidential IQ, Openness, Intellectual Brilliance, and Leadership."

2. Joshua Wolf Shenk, *Lincoln's Melancholy: How Depression Challenged a President and Fueled His Greatness* (Boston: Houghton Mifflin, 2005).

3. Dickerson, "Hardest Job in the World."

4. Tessa Ditonto, "A High Bar or a Double Standard? Gender, Competence, and Information in Political Campaigns," *Political Behavior* 39, no. 2 (June 2017); Nichole M. Bauer, "The Effects of Partisan Trespassing Strategies across Candidate Sex," *Political Behavior* 41, no. 4 (December 2019); Eric C. Cassese and Mirya R. Holman, "Party and Gender Stereotypes in Campaign Attacks," *Political Behavior* 40, no. 3 (September 2018); Caroline Heldman, Meredith Conroy, and Alissa R. Ackerman, *Sex and Gender in the 2016 Presidential Election* (Santa Barbara: ABC-CLIO, 2018); Regina Branton et al., "The Impact of Gender and Quality Opposition on the Relative Assessment of Candidate Competency," *Electoral Studies* 54 (August 2018).

5. Devah Pager, "The Mark of a Criminal Record," *American Journal of Sociology* 108, no. 5 (2003); Jamil Scott and Nadia Brown, "Reconsidering Gender Stereotypes with an Intersectional Lens," Online paper, November 26, 2018,

presented at 2019 National Conference of Black Political Scientists Annual Meeting, https://papers.ssrn.com/sol3/papers.cfm?abstract_id=3290902.

6. Gautam Mukunda and William J. Troy, "Caught in the Net: Lessons from the Financial Crisis for a Networked Future," *Parameters* 39, no. 2 (Summer 2009).

7. Groysberg, *Chasing Stars;* Groysberg, McLean, and Nohria, "Are Leaders Portable?"; Groysberg, Nanda, and Nohria, "Risky Business of Hiring Stars"; Huckman and Pisano, "Firm Specificity of Individual Performance."

8. George, *Presidential Decisionmaking in Foreign Policy;* Fred I. Greenstein and Dale Anderson, *Presidents and the Dissolution of the Union: Leadership Style from Polk to Lincoln* (Princeton, NJ: Princeton University Press, 2013); Elizabeth N. Saunders, "Leaders, Advisers, and the Political Origins of Elite Support for War," *Journal of Conflict Resolution* 62, no. 10 (November 2018).

9. Morris, *Rise of Theodore Roosevelt*, 366.

10. Dalton, *Theodore Roosevelt*, 15–35; Morris, *Rise of Theodore Roosevelt*, 4–20; David McCullough, *Mornings on Horseback: The Story of an Extraordinary Family, a Vanished Way of Life and the Unique Child Who Became Theodore Roosevelt* (New York: Simon & Schuster, 1982).

11. Dalton, *Theodore Roosevelt*, 35–64; Morris, *Rise of Theodore Roosevelt*, 20; McCullough, *Mornings on Horseback*.

12. Dalton, *Theodore Roosevelt*, 65–84; Morris, *Rise of Theodore Roosevelt*, 57–135; Theodore Roosevelt, *The Naval War of 1812, or, The History of the United States Navy during the Last War with Great Britain, to Which Is Appended an Account of the Battle of New Orleans* (Philadelphia: Gebbie and Co., 1902).

13. Dalton, *Theodore Roosevelt*, 81–91; Morris, *Rise of Theodore Roosevelt*, 131–255.

14. Dalton, *Theodore Roosevelt*, 98–100; Morris, *Rise of Theodore Roosevelt*, 275–322; Roger L. DiSilvestro, *Theodore Roosevelt in the Badlands: A Young Politician's Quest for Recovery in the American West* (New York: Walker, 2011).

15. Dalton, *Theodore Roosevelt*, 102–8; Morris, *Rise of Theodore Roosevelt*, 342–92; Theodore Roosevelt, *The Winning of the West: An Account of the Exploration and Settlement of Our Country from the Alleghanies to the Pacific* (Philadelphia: Gebbie and Co., 1903).

16. Dalton, *Theodore Roosevelt*, 117–47; Morris, *Rise of Theodore Roosevelt*, 393–491.

17. Dalton, *Theodore Roosevelt*, 149–62; Morris, *Rise of Theodore Roosevelt*, 491–568; H. Paul Jeffers, *Commissioner Roosevelt: The Story of Theodore Roosevelt and the New York City Police, 1895-1897* (New York: J. Wiley & Sons, 1994).

18. Dalton, *Theodore Roosevelt*, 149–62; Morris, *Rise of Theodore Roosevelt*, 491–568; Jeffers, *Commissioner Roosevelt*.

19. Dalton, *Theodore Roosevelt*, 162–63; Morris, *Rise of Theodore Roosevelt*, 568–605.

20. Dalton, *Theodore Roosevelt*, 163–65; Morris, *Rise of Theodore Roosevelt*, 606–24.

21. Dalton, *Theodore Roosevelt*, 169–71; Morris, *Rise of Theodore Roosevelt*, 627–80; Mark Lee Gardner, *Rough Riders: Theodore Roosevelt, His Cowboy Regiment, and the Immortal Charge up San Juan Hill* (New York: William Morrow, 2016); Theodore Roosevelt, *The Rough Riders: An Autobiography*, ed. Louis Auchincloss (New York: Library of America, 2004).

22. Dalton, *Theodore Roosevelt*, 171–74; Morris, *Rise of Theodore Roosevelt*, 680–87; Gardner, *Rough Riders;* Roosevelt, *Rough Riders*.

23. Dalton, *Theodore Roosevelt*, 176–79; Morris, *Rise of Theodore Roosevelt*, 687–709.

24. Dalton, *Theodore Roosevelt*, 176–79; Morris, *Rise of Theodore Roosevelt*, 687–709; Gardner, *Rough Riders;* Roosevelt, *Rough Riders*.

25. Dalton, *Theodore Roosevelt*, 179–80; Morris, *Rise of Theodore Roosevelt*, 709–21.

26. Dalton, *Theodore Roosevelt*, 182–90; Morris, *Rise of Theodore Roosevelt*, 729–42.

27. Dalton, *Theodore Roosevelt*, 190–91; Morris, *Rise of Theodore Roosevelt*, 747–67.

28. Dalton, *Theodore Roosevelt*, 197–201; Morris, *Rise of Theodore Roosevelt*, 775–80.

29. Lewis L. Gould, *The Presidency of William McKinley* (Lawrence: Regents Press of Kansas, 1980); Lewis L. Gould, *The Modern American Presidency*, foreword by Richard Norton Smith, 2nd ed., rev. and updated (Lawrence: University Press of Kansas, 2009).

30. Gould, *Presidency of William McKinley;* Gould, *Modern American Presidency*, 25 of 7373, Kindle; Dalton, *Theodore Roosevelt;* Lewis L. Gould, *Theodore Roosevelt* (New York: Oxford University Press, 2012).

31. Nye, *Presidential Leadership*, 62.

32. Morris, *Theodore Rex;* Dalton, *Theodore Roosevelt*.

33. Dalton, *Theodore Roosevelt;* Robert W. Merry, *President McKinley: Architect of the American Century* (New York: Simon & Schuster, 2017), 170 of 12717, Kindle; Morris, *Theodore Rex*.

34. Jean Strouse, *Morgan: American Financier* (New York: HarperPerennial, 2000); Ron Chernow, *The House of Morgan: An American Banking Dynasty and the Rise of Modern Finance* (New York: Simon & Schuster, 1991).

35. Morris, *Theodore Rex*, 2243 of 21341, Kindle.

36. Morris, *Theodore Rex*, 7463 of 21341, Kindle.

37. Dalton, *Theodore Roosevelt;* Gould, *Theodore Roosevelt*, 44–45 of 961, Kindle; Morris, *Theodore Rex*, 12676 of 21341, Kindle.

38. Zachary Karabell, *Chester Alan Arthur* (New York: Times Books, 2004).

39. Charles Fanning, "Dunne, Finley Peter," *American National Biography*, 1999; Roosevelt, *Rough Riders*.

40. Fanning, "Dunne, Finley Peter."

41. Lilienfeld et al., "Fearless Dominance and the US Presidency."

42. Morris, *Rise of Theodore Roosevelt*, 447.

43. Morris, *Rise of Theodore Roosevelt*, 296.

44. Fred I. Greenstein, *The Hidden-Hand Presidency: Eisenhower as Leader* (Baltimore: Johns Hopkins University Press, 1994), ix.

45. Jean Edward Smith, *Eisenhower: In War and Peace* (New York: Random House, 2012), 202–593 of 18959, Kindle; Tom Wicker, *Dwight D. Eisenhower* (New York: Times Books, 2002), 4–6 of 2817, Kindle.

46. Smith, *Eisenhower*, 317–1581 of 18959, Kindle; Wicker, *Dwight D. Eisenhower*, 7 of 2817, Kindle.

47. Smith, *Eisenhower*, 1419–5641 of 18959, Kindle; Wicker, *Dwight D. Eisenhower*, 7–8 of 2817, Kindle.

48. Rick Atkinson, *An Army at Dawn: The War in North Africa, 1942–1943* (New York: Henry Holt, 2002); Rick Atkinson, *The Day of Battle: The War in Sicily and Italy, 1943–1944* (New York: Henry Holt, 2007); Smith, *Eisenhower*, 4260–5971 of 18959, Kindle; Wicker, *Dwight D. Eisenhower*, 7–8 of 2817, Kindle.

49. Rick Atkinson, *The Guns at Last Light: The War in Western Europe, 1944–1945* (New York: Henry Holt, 2013); Smith, *Eisenhower*, 5971–6796 of 18959, Kindle; Wicker, *Dwight D. Eisenhower*, 8 of 2817, Kindle.

50. Smith, *Eisenhower*, 7598–8534 of 18959, Kindle; Wicker, *Dwight D. Eisenhower*, 8 of 2817, Kindle.

51. Dwight D. Eisenhower, *Crusade in Europe* (Garden City, NY: Doubleday, 1948); Smith, *Eisenhower*, 8826–9193 of 18959, Kindle; Ulysses S. Grant, *The Personal Memoirs of General Ulysses S. Grant* (New York: Sheba Blake, 2014).

52. Smith, *Eisenhower*, 8992–10451 of 18959, Kindle; Wicker, *Dwight D. Eisenhower*, 8–14 of 2817, Kindle.

53. Smith, *Eisenhower*, 9419–44 of 18959, Kindle.

54. Smith, *Eisenhower*, 9588–893 of 18959, Kindle; Wicker, *Dwight D. Eisenhower*, 14 of 2817, Kindle.

55. Smith, *Eisenhower*, 10096–457 of 18959, Kindle; Wicker, *Dwight D. Eisenhower*, 19 of 2817, Kindle.

56. David A. Nichols, *A Matter of Justice: Eisenhower and the Beginning of the Civil Rights Revolution* (New York: Simon and Schuster, 2008); David A. Nichols, *Ike and McCarthy: Dwight Eisenhower's Secret Campaign against Joseph McCarthy* (New York: Simon and Schuster, 2017).

57. Stephen E. Ambrose, *Eisenhower: Soldier and President* (New York: Simon & Schuster, 1990); Smith, *Eisenhower*; Wicker, *Dwight D. Eisenhower*.

58. Ambrose, *Eisenhower*; Smith, *Eisenhower*; Wicker, *Dwight D. Eisenhower*.

59. Nye, *Presidential Leadership*, 68; Smith, *Eisenhower*, 9731, 12341–93 of 18959, Kindle.

60. Gaddis, *Cold War*, 66–68; Priscilla Johnson McMillan, "Cold Warmonger," *New York Times*, May 25, 1997, www.nytimes.com/1997/05/25/books/cold-warmonger.html.

61. Evan Thomas, *Ike's Bluff: President Eisenhower's Secret Battle to Save the World* (New York: Little, Brown, 2012); Thomas C. Schelling, *The Strategy of Conflict* (Cambridge, MA: Harvard University Press, 1960).

62. Samuel P. Huntington, *The Common Defense: Strategic Programs in National Politics* (New York: Columbia University Press, 1961).

63. David A. Stockman, "Yes We Can: How Eisenhower Wrestled Down the U.S. Warfare State," *The Globalist*, April 29, 2014, www.theglobalist.com/yes-we-can-how-eisenhower-wrestled-down-the-u-s-warfare-state/; Nye, *Presidential Leadership*, 68.

64. Stephen G. Rabe, "Eisenhower Revisionism: A Decade of Scholarship," *Diplomatic History* 17, no. 1 (1993): 100; Smith, *Eisenhower*, 8554, 11759 of 18959, Kindle.

65. Scott Horton, "Eisenhower on the Opportunity Cost of Defense Spending," *Browsings: The Harper's Blog*, November 12, 2007, https://harpers.org/blog/2007/11/eisenhower-on-the-opportunity-cost-of-defense-spending/.

66. "Dwight David Eisenhower Chronology," Dwight D. Eisenhower Presidential Library, Museum, and Boyhood Home, accessed January 5, 2019, www.eisenhower.archives.gov/all_about_ike/chronologies.html.

67. Simonton, "Presidential Style."

68. Smith, *Eisenhower*, 9813 of 18959, Kindle.

69. David Mendell, *Obama: From Promise to Power* (New York: Amistad/HarperCollins, 2007); David J. Garrow, *Rising Star: The Making of Barack Obama* (New York: William Morrow, 2017); David Remnick, *The Bridge: The Life and Rise of Barack Obama* (New York: Alfred A. Knopf, 2010); David Maraniss, *Barack Obama: The Story* (New York: Simon & Schuster, 2012).

70. Mendell, *Obama;* Barack Obama, *Dreams from My Father: A Story of Race and Inheritance* (New York: Times Books, 1995); Garrow, *Rising Star;* Remnick, *Bridge;* Maraniss, *Barack Obama.*

71. Mendell, *Obama;* Garrow, *Rising Star;* Remnick, *Bridge;* Maraniss, *Barack Obama;* Colin Mcnulty and Jennifer White, *Making Obama* (podcast audio, 2018), www.wbez.org/shows/making-obama-podcast/.

72. Mendell, *Obama,* 2 of 7851, Kindle; Garrow, *Rising Star;* Remnick, *Bridge;* Maraniss, *Barack Obama.*

73. Mendell, *Obama;* Garrow, *Rising Star;* Remnick, *Bridge;* Maraniss, *Barack Obama.*

74. John Whitesides, "Black Voters Still Unsure about Obama," Reuters, February 8, 2007, www.reuters.com/article/us-usa-politics-obama/black-voters-

still-unsure-about-obama-idUSN0829251720070208; Jeff Berman, *The Magic Number* (Ordway House, 2012); Garrow, *Rising Star;* Maraniss, *Barack Obama;* Mendell, *Obama;* Remnick, *Bridge;* Michelle Peltier, "Why Black Women Prefer Clinton to Obama," CBS News, December 3, 2007, www.cbsnews.com/news /why-black-women-prefer-clinton-to-obama/; Paul Steinhauser, "Poll: Obama Makes Big Gains among Black Voters," *CNN Politics,* January 19, 2008, www .cnn.com/2008/POLITICS/01/18/poll.2008/index.html; Dan Balz, Anne E. Kornblut, and Shailagh Murray, "Obama Wins Iowa's Democratic Caucuses," *Washington Post,* January 4, 2008, www.washingtonpost.com/wp-dyn/content /article/2008/01/03/AR2008010304441.html.

75. Mendell, *Obama;* Garrow, *Rising Star;* Remnick, *Bridge;* Maraniss, *Barack Obama;* Chuck Todd and Sheldon R. Gawiser, with Ana Maria Arumi and G. Evans Witt, *How Barack Obama Won: A State-By-State Guide to the Historic 2008 Presidential Election* (New York: Vintage Books, 2009).

76. Jonathan Chait, *Audacity: How Barack Obama Defied His Critics and Created A Legacy That Will Prevail* (New York: Custom House, 2017).

77. Julie Kliegman, "Obamacare 'Has Never Been Favored by a Majority of Americans,' Gingrich Says," Politifact, September 26, 2013, www.politifact.com /truth-o-meter/statements/2013/sep/26/newt-gingrich/obamacare-has-never-been-favored-majority-american/; Robert J. Blendon et al., "Voters and Health Reform in the 2008 Presidential Election," *New England Journal of Medicine* 359, no. 19 (2008); "ACA at Age 4: More Disapproval Than Approval," U.S. Politics & Policy, Pew Research Center, March 20, 2014, www.people-press .org/2014/03/20/aca-at-age-4-more-disapproval-than-approval/.

78. Haynes Johnson and David S. Broder, *The System: The American Way of Politics at the Breaking Point* (Boston: Little, Brown, 1996).

79. Jonathan Freedland, "US Elections: Obama Wows Berlin Crowd with Historic Speech," *The Guardian,* July 24, 2008, www.theguardian.com /global/2008/jul/24/barackobama.uselections2008.

80. Branch Rickey, Wikiquote, accessed June 27, 2019, https://en.wikiquote .org/wiki/Branch_Rickey; Louis Pasteur, Wikiquote, accessed June 27, 2019, https://en.wikiquote.org/wiki/Louis_Pasteur.

CHAPTER 6

1. Gautam Mukunda, "Why Donald Trump Might Be the Most Dangerous Presidential Candidate in History," *HuffPost,* January 22, 2016, www.huffing-tonpost.com/entry/why-donald-trump-might-be_b_9368144.

2. Jonathan Allen and Amie Parnes, *Lucky: How Joe Biden Barely Won the Presidency* (New York: Crown, 2021).

3. Allen and Parnes, *Lucky;* Glenn Kessler, "How Liberal Was Joe Biden?," Fact Checker Analysis, *Washington Post,* May 17, 2019, www.washingtonpost. com/politics/2019/05/17/how-liberal-was-joe-biden/.

4. Lindsay Kalter, "A Closer Look at Joe Biden's Health," WebMD, October 28, 2020, www.webmd.com/a-to-z-guides/news/20201028/a-closer-look-at-joe-bidens-health.

5. Mukunda, "Don't Trust Anyone over 70"; McDermott, *Presidential Leadership, Illness, and Decision Making;* Park, *Impact of Illness on World Leaders;* Park, "Presidential Disability"; Post and Robins, "Captive King and His Captive Court"; Post and Robins, *When Illness Strikes the Leader;* Sumit Agarwal et al., "What Is the Age of Reason?," *Center for Retirement Research at Boston College,* no. 10–12 (July 2010), https://scholar.harvard.edu/files/laibson/files/ageofreason_supplement.pdf.

6. Donald J. Trump, tweet, @realdonaldtrump (suspended account), 2013, accessed January 24, 2019, https://twitter.com/realDonaldTrump/status/329390667438624768; Donald J. Trump, tweet, @realdonaldtrump (suspended account), 2018, accessed January 24, 2019, https://twitter.com/realDonaldTrump/status/949619270631256064; "Trump Again Calls Himself 'a Very Stable Genius,'" *Axios,* July 12, 2018, www.axios.com/donald-trump-very-stable-genius-nato-summit-twitter-30f4da11-9857-4fe4-b33f-ae1061cbfb46.html; Dan Spinelli, "Why Penn Won't Talk about Donald Trump," *Politico,* November 6, 2016, www.politico.com/magazine/story/2016/11/donald-trump-2016-wharton-pennsylvania-214425; Justin Elliott, "Just What Kind of Student Was Donald Trump?," *Salon,* May 3, 2011, www.salon.com/2011/05/03/donald_trump_wharton/.

7. Carlos Lozada, "I Just Binge-Read Eight Books by Donald Trump. Here's What I Learned," *Washington Post,* July 30, 2015, www.washingtonpost .com/news/book-party/wp/2015/07/30/i-just-binge-read-eight-books-by-donald-trump-heres-what-i-learned/; Michael Kranish, "A Fierce Will to Win Pushed Donald Trump to the Top," *Washington Post,* January 19, 2017, www .washingtonpost.com/politics/a-fierce-will-to-win-pushed-donald-trump-to-the-top/2017/01/17/6b36c2ce-c628-11e6-8bee-54e800ef2a63_story.html?utm_term =.4793df10607e; Donald J. Trump with Charles Leerhsen, *Trump: Surviving at the Top* (New York: Random House, 1990); Donald J. Trump with Dave Shiflett, *The America We Deserve* (Los Angeles: Renaissance Books, 2000); Donald J. Trump, *The Way to the Top: The Best Business Advice I Ever Received* (New York: Crown, 2004); Donald J. Trump, *Time to Get Tough: Making America #1 Again* (Washington, DC: Regnery, 2011); Donald J. Trump, *Crippled America: How to Make America Great Again* (New York: Threshold Editions, 2015); Donald Trump with Meredith McIver, *Trump: Think like a Billionaire: Everything You Need to Know about Success, Real Estate, and Life* (New York: Random House,

2004); Donald Trump with Tony Schwartz, *Trump: The Art of the Deal* (New York: Random House, 1987); Jane Mayer, "Donald Trump's Ghostwriter Tells All," *The New Yorker*, July 25, 2016, www.newyorker.com/magazine/2016/07/25/donald-trumps-ghostwriter-tells-all.

8. "FactChecking the 11th GOP Debate," FactCheck.Org, March 4, 2016, www.factcheck.org/2016/03/factchecking-the-11th-gop-debate/; David Barstow, Susanne Craig, and Russ Buettner, "Trump Engaged in Suspect Tax Schemes as He Reaped Riches from His Father," Special Investigation, *New York Times*, October 2, 2018, www.nytimes.com/interactive/2018/10/02/us/politics/donald-trump-tax-schemes-fred-trump.html; Russ Buettner, Susanne Craig, and Mike McIntire, "Long-Concealed Records Show Trump's Chronic Losses and Years of Tax Avoidance," *New York Times*, September 27, 2020, www.nytimes.com/interactive/2020/09/27/us/donald-trump-taxes.html.

9. Julie Pace and Jill Colvin, "Life in the White House Bubble? Trump's Had Practice," AP News, November 16, 2016, www.apnews.com/f4cb3d-c8949a447695edd65f7aba2108; James Hamblin, "Trump's Food Choices Grow More Disconcerting," *The Atlantic*, December 3, 2017, www.theatlantic.com/health/archive/2017/12/trump-eats/547355/; Alex Shephard, "Donald Trump Doesn't Read Books," *New Republic*, May 17, 2016, https://newrepublic.com/minutes/133566/donald-trump-doesnt-read-books.

10. Wayne Barrett, "Inside Donald Trump's Empire: Why He Didn't Run for President in 2012," *Daily Beast*, May 26, 2011, updated June 23, 2020, www.thedailybeast.com/inside-donald-trumps-empire-why-he-didnt-run-for-president-in-2012; Buettner, Craig, and McIntire, "Long-Concealed Records Show Trump's Chronic Losses"; Michael Daly, "Trump Tower Was Built on Undocumented Polish Immigrants' Backs," *Daily Beast*, July 8, 2015, updated April 14, 2017, www.thedailybeast.com/trump-tower-was-built-on-undocumented-polish-immigrants-backs; David W. Dunlap, "1973: Meet Donald Trump," *New York Times*, July 30, 2015, Looking Back, www.nytimes.com/times-insider/2015/07/30/1973-meet-donald-trump/; David A. Graham, "The Many Scandals of Donald Trump: A Cheat Sheet," *The Atlantic*, January 23, 2017, www.theatlantic.com/politics/archive/2017/01/donald-trump-scandals/474726/; James Hohmann, "The Daily 202: Lessons from My Search for Donald Trump's Personal Giving to Charity," *Washington Post*, August 5, 2016, www.washingtonpost.com/news/powerpost/paloma/daily-202/2016/08/05/daily-202-lessons-from-my-search-for-donald-trump-s-personal-giving-to-charity/57a3eb5fcd249a7e29d0cf7a/; Tom McNichol, "The Art of the Upsell: How Donald Trump Profits from 'Free' Seminars," *The Atlantic*, March 17, 2014, www.theatlantic.com/business/archive/2014/03/the-art-of-the-upsell-how-donald-trump-profits-from-free-seminars/284450/; Steve Reilly, "USA TODAY Exclusive: Hundreds Allege Donald Trump Doesn't Pay His Bills," *USA Today*, June 9, 2016, www.usatoday.com/story/news/politics/elections/2016/06/09/donald-

trump-unpaid-bills-republican-president-laswuits/85297274/; Megan Twohey and Michael Barbaro, "Two Women Say Donald Trump Touched Them Inappropriately," *New York Times,* October 12, 2016, www.nytimes.com/2016/10/13/us/politics/donald-trump-women.html.

11. Heather Long, "Trump Organization Is Now America's 48th Largest Private Company,"CNN,December15,2016,https://money.cnn.com/2016/12/15/investing/trump-organization-48th-largest-private-company/; Michael D'Antonio, *Never Enough: Donald Trump and the Pursuit of Success* (New York: Thomas Dunne Books/St. Martin's Press, 2015).

12. David S. Hilzenrath and Michelle Singletary, "Trump Went Broke, but Stayed on Top," *Washington Post,* November 29, 1992, www.washingtonpost.com/archive/politics/1992/11/29/trump-went-broke-but-stayed-on-top/e1685555–1de7–400c-99a8–9cd9c0bca9fe/?utm_term=.69921354a6ac.

13. Nassim Nicholas Taleb, various tweets, Twitter, 2016, https://twitter.com/nntaleb.

14. Jenna Johnson, "Donald Trump: They Say I Could 'Shoot Somebody' and Still Have Support," *Washington Post,* January 23, 2016, www.washingtonpost.com/news/post-politics/wp/2016/01/23/donald-trump-i-could-shoot-somebody-and-still-have-support/?utm_term=.fb8f88dbb739.

15. Emily Nussbaum, "The TV That Created Donald Trump," *The New Yorker,* July 31, 2017, www.newyorker.com/magazine/2017/07/31/the-tv-that-created-donald-trump; Patrick Radden Keefe, "How Mark Burnett Resurrected Donald Trump as an Icon of American Success," *The New Yorker,* January 7, 2019, www.newyorker.com/magazine/2019/01/07/how-mark-burnett-resurrected-donald-trump-as-an-icon-of-american-success; Barstow, Craig, and Buettner, "Trump Engaged in Suspect Tax Schemes"; David Axelrod, "Reality TV Bites: 'The Apprentice' Effect Aids Trump," CNN, March 9, 2016, www.cnn.com/2015/09/27/opinions/axelrod-trump-the-apprentice/index.html.

16. Charles V. Bagli, "A Trump Empire Built on Inside Connections and $885 Million in Tax Breaks," *New York Times,* September 17, 2016, www.nytimes.com/2016/09/18/nyregion/donald-trump-tax-breaks-real-estate.html.

17. Beth A. Visser, Angela S. Book, and Anthony A. Volk, "Is Hillary Dishonest and Donald Narcissistic? A HEXACO Analysis of the Presidential Candidates' Public Personas," *Personality and Individual Differences* 106 (2017).

18. Matt Labash, "Nine Tales of Trump at His Trumpiest," *The Weekly Standard,* January 22, 2016, www.weeklystandard.com/matt-labash/nine-tales-of-trump-at-his-trumpiest; Michael Kruse, "The 199 Most Donald Trump Things Donald Trump Has Ever Said," *Politico,* August 14, 2015, www.politico.com/magazine/story/2015/08/the-absolute-trumpest-121328; Philip Bump, "The Foremost Experts on Various Topics According to Trump, Most of Whom Are Trump," *Washington Post,* January 2, 2018, www.washingtonpost.com/politics/2019/01/02/foremost-experts-various-topics-according-trump-most

-whom-are-trump/; Henry Alford, "Is Donald Trump Actually a Narcissist? Therapists Weigh In!," *Vanity Fair*, November 11, 2015, www.vanityfair.com /news/2015/11/donald-trump-narcissism-therapists.

19. Trump, *Art of the Deal*; Josh Barro, "10 Things I Learned about Donald Trump in 'The Art of the Deal,'" *New York Times*, September 22, 2015, The Upshot, www.nytimes.com/2015/09/22/upshot/10-things-i-learned-about-donald-trump-in-the-art-of-the-deal.html; Josh Barro, "A Quote from 'The Art of the Deal' Perfectly Explains Trump's Presidency," *Business Insider*, April 20, 2017, www.businessinsider.com/art-of-the-deal-trump-presidency-2017–4; Callum Borchers, "The Amazing Story of Donald Trump's Old Spokesman, John Barron—Who Was Actually Donald Trump Himself," *Washington Post*, May 13, 2016, www.washingtonpost.com/news/the-fix/wp/2016/03/21/the-amazing-story-of-donald-trumps-old-spokesman-john-barron-who-was-actually-donald-trump-himself/.

20. Angie Drobnic Holan and Linda Qiu, "2015 Lie of the Year: The Campaign Misstatements of Donald Trump," PolitiFact, December 21, 2015, www .politifact.com/truth-o-meter/article/2015/dec/21/2015-lie-year-donald-trump-campaign-misstatements/; Nolan D. McCaskill, "Trump Accuses Cruz's Father of Helping JFK's Assassin," *Politico*, May 3, 2016, www.politico.com/blogs /2016-gop-primary-live-updates-and-results/2016/05/trump-ted-cruz-father-222730.

21. Visser, Book, and Volk, "Is Hillary Dishonest and Donald Narcissistic?"; Witt et al., "Assessment of Fearless Dominance and Impulsive Antisociality."

22. Libby Cathey and Meghan Keneally, "A Look Back at Trump Comments Perceived by Some as Encouraging Violence," ABC News, May 30, 2020, https:// abcnews.go.com/Politics/back-trump-comments-perceived-encouraging-violence /story?id=48415766; Maggie Haberman, "Donald Trump Says His Mocking of New York Times Reporter Was Misread," *New York Times*, November 26, 2015, www.nytimes.com/2015/11/27/us/politics/donald-trump-says-his-mocking-of-new-york-times-reporter-was-misread.html; Steve Turnham, "Donald Trump to Father of Fallen Soldier: 'I've Made a Lot of Sacrifices,'" ABC News, July 30, 2016, https://abcnews.go.com/Politics/donald-trump-father-fallen-soldier-ive-made-lot/story?id=41015051; Felicia Sonmez, "Donald Trump on John McCain in 1999: 'Does Being Captured Make You a Hero?,'" *Washington Post*, August 7, 2018, www.washingtonpost.com/politics/donald-trump-on-john-mccain-in-1999-does-being-captured-make-you-a-hero/2018/08/07/a2849b1c-9a56-11e8–8d5e-c6c594024954_story.html; Reveszm Rachael, "9/11: Donald Trump's Bizarre Quotes about September 11 Attacks Prior to Becoming President," *The Independent*, September 11, 2018, www.independent.co.uk/news/world /americas/donald-trump-bizarre-quotes-911-attacks-tallest-building-higher-ratings-muslims-cheering-george-w-a8530571.html.

23. Eliza Relman, "The 22 Women Who Have Accused Trump of Sexual Misconduct," *Business Insider*, updated September 26, 2018, accessed February 8,

2019, www.businessinsider.com/women-accused-trump-sexual-misconduct-list-2017–12; David A. Fahrenthold, "Trump Boasts about His Philanthropy. But His Giving Falls Short of His Words," *Washington Post,* October 29, 2016, www.washingtonpost.com/politics/trump-boasts-of-his-philanthropy-but-his-giving-falls-short-of-his-words/2016/10/29/b3c03106–9ac7–11e6-a0ed-ab0774c1eaa5_story.html.

24. Timothy L. O'Brien, *TrumpNation: The Art of Being the Donald* (New York: Warner Business Books, 2005).

25. Michelle Lee, "Fact Check: Has Trump Declared Bankruptcy Four or Six Times?," *Washington Post,* September 26, 2016, www.washingtonpost.com/politics/2016/live-updates/general-election/real-time-fact-checking-and-analysis-of-the-first-presidential-debate/fact-check-has-trump-declared-bankruptcy-four-or-six-times/.

26. Karen S. Schneider, "The Donald Ducks Out," *People,* May 19, 1997, https://people.com/archive/cover-story-the-donald-ducks-out-vol-47-no-19/; Susanne Craig, "Trump Boasts of Rapport with Wall St., but the Feeling Is Not Quite Mutual," *New York Times,* May 23, 2016, Dealbook, www.nytimes.com/2016/05/24/business/dealbook/donald-trump-relationship-bankers.html.

27. Matt Viser, "Donald Trump's Airline Went from Opulence in the Air to Crash Landing," *Boston Globe,* May 27, 2016, www.bostonglobe.com/news/politics/2016/05/27/donald-trump-airline-went-from-opulence-air-crash-landing/zEf1Er2Hok2dPTVVmZT6NP/story.html.

28. Joe Nocera, "Donald Trump's Less-Than-Artful Failure in Pro Football," *New York Times,* February 19, 2016, www.nytimes.com/2016/02/20/sports/football/donald-trumps-less-than-artful-failure-in-pro-football.html.

29. David Segal, "What Donald Trump's Plaza Hotel Deal Reveals about His White House Bid," *New York Times,* January 16 2016, www.nytimes.com/2016/01/17/business/what-donald-trumps-plaza-deal-reveals-about-his-white-house-bid.html.

30. Joshua Green, *Devil's Bargain: Steve Bannon, Donald Trump, and the Storming of the Presidency* (New York: Penguin, 2017).

31. Cas Mudde and Cristóbal Rovira Kaltwasser, *Populism: A Very Short Introduction* (New York: Oxford University Press, 2017), 6.

32. Green, *Devil's Bargain;* Uri Friedman, "What Is a Populist?," *The Atlantic* (Global), February 27, 2017, www.theatlantic.com/international/archive/2017/02/what-is-populist-trump/516525/.

33. Yoni Appelbaum, "'I Alone Can Fix It,'" *The Atlantic,* July 21, 2016. www.theatlantic.com/politics/archive/2016/07/trump-rnc-speech-alone-fix-it/492557/; Friedman, "What Is a Populist?"

34. German Lopez, "Donald Trump's Long History of Racism, from the 1970s to 2019," *Vox,* February 14, 2019, www.vox.com/2016/7/25/12270880/donald-trump-racist-racism-history.

35. Michael Tesler and John Sides, "How Political Science Helps Explain the Rise of Trump: The Role of White Identity and Grievances," *Washington Post*, March 3, 2016, www.washingtonpost.com/news/monkey-cage/wp/2016/03/03 /how-political-science-helps-explain-the-rise-of-trump-the-role-of-white-identity-and-grievances/.

36. Tyler T. Reny, Loren Collingwood, and Ali Valenzuela, "Vote Switching in the 2016 Election: How Racial and Immigration Attitudes, Not Economics, Explain Shifts in White Voting," *Public Opinion Quarterly* 8, no. 1 (Spring 2019); Zack Beauchamp, "A New Study Reveals the Real Reason Obama Voters Switched to Trump," *Vox*, October 16, 2018, www.vox.com/policy-and-poli-tics/2018/10/16/17980820/trump-obama-2016-race-racism-class-economy-2018-midterm; John Sides, Michael Tesler, and Lynn Vavreck, *Identity Crisis: The 2016 Presidential Campaign and the Battle for the Meaning of America* (Princeton, NJ: Princeton University Press, 2018); Diana C. Mutz, "Status Threat, Not Economic Hardship, Explains the 2016 Presidential Vote," *Proceedings of the National Academy of Sciences* 115, no. 19 (2018), www.pnas.org/content/pnas /115/19/E4330.full.pdf.

37. Lawrence K. Altman, "Parsing Ronald Reagan's Words for Early Signs of Alzheimer's," *New York Times*, March 30, 2015, The Doctor's World, www .nytimes.com/2015/03/31/health/parsing-ronald-reagans-words-for-early-signs-of-alzheimers.html; Visar Berisha et al., "Tracking Discourse Complexity Preceding Alzheimer's Disease Diagnosis: A Case Study Comparing the Press Conferences of Presidents Ronald Reagan and George Herbert Walker Bush," *Journal of Alzheimer's Disease* 45, no. 3 (March 2015); Rick Tetzeli, "Could This Radical New Approach to Alzheimer's Lead to a Breakthrough?," *Forbes*, January 18, 2019, http://fortune.com/longform/alzheimers-disease-cure-break-through/; Mukunda, "Don't Trust Anyone over 70"; Philip Weiss, "The Lives They Lived: Fred C. Trump, b. 1905; The Fred," *New York Times*, January 2, 2000, www.nytimes.com/2000/01/02/magazine/the-lives-they-lived-fred-c-trump-b-1905-the-fred.html.

38. Scott Neuman, "Doctor: Trump Dictated Letter Attesting to his 'Extraordinary' Health," *The Two-Way*, NPR, May 2, 2018, www.npr.org/sections /thetwo-way/2018/05/02/607638733/doctor-trump-dictated-letter-attesting-to-his-extraordinary-health; Kyle Swenson, "Harold Bornstein: Exiled from Trumpland, Doctor Now 'Frightened and Sad,'" *Washington Post*, May 2, 2018, www .washingtonpost.com/news/morning-mix/wp/2018/05/02/harold-bornstein-exiled-from-trumpland-former-doctor-now-frightened-and-sad/.

39. James Hanblin, "Is Something Neurologically Wrong with Donald Trump?," *The Atlantic*, January 3, 2018, www.theatlantic.com/health/archive /2018/01/trump-cog-decline/548759/; Sharon Begley, "Trump Wasn't Always So Linguistically Challenged. What Could Explain the Change?," *Stat*, May 23,

2017, www.statnews.com/2017/05/23/donald-trump-speaking-style-interviews/.

40. Jeva Lange, "Donald Trump Flies Back to New York Every Night to Sleep in His Own Bed," *The Week*, January 8, 2016, https://theweek.com/speedreads /598324/donald-trump-flies-back-new-york-every-night-sleep-bed.

41. Green, *Devil's Bargain*.

42. Katie Benner, "Trump Pressed Justice Dept. to Declare Election Results Corrupt, Notes Show," *New York Times*, July 30, 2021, www.nytimes.com/2021/07 /30/us/politics/trump-justice-department-election.html.

43. "Global Health Security Index," Nuclear Threat Initiative, Johns Hopkins Center for Health Security, 2019, accessed August 18, 2021, www.ghsindex.org/; Adam Geller and Janie Har, "'Shameful': US Virus Deaths Top 400K as Trump Leaves Office," AP News, January 19, 2021, https://apnews.com/article/donald-trump-pandemics-public-health-coronavirus-pandemic-f6e976f34a6971c889ca8a 4c5e1c0068.

44. "Excess Deaths Associated with Covid-19," Centers for Disease Control and Prevention, National Center for Health Statistics, accessed August 18, 2021, www.cdc.gov/nchs/nvss/vsrr/covid19/excess_deaths.htm; James Fallows, "The 3 Weeks That Changed Everything," *The Atlantic*, June 29, 2020, www.theatlantic.com/politics/archive/2020/06/how-white-house-coronavirus-response-went-wrong/613591/; Ed Yong, "How the Pandemic Defeated America," *The Atlantic*, September 2020, www.theatlantic.com/magazine/archive /2020/09/coronavirus-american-failure/614191/.

45. David Nakamura, "'Maybe I Have a Natural Ability': Trump Plays Medical Expert on Coronavirus by Second-Guessing the Professionals," *Washington Post*, March 6, 2020, www.washingtonpost.com/politics/maybe-i-have-a-natural-ability-trump-plays-medical-expert-on-coronavirus-by-second-guessing-the-professionals/2020/03/06/3ee0574c-5ffb-11ea-9055-5fa12981bbbf_story .html; Angie Drobnic Holan, "In Context: Donald Trump's 'Very Fine People on Both Sides' Remarks (Transcript)," Politifact, April 26, 2019, www .politifact.com/article/2019/apr/26/context-trumps-very-fine-people-both-sides-remarks/; William J. Broad and Dan Levin, "Trump Muses about Light as Remedy, but Also Disinfectant, Which Is Dangerous," *New York Times*, April 24, 2020. www.nytimes.com/2020/04/24/health/sunlight-coronavirus-trump .html.

46. Noah Weiland et al., "Trump Was Sicker Than Acknowledged with Covid-19," *New York Times*, February 11, 2021, www.nytimes.com/2021/02/11/us/politic s/trump-coronavirus.html; Libby Cathey, "Timeline: Tracking Trump alongside Scientific Developments on Hydroxychloroquine," ABC News, August 8, 2020, https://abcnews.go.com/Health/timeline-tracking-trump-alongside-scientific-developments-hydroxychloroquine/story?id=72170553.

CONCLUSION

1. Bruce Blair, "Strengthening Checks on Presidential Nuclear Launch Authority," *Arms Control Today,* January/February 2018.

2. Blair, "Strengthening Checks on Presidential Nuclear Launch Authority"; Geoff Brumfiel, "Ex-Missile Crew Members Say Cheating Is Part of the Culture," *All Things Considered,* National Public Radio, March 12, 2014, www.npr .org/2014/03/12/289423404/ex-missile-crew-members-say-cheating-is-part-of-the-culture.

3. Elizabeth Goitein, "The Alarming Scope of the President's Emergency Powers," *The Atlantic,* January/February 2019, www.theatlantic.com/magazine /archive/2019/01/presidential-emergency-powers/576418/; Korematsu v. United States, 323 US 214 (1944), Oyez, www.oyez.org/cases/1940–1955/323us214.

4. Goitein, "Alarming Scope of the President's Emergency Powers"; *A Guide to Emergency Powers and Their Use* (Washington, DC: Brennan Center for Justice, 2018), www.brennancenter.org/analysis/emergency-powers.

5. *Guide to Emergency Powers.*

6. Tim Weiner, *Enemies: A History of the FBI* (New York: Random House, 2012).

7. John T. Elliff, *The Reform of FBI Intelligence Operations* (Princeton, NJ: Princeton University Press, 1979).

8. Morgan Chalfant and Brett Samuels, "Trump Remarks Put Pressure on Barr," *The Hill,* October 20, 2020, https://thehill.com/homenews/administration /521942-trump-remarks-put-pressure-on-barr.

9. Barbara Norrander, "Presidential Politics in the Post-Reform Era," field essay, *Political Research Quarterly* 49, no. 4 (December 1996).

10. Scott Piroth, "Selecting Presidential Nominees," *Social Education* 64, no. 5 (2000); Jeffrey H. Anderson and Jay Cost, "A Republican Nomination Process," *National Affairs,* Winter 2019, www.nationalaffairs.com/publications/detail /a-republican-nomination-process.

11. Caroline Tolbert and Peverill Squire, "Reforming the Presidential Nomination Process," *PS: Political Science and Politics* 42, no. 1 (January 2009).

12. Jen O'Malley Dillon and Larry Cohen, *Report of the Unity Reform Commission,* Democratic National Committee, December 8 and 9, 2017, https:// democrats.org/wp-content/uploads/2018/10/URC_Report_FINAL.pdf; Seth Masket, "How to Improve the Primary Process? Make it Less Democratic," *Pacific Standard,* August 11, 2017, https://psmag.com/magazine/how-to-improve-the-primary-process; Adam Levy, "DNC Changes Superdelegate Rules in Presidential Nomination Process," *CNN Politics,* August 25, 2018, www.cnn .com/2018/08/25/politics/democrats-superdelegates-voting-changes/index.html.

13. Jimmy Carter, "Presidential Disability and the Twenty-Fifth Amendment: A President's Perspective," *JAMA* 272, no. 21 (1994).

14. Blair, "Strengthening Checks on Presidential Nuclear Launch Authority."

15. Scott Boston et al., *Assessing the Conventional Force Imbalance in Europe: Implications for Countering Russian Local Superiority* (Santa Monica, CA: The Rand Corporation, 2018), www.rand.org/pubs/research_reports/RR2402.html; Ankit Panda, "Backgrounder: 'No First Use' and Nuclear Weapons," Council on Foreign Relations, July 17, 2018, www.cfr.org/backgrounder/no-first-use-and-nuclear-weapons; Frank A. Rose, "As Russia and China Improve Their Conventional Military Capabilities, Should the US Rethink Its Assumptions on Extended Nuclear Deterrence?," *Order from Chaos,* Brookings Institution, October 23, 2018, www.brookings.edu/blog/order-from-chaos/2018/10/23/as-russia-and-china-improve-their-conventional-military-capabilities-should-the-us-rethink-its-assumptions-on-extended-nuclear-deterrence/.

16. Jamie Raskin, "Raskin Reintroduces 25th Amendment Legislation Establishing Independent Commission on Presidential Capacity," news release, October 9, 2020, https://raskin.house.gov/2020/10/raskin-reintroduces-25th-amendment-legislation-establishing-independent.

17. David Firestone and Philip Shenon, "A Hushed but Vital Issue: Thurmond's Health," *New York Times,* March 9, 2001, www.nytimes.com/2001/03/09/us/a-hushed-but-vital-issue-thurmond-s-health.html.

18. James Madison, "Federalist No. 10" and "Federalist No. 14," in *The Federalist Papers* (Seattle: AmazonClassics, 2017).

19. Dickerson, "Hardest Job in the World."

20. Walter Scheidel, "Demography," in *The Cambridge Economic History of the Greco-Roman World,* ed. Walter Scheidel, Ian Morris, and Richard P. Saller (Cambridge: Cambridge University Press, 2007).

APPENDIX

1. "Presidential Historians Survey 2017"; Rottinghaus and Vaughn, "Official Results of the 2018 Presidents & Executive Politics Presidential Greatness Survey"; "Siena's 6th Presidential Expert Poll."

2. Gary M. Maranell, "The Evaluation of Presidents: An Extension of the Schlesinger Polls," *Journal of American History* 57, no. 1 (June 1970); Arthur M. Schlesinger, "Our Presidents: A Rating by 75 Historians," *New York Times Magazine,* July 29, 1962; William J. Ridings Jr. and Stuart B. McIver, *Rating the Presidents: A Ranking of U.S. Leaders, from the Great and Honorable to the Dishonest and Incompetent* (New York: Carol Publishing Group, 1997); Arthur M. Schlesinger Jr., "Rating the Presidents: Washington to Clinton," *Political Science Quarterly* 112, no. 2 (1997); James Taranto, "The Rankings," *Wall Street Journal,* September 12, 2005; "American Presidents: Greatest and Worst," Siena Research Institute, July 1, 2010, https://web.archive.org/web/20150707011431/http://

www2.siena.edu/uploadedfiles/home/parents_and_community/community_
page/sri/independent_research/Presidents%20Release_2010_final.pdf; Iwan
Morgan, "UK Survey of US Presidents: Results and Analysis," Institute for the
Study of the Americas: United States Presidency Centre, accessed June 18,
2019, www.community-languages.org.uk/US-presidency-survey/pdf/analysis
.pdf; Brandon Rottinghaus and Justin S. Vaughn, "Measuring Obama against
the Great Presidents," The Brookings Institution, updated April 2, 2015, www
.brookings.edu/blog/fixgov/2015/02/13/measuring-obama-against-the-great-
presidents/; Brandon Rottinghaus and Justin S. Vaughn, "How Does Trump
Stack Up Against the Best—and Worst—Presidents?," *New York Times*, February
19, 2018, www.nytimes.com/interactive/2018/02/19/opinion/how-does-trump-
stack-up-against-the-best-and-worst-presidents.html; "Historical Rankings of
Presidents of the United States," Wikipedia, accessed June 18, 2019, https://en
.wikipedia.org/wiki/Historical_rankings_of_presidents_of_the_United_States.

3. Alan S. Blinder and Mark W. Watson, "Presidents and the US Economy: An
Econometric Explanation," *American Economic Review* 106, no. 4 (2016).

4. Taylor, "Economic Ranking of the US Presidents."

5. Eshbaugh-Soha and Peake, "Presidents and the Economic Agenda."

6. Neil Irwin, "Presidents Have Less Power over the Economy Than You Might
Think," The Upshot, *New York Times*, January 16, 2017, www.nytimes.com/2017
/01/17/upshot/presidents-have-less-power-over-the-economy-than-you-might-
think.html.

7. Richard Vedder and Lowell Gallaway, "Rating Presidential Performance,"
in *Reassessing the Presidency: The Rise of the Executive State and the Decline of
Freedom*, ed. John V. Denson (Auburn, AL: Ludwig von Mises Institute, 2001).

8. Charles F. Faber and Richard B. Faber, *The American Presidents Ranked
by Performance, 1789–2012* (Jefferson: McFarland & Company, Incorporated
Publishers, 2012).

9. Tim H. Blessing, "Presidents and Significance: Partisanship as a Source of
Perceived Greatness," *White House Studies* 3, no. 1 (2003).

10. David Nice, "The Influence of War and Party System Aging on the Ranking of Presidents," *Western Political Quarterly* 37, no. 3 (September 1984).

11. David R. Henderson and Zachary Grochenour, "War and Presidential
Greatness," *The Independent Review* 17, no. 4 (2013).

12. Jill Curry and Irwin L. Morris, "The Contemporary Presidency: Explaining Presidential Greatness: The Roles of Peace and Prosperity," *Presidential
Studies Quarterly* 40, no. 3 (September 2010).

13. David Gray Adler, "Presidential Greatness as an Attribute of Warmaking,"
Presidential Studies Quarterly 33, no. 3 (September 2003).

14. David A. Crockett, *The Opposition Presidency: Leadership and the Constraints of History* (College Station: Texas A&M University Press, 2002).

15. Mukunda, *Indispensable*.

16. Stephen Van Evera, *Guide to Methods for Students of Political Science* (Ithaca, NY: Cornell University Press, 1997).

17. Robert W. Merry, *Where They Stand: The American Presidents in the Eyes of Voters and Historians* (New York: Simon & Schuster, 2012), 3–16; Simonton, "Presidential Greatness and Performance"; Simonton, "Presidential IQ, Openness, Intellectual Brilliance, and Leadership"; Dean Keith Simonton, "Presidential Greatness: The Historical Consensus and Its Psychological Significance," *Political Psychology* 7, no. 2 (June 1986); Alvin S. Felzenberg, *The Leaders We Deserved (and a Few We Didn't): Rethinking the Presidential Rating Game* (New York: Basic Books, 2010).

18. James Tilley and Sara B. Hobolt, "Is the Government to Blame? An Experimental Test of How Partisanship Shapes Perceptions of Performance and Responsibility," *Journal of Politics* 73, no. 2 (April 2011).

19. David Mervin, "Political Science and the Study of the Presidency," *Presidential Studies Quarterly* 25, no. 4 (Fall 1995).

20. Philip E. Tetlock, "Agreeing to Disagree: A Respectful Reply to a Senior Statesman of Political Psychology," *Political Psychology* 16, no. 3 (1995); Philip E. Tetlock, "How Politicized Is Political Psychology and Is There Anything We Should Do about It?," *Political Psychology* 15, no. 3 (1994); Philip E. Tetlock, "Political Psychology or Politicized Psychology: Is the Road to Scientific Hell Paved with Good Moral Intentions?," *Political Psychology* 15, no. 3 (1994).

21. Joseph E. Uscinski and Arthur Simon, "Partisanship as a Source of Presidential Rankings," *White House Studies* 11, no. 1 (2010).

22. Meena Bose, "Presidential Ratings: Lessons and Liabilities," *White House Studies* 3, no. 1 (2003): 6.

23. Tetlock, *Expert Political Judgment;* Philip E. Tetlock, "Good Judgment in International Politics: Three Psychological Perspectives," *Political Psychology* 13, no. 3 (September 1992).

24. Philip E. Tetlock and Dan Gardner, *Superforecasting: The Art and Science of Prediction* (New York: Crown, 2015).

25. James Surowiecki, *The Wisdom of Crowds* (New York: Random House, 2005).

26. Charles C. Ragin, *Fuzzy-Set Social Science* (Chicago: University of Chicago Press, 2000).

27. Gerring and Cojocaru, "Selecting Cases for Intensive Analysis."

28. Taleb, *Fooled by Randomness;* Taleb, *Black Swan;* Nassim Nicholas Taleb, *Antifragile: Things That Gain from Disorder* (New York: Random House, 2012); Gerring and Cojocaru, "Selecting Cases for Intensive Analysis."

29. Sam Jones, "Wednesday Catastrophe: Breaking the Buck," *Alphaville* (blog of *Financial Times*), September 17, 2008, http://ftalphaville.ft.com /blog/2008/09/17/15992/wednesday-catastrophe-breaking-the-buck/; Sam Jones, "Why Letting Lehman Go Did Crush the Financial Markets," *Alphaville*

(blog of *Financial Times*), March 12, 2009, http://ftalphaville.ft .com/blog/2009/03/12/53515/why-letting-lehman-go-did-crush-the-financial-markets/; Hyman P. Minsky, "The Modeling of Financial Instability: An Introduction," *Modeling and Simulation* 5, no. 1, Proceedings of the Fifth Annual Pittsburgh Conference, April 24–26, 1974; Nicola Gennaioli, Andrei Shleifer, and Robert Vishny, "Neglected Risks, Financial Innovation, and Financial Fragility," *Journal of Financial Economics* 104, no. 3 (2012); Financial Crisis Inquiry Commission, *The Financial Crisis Inquiry Report: Final Report of the National Commission on the Causes of the Financial and Economic Crisis in the United States* (New York: Public Affairs, 2011); Jeffrey Friedman, *What Caused the Financial Crisis* (Philadelphia: University of Pennsylvania Press, 2009).

30. Francis Russell, *The Shadow of Blooming Grove: Warren G. Harding in His Times* (New York: McGraw-Hill, 1968); Laton McCartney, *The Teapot Dome Scandal: How Big Oil Bought the Harding White House and Tried to Steal the Country* (New York: Random House, 2008); Eugene P. Trani and David L. Wilson, *The Presidency of Warren G. Harding* (Lawrence: Regents Press of Kansas, 1977).

31. Simonton, "Presidential IQ, Openness, Intellectual Brilliance, and Leadership," 516.

32. Randolph C. Downes, *The Rise of Warren Gamaliel Harding, 1865–1920* (Columbus: Ohio State University Press, 1970); Robert K. Murray, *The Harding Era: Warren G. Harding and His Administration* (Minneapolis: University of Minnesota Press, 1969); Robert K. Murray, *The Politics of Normalcy: Governmental Theory and Practice in the Harding-Coolidge Era* (New York: Norton, 1973).

33. John W. Dean, *Warren G. Harding* (New York: Times Books, 2004).

34. Sylvia Ellis, *Freedom's Pragmatist: Lyndon Johnson and Civil Rights* (Gainesville: University Press of Florida, 2013); Clay Risen, *The Bill of the Century: The Epic Battle for the Civil Rights Act* (New York: Bloomsbury Press, 2014).

35. John A. Farrell, *Richard Nixon: The Life* (New York: Doubleday, 2017).

36. Scott S. Greenberger, *The Unexpected President: The Life and Times of Chester A. Arthur* (New York: Da Capo Press, Hachette Book Group, 2017).

Bibliography

"ACA at Age 4: More Disapproval Than Approval." U.S. Politics & Policy, Pew Research Center, March 20, 2014. www.people-press.org/2014/03/20/aca-at-age-4-more-disapproval-than-approval/.

Adler, David Gray. "Presidential Greatness as an Attribute of Warmaking." *Presidential Studies Quarterly* 33, no. 3 (September 2003): 466–83.

Agarwal, Sumit, John C. Driscoll, Xavier Gabaix, and David Laibson. "What Is the Age of Reason?" *Center for Retirement Research at Boston College*, no. 10–12 (July 2010): 1–8. https://scholar.harvard.edu/files/laibson/files/ageofreason_supplement.pdf.

Alford, Henry. "Is Donald Trump Actually a Narcissist? Therapists Weigh In!" *Vanity Fair*, November 11, 2015. www.vanityfair.com/news/2015/11/donald-trump-narcissism-therapists.

Allen, Jonathan, and Amie Parnes. *Lucky: How Joe Biden Barely Won the Presidency.* New York: Crown, 2021.

Allison, Graham T., and Philip Zelikow. *Essence of Decision: Explaining the Cuban Missile Crisis.* 2nd ed. New York: Longman, 1999.

Altman, Lawrence K. "Parsing Ronald Reagan's Words for Early Signs of Alzheimer's." *New York Times*, March 30, 2015, The Doctor's World. www.nytimes.com/2015/03/31/health/parsing-ronald-reagans-words-for-early-signs-of-alzheimers.html.

Ambrose, Stephen E. *Eisenhower: Soldier and President.* New York: Simon & Schuster, 1990.

"American Presidents: Greatest and Worst." Siena Research Institute, July 1, 2010. https://web.archive.org/web/20150707011431/http://www2.siena.edu /uploadedfiles/home/parents_and_community/community_page/sri /independent_research/Presidents%20Release_2010_final.pdf.

Anderson, Jeffrey H., and Jay Cost. "A Republican Nomination Process." *National Affairs*, Winter 2019. www.nationalaffairs.com/publications/detail/a-republican-nomination-process.

Ansolabehere, Stephen. "The Paradox of Minimal Effects." In *Do Campaigns Matter?*, edited by Brady Henry and Johnson Richard. Ann Arbor: University of Michigan Press, 2001.

Anson, Ian G. "Partisanship, Political Knowledge, and the Dunning-Kruger Effect." *Political Psychology* 39, no. 5(2018): 1173–92.

Antonovsky, Aaron. "Social Class, Life Expectancy and Overall Mortality." *Milbank Memorial Fund Quarterly* 45, no. 2 (1967): 31–73.

Appelbaum, Yoni. "'I Alone Can Fix It.'" *The Atlantic*, July 21, 2016. www .theatlantic.com/politics/archive/2016/07/trump-rnc-speech-alone-fix-it /492557/.

Atkinson, Rick. *An Army at Dawn: The War in North Africa, 1942–1943*. New York: Henry Holt, 2002.

———. *The Day of Battle: The War in Sicily and Italy, 1943–1944*. New York: Henry Holt, 2007.

———. *The Guns at Last Light: The War in Western Europe, 1944–1945*. New York: Henry Holt, 2013.

Axelrod, David. "Reality TV Bites: 'The Apprentice' Effect Aids Trump." CNN, March 9, 2016. www.cnn.com/2015/09/27/opinions/axelrod-trump-the-apprentice/index.html.

Babiak, Paul, and Robert D Hare. *Snakes in Suits: When Psychopaths Go to Work*. New York: HarperCollins Publishers, 2006.

Bagli, Charles V. "A Trump Empire Built on Inside Connections and $885 Million in Tax Breaks." *New York Times*, September 17, 2016. www.nytimes .com/2016/09/18/nyregion/donald-trump-tax-breaks-real-estate.html.

Baime, A. J. *The Accidental President: Harry S. Truman and the Four Months That Changed the World*. Boston: Houghton Mifflin Harcourt, 2017.

Baker, Catherine. *The Yugoslav Wars of the 1990s*. New York: Palgrave, 2015.

Baker, Jean H. *James Buchanan*. New York: Times Books, 2004.

Balz, Dan, Anne E. Kornblut, and Shailagh Murray. "Obama Wins Iowa's Democratic Caucuses." *Washington Post*, January 4, 2008. www.washingtonpost .com/wp-dyn/content/article/2008/01/03/AR2008010304441.html.

Balz, John. "Ready to Lead on Day One: Predicting Presidential Greatness from Experience." *PS: Political Science and Politics* 43 (July 2010): 487–92.

Bardach, Eugene. *The Implementation Game: What Happens After a Bill Becomes a Law*. Cambridge, MA: MIT Press, 1977.

Barnichon, Regis, Christian Matthes, and Alexander Ziegenbein. "The Financial Crisis at 10: Will We Ever Recover?" Federal Reserve Bank of San Francisco Economic Letter, August 13, 2018. www.frbsf.org/economic-research /publications/economic-letter/2018/august/financial-crisis-at-10-years-will-we-ever-recover/.

Barrett, Wayne. "Inside Donald Trump's Empire: Why He Didn't Run for President in 2012." *Daily Beast,* May 26, 2011, updated June 23, 2020. www.thedailybeast.com/inside-donald-trumps-empire-why-he-didnt-run-for-president-in-2012.

Barro, Josh. "10 Things I Learned about Donald Trump in 'The Art of the Deal.'" *New York Times,* September 22, 2015, The Upshot. www.nytimes .com/2015/09/22/upshot/10-things-i-learned-about-donald-trump-in-the-art-of-the-deal.html.

———. "A Quote from 'The Art of the Deal' Perfectly Explains Trump's Presidency." *Business Insider,* April 20, 2017. www.businessinsider.com/art-of-the-deal-trump-presidency-2017-4.

Barstow, David, Susanne Craig, and Russ Buettner. "Trump Engaged in Suspect Tax Schemes as He Reaped Riches from His Father." Special Investigation, *New York Times,* October 2, 2018. www.nytimes.com/interactive/2018/10/02 /us/politics/donald-trump-tax-schemes-fred-trump.html.

Bauer, Nichole M. "The Effects of Partisan Trespassing Strategies across Candidate Sex." *Political Behavior* 41, no. 4 (2019): 897–915.

Baumeister, Roy F., and Steven J. Scher. "Self-Defeating Behavior Patterns among Normal Individuals: Review and Analysis of Common Self-Destructive Tendencies." *Psychological Bulletin* 104, no. 1 (1988): 3–22.

Beatty, Randolph P, and Edward J Zajac. "CEO Change and Firm Performance in Large Corporations: Succession Effects and Manager Effects." *Strategic Management Journal* 8, no. 4 (1987): 305–17.

Beauchamp, Zack. "A New Study Reveals the Real Reason Obama Voters Switched to Trump." *Vox,* October 16, 2018. www.vox.com/policy-and-politics/2018/10/16/17980820/trump-obama-2016-race-racism-class-economy-2018-midterm.

Begley, Sharon. "Trump Wasn't Always So Linguistically Challenged. What Could Explain the Change?" *Stat,* May 23, 2017. www.statnews.com/2017/05 /23/donald-trump-speaking-style-interviews/.

Bennedsen, Morten, Francisco Pérez-González, and Daniel Wolfenzon. "Do CEOs Matter?" Online paper at Columbia University, 2006. www0 .gsb.columbia.edu/mygsb/faculty/research/pubfiles/3177/valueceos .pdf.

Benner, Katie. "Trump Pressed Justice Dept. To Declare Election Results Corrupt, Notes Show." *New York Times,* July 30, 2021. www.nytimes .com/2021/07/30/us/politics/trump-justice-department-election.html.

Bennett, W. Lance, and Shanto Iyengar. "A New Era of Minimal Effects? The Changing Foundations of Political Communication." *Journal of Communication* 58, no. 4 (2008): 707–31.

Berelson, Bernard. *Voting: A Study of Opinion Formation in a Presidential Campaign*. Chicago: University of Chicago Press, 1954.

Berisha, Visar, Shuai Wang, Amy LaCross, and Julie Liss. "Tracking Discourse Complexity Preceding Alzheimer's Disease Diagnosis: A Case Study Comparing the Press Conferences of Presidents Ronald Reagan and George Herbert Walker Bush." *Journal of Alzheimer's Disease* 45, no. 3 (March 2015): 959–63.

Berman, Jeff. *The Magic Number*. Ordway House, 2012.

Bernanke, Ben S. "Economic Policy: Lessons from History." Board of Governors of the Federal Reserve System, 2010, accessed August 15, 2018. www .federalreserve.gov/newsevents/speech/bernanke20100408a.htm.

Bernanke, Ben S., and Harold James. "The Gold Standard, Deflation, and Financial Crisis in the Great Depression: An International Comparison." In *Financial Markets and Financial Crises*, edited by R. Glenn Hubbard, 33–68. Chicago: University of Chicago Press, 1990.

Bismarck, Otto von. Wikiquote, accessed May 13, 2018. https://en.wikiquote .org/wiki/Otto_von_Bismarck.

Black, William K. *The Best Way to Rob a Bank Is to Own One: How Corporate Executives and Politicians Looted the S&L Industry*. Austin: University of Texas Press, 2005.

Blair, Bruce. "Strengthening Checks on Presidential Nuclear Launch Authority." *Arms Control Today*, January/February 2018, 6–13.

Blendon, Robert J., Drew E. Altman, John M. Benson, Mollyann Brodie, Tami Buhr, Claudia Deane, and Sasha Buscho. "Voters and Health Reform in the 2008 Presidential Election." *New England Journal of Medicine* 359, no. 19 (2008): 2050–61.

Blessing, Tim H. "Presidents and Significance: Partisanship as a Source of Perceived Greatness." *White House Studies* 3, no. 1 (2003): 41–51.Blinder, Alan S., and Mark Zandi. *How the Great Recession Was Brought to an End*. Moody's Analytics, 2010.

Blinder, Alan S., and Mark W. Watson. "Presidents and the US Economy: An Econometric Explanation." *American Economic Review* 106, no. 4 (2016): 1015–45.

Blonigen, Daniel M., Brian M. Hicks, Robert F. Krueger, Christopher J. Patrick, and William G. Iacono. "Psychopathic Personality Traits: Heritability and Genetic Overlap with Internalizing and Externalizing Psychopathology." *Psychological Medicine* 35, no. 5 (May 2005): 637–48.

Blustein, Paul. *The Chastening: Inside the Crisis That Rocked the Global Financial System and Humbled the IMF*. New York: PublicAffairs, 2001.

Borchers, Callum. "The Amazing Story of Donald Trump's Old Spokesman, John Barron—Who Was Actually Donald Trump Himself." *Washington Post,* May 13, 2016. www.washingtonpost.com/news/the-fix/wp/2016/03/21/the-amazing-story-of-donald-trumps-old-spokesman-john-barron-who-was-actually-donald-trump-himself/.

Bose, Meena. "Presidential Ratings: Lessons and Liabilities." *White House Studies* 3, no. 1 (2003): 3–19.

Boston, Scott, Michael Johnson, Nathan Beauchamp-Mustafaga, and Yvonne K. Crane. *Assessing the Conventional Force Imbalance in Europe: Implications for Countering Russian Local Superiority.* (Santa Monica, CA: The Rand Corporation, 2018). www.rand.org/pubs/research_reports/RR2402.html.

Boulard, Garry. *The Worst President—The Story of James Buchanan.* Bloomington, IN: iUniverse, 2015.

Bourne, Peter G. *Jimmy Carter: A Comprehensive Biography from Plains to Post-Presidency.* New York: Scribner, 1997.

Branton, Regina, Ashley English, Samantha Pettey, and Tiffany D. Barnes. "The Impact of Gender and Quality Opposition on the Relative Assessment of Candidate Competency." *Electoral Studies* 54 (August 2018): 35–43.

Braybrooke, David, and Charles E. Lindblom. *A Strategy of Decision.* London: The Free Press of Glencoe, 1963.

Broad, William J., and Dan Levin. "Trump Muses about Light as Remedy, but Also Disinfectant, Which Is Dangerous." *New York Times,* April 24, 2020. www.nytimes.com/2020/04/24/health/sunlight-coronavirus-trump.html.

Brumfiel, Geoff. "Ex-Missile Crew Members Say Cheating Is Part of the Culture." *All Things Considered,* National Public Radio, March 12, 2014. www.npr.org/2014/03/12/289423404/ex-missile-crew-members-say-cheating-is-part-of-the-culture.

Buchanan, James. "First Annual Message to Congress on the State of the Union." December 8, 1857. The American Presidency Project, University of California, Santa Barbara. www.presidency.ucsb.edu/documents/first-annual-message-congress-the-state-the-union.

Buettner, Russ, Susanne Craig, and Mike McIntire. "Long-Concealed Records Show Trump's Chronic Losses and Years of Tax Avoidance." *New York Times,* September 27, 2020. www.nytimes.com/interactive/2020/09/27/us/donald-trump-taxes.html.

Bump, Philip. "The Foremost Experts on Various Topics According to Trump, Most of Whom Are Trump." *Washington Post,* January 2, 2018. www.washingtonpost.com/politics/2019/01/02/foremost-experts-various-topics-according-trump-most-whom-are-trump/.

Burlingame, Michael. *Abraham Lincoln: A Life.* Baltimore: Johns Hopkins University Press, 2008.

Burns, James MacGregor. *Roosevelt: The Soldier of Freedom*. New York: Open Road Media, 2012.

Burt, Ronald S. *Brokerage and Closure: An Introduction to Social Capital*. New York: Oxford University Press, 2005.

Bush, George, and Brent Scowcroft. *A World Transformed*. New York: Knopf, 1998.

Byman, Daniel L., and Kenneth M. Pollack. "Let Us Now Praise Great Men: Bringing the Statesman Back In." *International Security* 25, no. 4 (Spring 2001): 107–46.

Cabane, Olivia Fox. *The Charisma Myth: How Anyone Can Master the Art and Science of Personal Magnetism*. New York, 2012.

Cable, Daniel M, and Charles K Parsons. "Socialization Tactics and Person-Organization Fit." *Personnel Psychology* 54, no. 1 (2001): 1–23.

Campos, Paul. "The Truman Show." *New York Magazine*, July 24, 2021. https://nymag.com/intelligencer/2021/07/the-truman-show.html.

Cannon, Lou. *President Reagan: The Role of a Lifetime*. New York: Public Affairs, 2000.

Carter, Jimmy. "Presidential Disability and the Twenty-Fifth Amendment: A President's Perspective." *JAMA* 272, no. 21 (1994): 1698.

Cassese, Eric C., and Mirya R. Holman. "Party and Gender Stereotypes in Campaign Attacks." *Political Behavior* 40, no. 3 (September 2018): 785–807.

Cathey, Libby. "Timeline: Tracking Trump alongside Scientific Developments on Hydroxychloroquine." ABC News, August 8, 2020. https://abcnews.go.com/Health/timeline-tracking-trump-alongside-scientific-developments-hydroxychloroquine/story?id=72170553.

Cathey, Libby, and Meghan Keneally. "A Look Back at Trump Comments Perceived by Some as Encouraging Violence." ABC News, May 30, 2020. https://abcnews.go.com/Politics/back-trump-comments-perceived-encouraging-violence/story?id=48415766.

Ceaser, James W. *Presidential Selection: Theory and Development*. Princeton, NJ: Princeton University Press, 1979.

Chait, Jonathan. *Audacity: How Barack Obama Defied His Critics and Created a Legacy That Will Prevail*. New York: Custom House, 2017.

Chalfant, Morgan, and Brett Samuels. "Trump Remarks Put Pressure on Barr." *The Hill*, October 20, 2020. https://thehill.com/homenews/administration/521942-trump-remarks-put-pressure-on-barr.

Chandrasekaran, Rajiv. *Imperial Life in the Emerald City: Inside Iraq's Green Zone*. 1st ed. New York: Alfred A. Knopf, 2006.

Chang, Ailsa. "Critics of President George H. W. Bush Reflect on His Handling of the AIDS Crisis." *All Things Considered*, National Public Radio, December 4, 2018. www.npr.org/2018/12/04/673398013

/critics-of-president-george-h-w-bush-reflect-on-his-handling-of-the-aids-crisis.

Chase, James S. *Emergence of the Presidential Nominating Convention 1789–1832.* Urbana, IL: University of Illinois Press, 1973.

Chatman, Jennifer A. "Improving Interactional Organizational Research: A Model of Person-Organization Fit." *Academy of Management Review* 14, no. 3 (1989): 333–49.

Chatterjee, Arijit, and Donald C. Hambrick. "It's All about Me: Narcissistic Chief Executive Officers and Their Effects on Company Strategy and Performance." *Administrative Science Quarterly* 52, no. 3 (2007): 351–86.

Chen, S., A. Y. Lee-Chai, and J. A. Bargh. "Relationship Orientation as a Moderator of the Effects of Social Power." *Journal of Personality and Social Psychology* 80, no. 2 (February 2001): 173–87.

Chernow, Ron. *The House of Morgan: An American Banking Dynasty and the Rise of Modern Finance.* New York: Simon & Schuster, 1991.

Cherny, Andrei. *The Candy Bombers: The Untold Story of the Berlin Airlift and America's Finest Hour.* New York: G. P. Putnam's Sons, 2008.

Chwieroth, Jeffrey M. "Counterfactuals and the Study of the American Presidency." *Presidential Studies Quarterly* 32, no. 2 (April 2004): 293–327.

Cohen, Marty, David Karol, Hans Noel, and John Zaller. *The Party Decides: Presidential Nominations before and after Reform.* Chicago: University of Chicago Press, 2008.

Craig, Susanne. "Trump Boasts of Rapport with Wall St., but the Feeling Is Not Quite Mutual." *New York Times,* May 23, 2016, Dealbook. www.nytimes .com/2016/05/24/business/dealbook/donald-trump-relationship-bankers.html.

Cramer, Richard Ben. *What It Takes: The Way to the White House.* New York: Random House, 1992.

Crockett, David A. *The Opposition Presidency: Leadership and the Constraints of History.* College Station: Texas A&M University Press, 2002.

Culver, John C., and John Hyde. *American Dreamer: The Life and Times of Henry A. Wallace.* New York: W. W. Norton, 2001.

Curry, Jill, and Irwin L. Morris. "The Contemporary Presidency: Explaining Presidential Greatness: The Roles of Peace and Prosperity." *Presidential Studies Quarterly* 40, no. 3 (September 2010): 515–30.

Dallek, Robert. *Harry S. Truman.* New York: Times Books, 2008.

———. *An Unfinished Life: John F. Kennedy.* New York: Little, Brown, 2004.

Dalton, Kathleen. *Theodore Roosevelt: A Strenuous Life.* New York: Alfred A. Knopf, 2002.

Daly, Michael. "Trump Tower Was Built on Undocumented Polish Immigrants' Backs." *Daily Beast,* July 8, 2015, updated April 14, 2017. www.thedailybeast .com/trump-tower-was-built-on-undocumented-polish-immigrants-backs.

D'Antonio, Michael. *Never Enough: Donald Trump and the Pursuit of Success.* Donald Trump and the Pursuit of Success. First edition. ed. New York: Thomas Dunne Books/St. Martin's Press, 2015.

Darwin, Charles. *Origin of Species:150th Anniversary Edition.* Alachua, FL: Bridge-Logos, 2009.

Dean, John W. *Warren G. Harding.* New York: Times Books, 2004.

DeCelles, Katherine A., D. Scott DeRue, Joshua D. Margolis, and Tara L. Ceranic. "Does Power Corrupt or Enable? When and Why Power Facilitates Self-Interested Behavior." *Journal of Applied Psychology* 97, no. 3 (2012): 681–89.

DeLong, Bradford, "Henry A. Wallace (1952) on the Ruthless Nature and Utter Evil of Soviet Communism: Cold-War Era God-That-Failed Weblogging," *Grasping Reality* (blog), July 24, 2013. http://delong.typepad.com/sdj/2013 /02/henry-a-wallace-1952-on-the-ruthless-nature-of-communism-cold-war-era-god-that-failed-weblogging.html.

Deluga, Ronald J. "American Presidential Machiavellianism: Implications for Charismatic Leadership and Rated Performance." *The Leadership Quarterly* 12, no. 3 (2001): 339–63.

Dickerson, John. "The Hardest Job in the World." *The Atlantic,* May 2018. www .theatlantic.com/magazine/archive/2018/05/a-broken-office/556883/.

Dillon, Jen O'Malley, and Larry Cohen. *Report of the Unity Reform Commission.* Democratic National Committee, December 8 and 9, 2017. https://democrats .org/wp-content/uploads/2018/10/URC_Report_FINAL.pdf.

DiSilvestro, Roger L. *Theodore Roosevelt in the Badlands: A Young Politician's Quest for Recovery in the American West.* New York: Walker, 2011.

Ditonto, Tessa. "A High Bar or a Double Standard? Gender, Competence, and Information in Political Campaigns." *Political Behavior* 39, no. 2 (June 2017): 301–25.

Donald, David Herbert. *Lincoln.* New York: Touchstone, 1996.

Douglas, Stephen Arnold. "Kansas-Lecompton Convention: Speech of Senator Douglas, of Illinois, on the President's Message: Delivered in the Senate of the United States, December 9, 1857." Oberlin College Library Anti-Slavery Collection. https://archive.org/details/ASPC0005211000.

Downes, Randolph C. *The Rise of Warren Gamaliel Harding, 1865–1920.* Columbus: Ohio State University Press, 1970.

Downs, Anthony. *Inside Bureaucracy.* Boston: Little, Brown, 1991.

Downs, George W., and David M. Rocke. "Conflict, Agency, and Gambling for Resurrection: The Principal-Agent Problem Goes to War." *American Journal of Political Science* 38, no. 2 (May 1994): 362–80.

Dror, Yehezkel. "Statecraft as Prudent Risk-Taking: The Case of the Middle East Peace Process." *Journal of Contingencies and Crisis Management* 2, no. 3 (September 1994): 126–37.

Dunlap, David W. "1973: Meet Donald Trump." *New York Times,* July 30, 2015, LookingBack.www.nytimes.com/times-insider/2015/07/30/1973-meet-donald-trump/.

Dunning, David. "Chapter Five—the Dunning-Kruger Effect: On Being Ignorant of One's Own Ignorance." In *Advances in Experimental Social Psychology,* edited by James M. Olson and Mark P. Zanna, 247–96: Waltham, MA: Academic Press, 2011.

Dutton, Kevin. *The Wisdom of Psychopaths: Lessons in Life from Saints, Spies and Serial Killers.* London: William Heinemann, 2012.

"Dwight David Eisenhower Chronology." Dwight D. Eisenhower Presidential Library, Museum, and Boyhood Home, accessed January 5, 2019. www.eisenhower.archives.gov/all_about_ike/chronologies.html.

Ecelbarger, Gary L. *The Great Comeback: How Abraham Lincoln Beat the Odds to Win the 1860 Republican Nomination.* New York: Thomas Dunne Books, 2008.

Eichengreen, Barry, and Peter Temin. "The Gold Standard and the Great Depression." *Contemporary European History* 9, no. 2 (2000): 183–207.

Eisenhower, Dwight D. *Crusade in Europe.* Garden City, NY: Doubleday, 1948.

Elliff, John T. *The Reform of FBI Intelligence Operations.* Princeton University Press, 1979.

Elliott, Justin. "Just What Kind of Student Was Donald Trump?" *Salon,* May 3, 2011. www.salon.com/2011/05/03/donald_trump_wharton/.

Ellis, Sylvia. *Freedom's Pragmatist: Lyndon Johnson and Civil Rights.* Gainesville: University Press of Florida, 2013.

Epstein, Gerald A. *Financialization and the World Economy.* Cheltenham: Edward Elgar, 2005.

Eshbaugh-Soha, Matthew, and Jeffrey S. Peake. "Presidents and the Economic Agenda." *Political Research Quarterly* 58, no. 1 (2005): 127–38.

Estimates Group Office of Intelligence Research, Department of State. "Intelligence Estimate." *Foreign Relations of the United States* 7, no. Korea (1950): 149–54.

Etcheson, Nicole. "General Jackson Is Dead: James Buchanan, Stephen A. Douglas, and Kansas Policy." In *James Buchanan and the Coming of the Civil War,* edited by John W. Quist and Michael J. Birkner, 86–110. Gainesville: University Press of Florida, 2013.

Etcoff, Nancy L. *Survival of the Prettiest: The Science of Beauty.* 1st ed. New York: Anchor, 1999.

Excess Deaths Associated with Covid-19." Centers for Disease Control and Prevention, National Center for Health Statistics, accessed August 18, 2021. www.cdc.gov/nchs/nvss/vsrr/covid19/excess_deaths.htm.

Faber, Charles F., and Richard B. Faber. *The American Presidents Ranked by Performance, 1789–2012*. Jefferson: McFarland & Company, Incorporated Publishers, 2012.

"Factchecking the 11th GOP Debate." FactCheck.Org, March 4, 2016. www.factcheck.org/2016/03/factchecking-the-11th-gop-debate/.

Fahrenthold, David A. "Trump Boasts about His Philanthropy. But His Giving Falls Short of His Words." *Washington Post*, October 29, 2016. www.washingtonpost.com/politics/trump-boasts-of-his-philanthropy-but-his-giving-falls-short-of-his-words/2016/10/29/b3c03106–9ac7–11e6-a0ed-ab0774c1eaa5_story.html.

Fallows, James. "The 3 Weeks That Changed Everything." *The Atlantic*, June 29, 2020. www.theatlantic.com/politics/archive/2020/06/how-white-house-coronavirus-response-went-wrong/613591/.

Fanning, Charles. "Dunne, Finley Peter." American National Biography, 1999.

Farrell, John A. *Richard Nixon: The Life*. New York: Doubleday, 2017.

Fast, Nathanael J., Deborah H Gruenfeld, Niro Sivanathan, and Adam D. Galinsky. "Illusory Control: A Generative Force behind Power's Far-Reaching Effects." *Psychological Science* 20, no. 4 (2009): 502–8.

Fazal, Tanisha M. *State Death: The Politics and Geography of Conquest, Occupation, and Annexation*. Princeton, NJ: Princeton University Press, 2007.

Fearon, James D. "Counterfactuals and Hypothesis Testing in Political Science." *World Politics* 43, no. 2 (January 1991): 169–95.

Fehrenbacher, Don E., ed. *Abraham Lincoln: Speeches and Writings, 1832–1858*. New York: Penguin Books, 1989.

———, ed. *Abraham Lincoln: Speeches and Writings, 1859–1865*. New York: Penguin Books, 1989.

Felzenberg, Alvin S. *The Leaders We Deserved (and a Few We Didn't): Rethinking the Presidential Rating Game*. New York: Basic Books, 2010.

Ferrell, Robert H. *Choosing Truman: The Democratic Convention of 1944*. Columbia: University of Missouri Press, 1994.

———. *Harry S. Truman: A Life*. Columbia, Missouri: University of Missouri Press, 1994.

Financial Crisis Inquiry Commission. *The Financial Crisis Inquiry Report: Final Report of the National Commission on the Causes of the Financial and Economic Crisis in the United States*. New York: Public Affairs, 2011.

Finkel, Steven E. "Reexamining the 'Minimal Effects' Model in Recent Presidential Campaigns." *Journal of Politics* 55, no. 1 (1993): 1–21.

Finkelman, Paul. "James Buchanan, Dred Scott, and the Whisper of Conspiracy." In *James Buchanan and the Coming of the Civil War*, edited by John W. Quist and Michael J. Birkner, 20–45. Gainesville: University Press of Florida, 2013.

Fiorina, Morris P. *The Political Parties Have Sorted.* The Hoover Institution (Palo Alto: September 21 2016). www.hoover.org/sites/default/files/research /docs/fiorina_3_finalfile.pdf.

Firestone, David, and Philip Shenon. "A Hushed but Vital Issue: Thurmond's Health." *New York Times,* March 9, 2001. www.nytimes.com/2001/03/09 /us/a-hushed-but-vital-issue-thurmond-s-health.html.

Freedland, Jonathan. "US Elections: Obama Wows Berlin Crowd with Historic Speech." *The Guardian,* July 24, 2008. www.theguardian.com/global/2008 /jul/24/barackobama.uselections2008.

Freeman, Richard B. "It's Financialization!" *International Labour Review* 149, no. 2 (2010): 163–83.

Friedman, Jeffrey. *What Caused the Financial Crisis.* Philadelphia: University of Pennsylvania Press, 2009.

Friedman, Uri. "What Is a Populist?" *The Atlantic* (Global), February 27, 2017. www.theatlantic.com/international/archive/2017/02/what-is-populist-trump /516525/.

Furnham, Adrian. *The Elephant in the Boardroom: The Causes of Leadership Derailment.* Epub. London: Palgrave Macmillan, 2010.

Furnham, Adrian, Steven C. Richards, and Delroy L. Paulhus. "The Dark Triad of Personality: A 10 Year Review." *Social and Personality Psychology Compass* 7, no. 3 (2013): 199–216.

Gaddis, John Lewis. *The Cold War: A New History.* New York: Penguin Press, 2005.

Gaddis, John Lewis, and Paul Nitze. "NSC 68 and the Soviet Threat Reconsidered." *International Security* 4, no. 4 (Spring 1980): 164–76.

Galinsky, Adam D., Joe C. Magee, M. Ena Inesi, and Deborah H Gruenfeld. "Power and Perspectives Not Taken." *Psychological Science* 17, no. 12 (2006): 1068–74.

Gallagher, Maryann E., and Susan H. Allen. "Presidential Personality: Not Just a Nuisance." *Foreign Policy Analysis* 10, no. 1 (2014): 1–21.

Gallagher, Maryann E., and Bethany Blackstone. "Taking Matters into Their Own Hands: Presidents' Personality Traits and the Use of Executive Orders." *Presidential Studies Quarterly* 45, no. 2 (2015): 221–46.

Gara, Larry. *The Presidency of Franklin Pierce.* Lawrence: University Press of Kansas, 1991.

Gardner, Mark Lee. *Rough Riders: Theodore Roosevelt, His Cowboy Regiment, and the Immortal Charge up San Juan Hill.* New York: William Morrow, 2016.

Garrow, David J. *Rising Star: The Making of Barack Obama.* New York: William Morrow, 2017.

Geller, Adam, and Janie Har. "'Shameful': US Virus Deaths Top 400k as Trump Leaves Office." AP News, January 19, 2021. https://apnews.com

/article/donald-trump-pandemics-public-health-coronavirus-pandemic-f6e976f34a6971c889ca8a4c5e1c0068.

Gennaioli, Nicola, Andrei Shleifer, and Robert Vishny. "Neglected Risks, Financial Innovation, and Financial Fragility." *Journal of Financial Economics* 104, no. 3 (2012): 452–68.

George, Alexander L. "American Policy-Making and the North Korean Aggression." *World Politics* 7, no. 2 (January 1955): 209–32.

———. *Presidential Decisionmaking in Foreign Policy: The Effective Use of Information and Advice.* Boulder, CO: Westview Press, 1980.

Gerring, John. "Case-Selection for Case Study Analysis: Qualitative and Quantitative Techniques." In *Oxford Handbook on Political Methodology,* edited by Janet M. Box-Steffensmeier, Henry E. Brady, and David Collier, 645–84. Oxford: Oxford University Press, 2006.

———. *Case Study Research: Principles and Practices.* New York: Cambridge University Press, 2007.

Gerring, John, and Lee Cojocaru. "Selecting Cases for Intensive Analysis: A Diversity of Goals and Methods." *Sociological Methods & Research* 45, no. 3 (2016): 392–423.

Gienapp, William E. "'No Bed of Roses': James Buchanan, Abraham Lincoln, and Presidential Leadership in the Civil War Era." In *James Buchanan and the Political Crisis of the 1850s,* edited by Michael J. Birkner, 93–122. Cransbury, NJ: Associated University Presses, 1996.

Gilpin, Robert. *War and Change in World Politics.* New York: Cambridge University Press, 1981. http://discovery.lib.harvard.edu//?itemid=%7clibrary%2fm%2faleph%7c000392138.

Gladwell, Malcolm. *Blink: The Power of Thinking without Thinking.* New York: Little, Brown, 2005.

"Global Health Security Index." Nuclear Threat Initiative, Johns Hopkins Center for Health Security, 2019, accessed August 18, 2021. www.ghsindex.org/.

Goitein, Elizabeth. "The Alarming Scope of the President's Emergency Powers." *The Atlantic,* January/February 2019. www.theatlantic.com/magazine/archive/2019/01/presidential-emergency-powers/576418/.

Goodwin, Doris Kearns. *Team of Rivals: The Political Genius of Abraham Lincoln.* New York: Simon & Schuster, 2005.

Gordon, Michael R., and Bernard E. Trainor. *Cobra II: The inside Story of the Invasion and Occupation of Iraq.* New York: Pantheon Books, 2006.

Gordon-Reed, Annette. *Andrew Johnson.* New York: Times Books, Henry Holt, 2011.

Gould, Lewis L. *The Modern American Presidency.* Foreword by Richard Norton Smith. 2nd ed., rev. and updated. Lawrence: University Press of Kansas, 2009.

———. *The Presidency of William McKinley.* Lawrence: Regents Press of Kansas, 1980.

———. *Theodore Roosevelt.* New York: Oxford University Press, 2012.

Graham, David A. "The Many Scandals of Donald Trump: A Cheat Sheet." *The Atlantic,* January 23, 2017. www.theatlantic.com/politics/archive/2017/01 /donald-trump-scandals/474726/.

Grant, Ulysses S. *The Personal Memoirs of General Ulysses S. Grant.* New York: Sheba Blake, 2014.

Green, Joshua. *Devil's Bargain: Steve Bannon, Donald Trump, and the Storming of the Presidency.* New York: Penguin, 2017.

Greenberger, Scott S. *The Unexpected President: The Life and Times of Chester A. Arthur.* New York: Da Capo Press, Hachette Book Group, 2017.

Greenstein, Fred I. *The Hidden-Hand Presidency: Eisenhower as Leader.* Baltimore: Johns Hopkins University Press, 1994.

———. "The Impact of Personality on the End of the Cold War: A Counterfactual Analysis." *Political Psychology* 19, no. 1 (1998): 1–16.

Greenstein, Fred I., and Dale Anderson. *Presidents and the Dissolution of the Union: Leadership Style from Polk to Lincoln.* Princeton, NJ: Princeton University Press, 2013.

Groysberg, Boris. *Chasing Stars: The Myth of Talent and the Portability of Performance.* Princeton, NJ: Princeton University Press, 2010.

Groysberg, Boris, Andrew N. McLean, and Nitin Nohria. "Are Leaders Portable?" *Harvard Business Review* 84, no. 5 (2006): 92–100.

Groysberg, Boris, Ashish Nanda, and Nitin Nohria. "The Risky Business of Hiring Stars." *Harvard Business Review* 82 (2004): 92–100.

A Guide to Emergency Powers and Their Use. Washington, DC: Brennan Center for Justice, 2018. www.brennancenter.org/analysis/emergency-powers.

Haberman, Maggie. "Donald Trump Says His Mocking of New York Times Reporter Was Misread." *New York Times,* November 26, 2015. www.nytimes .com/2015/11/27/us/politics/donald-trump-says-his-mocking-of-new-york- times-reporter-was-misread.html.

Hager, G. L., and T. Sullivan. "President-Centered and Presidency-Centered Explanations of Presidential Public Activity." *American Journal of Political Science* 38, no. 4 (1994): 1079–1103.

Hamblin, James. "Trump's Food Choices Grow More Disconcerting." *The Atlantic,* December 3, 2017. www.theatlantic.com/health/archive/2017/12 /trump-eats/547355/.

Hambrick, Donald C. "Upper Echelons Theory: An Update." *Academy of Management Review* 32, no. 2 (April 2007): 334–43.

Hambrick, Donald C., and Eric Abrahamson. "Assessing Managerial Discretion across Industries: A Multimethod Approach." *Academy of Management Journal* 38, no. 5 (October 1995): 1427–41.

Hambrick, Donald C., and Phyllis A. Mason. "Upper Echelons: The Organization as a Reflection of Its Top Managers." *Academy of Management Review* 9, no. 2 (1984): 193–206.

Hamby, Alonzo L. *Man of the People: A Life of Harry S. Truman.* New York: Oxford University Press, 1995.

Hamermesh, Daniel, and Amy M. Parker. "Beauty in the Classroom: Professors' Pulchritude and Putative Pedagogical Productivity." *Economics of Education Review* 24 (2005): 369–76.

Hamermesh, Daniel S. *Beauty Pays: Why Attractive People Are More Successful.* Princeton, NJ: Princeton University Press, 2011.

Hamermesh, Daniel S., and Jeff E. Biddle. "Beauty and the Labor Market." *The American Economic Review* 84, no. 5 (1994): 1174–94.

Hamilton, Alexander. "Federalist No. 68." 501–06. Seattle: AmazonClassics, 2017.

Hanblin, James. "Is Something Neurologically Wrong with Donald Trump?" *The Atlantic,* January 3, 2018. www.theatlantic.com/health/archive/2018/01/trump-cog-decline/548759/.

Hannan, Michael T., and John H. Freeman. *Organizational Ecology.* Cambridge, MA: Harvard University Press, 1989.

Harris, William C. *Lincoln's Rise to the Presidency.* Lawrence: University Press of Kansas, 2007.

Haynes, John Earl, and Harvey Klehr. *Venona: Decoding Soviet Espionage in America.* New Haven, CT: Yale University Press, 1999.

Heldman, Caroline, Meredith Conroy, and Alissa R. Ackerman. *Sex and Gender in the 2016 Presidential Election.* Santa Barbara: ABC-CLIO, 2018.

Henderson, David R., and Zachary Grochenour. "War and Presidential Greatness." *The Independent Review* 17, no. 4 (2013): 505–16.

Hess, Gary R. *Presidential Decisions for War: Korea, Vietnam, the Persian Gulf, and Iraq.* 2nd ed. Baltimore: Johns Hopkins University Press, 2009.

Higgins, Monica C. *Career Imprints: Creating Leaders across an Industry.* San Francisco: Jossey-Bass, 2005.

Hillygus, D. Sunshine, and Simon Jackman. "Voter Decision Making in Election 2000: Campaign Effects, Partisan Activation, and the Clinton Legacy." *American Journal of Political Science* 47, no. 4 (2003): 583–96.

Hilzenrath, David S., and Michelle Singletary. "Trump Went Broke, but Stayed on Top." *Washington Post,* November 29, 1992. www.washingtonpost.com/archive/politics/1992/11/29/trump-went-broke-but-stayed-on-top/e1685555-1de7-400c-99a8-9cd9c0bca9fe/?utm_term=.69921354a6ac.

"Historical Rankings of Presidents of the United States." Wikipedia, accessed June 18, 2019. https://en.wikipedia.org/wiki/Historical_rankings_of_presidents_of_the_United_States.

Hoekstra, Douglas J. "The Politics of *Politics:* Skowronek and Presidential Research." *Presidential Studies Quarterly* 29, no. 3 (1999): 657–71.

Hogan, Robert. *Personality and the Fate of Organizations*. Mahwah, NJ: Psychology Press, 2007.

Hogan, Robert, Gordon J. Curphy, and Joyce Hogan. "What We Know about Leadership: Effectiveness and Personality." *American Psychologist* 49, no. 6 (June 1994): 493–504.

Hogan, Robert, and Robert B. Kaiser. "What We Know about Leadership." *Review of General Psychology* 9, no. 2 (June 2005): 169–80.

Hohmann, James. "The Daily 202: Lessons from My Search for Donald Trump's Personal Giving to Charity." *Washington Post*, August 5, 2016. www .washingtonpost.com/news/powerpost/paloma/daily-202/2016/08/05 /daily-202-lessons-from-my-search-for-donald-trump-s-personal-giving-to-charity/57a3eb5fcd249a7e29d0cf7a/.

Holan, Angie Drobnic. "In Context: Donald Trump's 'Very Fine People on Both Sides' Remarks (Transcript)." Politifact, April 26, 2019. www.politifact .com/article/2019/apr/26/context-trumps-very-fine-people-both-sides-remarks/.

Holan, Angie Drobnic, and Linda Qiu. "2015 Lie of the Year: The Campaign Misstatements of Donald Trump." PolitiFact, December 21, 2015. www .politifact.com/truth-o-meter/article/2015/dec/21/2015-lie-year-donald-trump-campaign-misstatements/.

Holmes, Jack E., and Robert E. Elder Jr. "Our Best and Worst Presidents: Some Possible Reasons for Perceived Performance." *Presidential Studies Quarterly* 19, no. 3 (1989): 529–57.

Holsti, Ole R. "Foreign Policy Decision Makers Viewed Psychologically: 'Cognitive Process' Approaches." In *In Search of Global Patterns*, edited by James N. Rosenau, 120–44. New York: The Free Press, 1976.

Holt, Michael F. "Another Look at the Election of 1856." In *James Buchanan and the Political Crisis of the 1850s*, edited by Michael J. Birkner, 37–67. Cransbury, NJ: Associated University Presses, 1996.

———. *Franklin Pierce*. New York: Times Books, 2010.

Horton, Scott. "Eisenhower on the Opportunity Cost of Defense Spending." *Browsings: The Harper's Blog*, November 12, 2007. https://harpers.org /blog/2007/11/eisenhower-on-the-opportunity-cost-of-defense-spending/.

House, Robert J., and Ram N. Aditya. "The Social Scientific Study of Leadership: Quo Vadis?" *Journal of Management* 23, no. 3 (1997): 409–73.

"How Selecting U.S. Presidential Candidates Became the People's Choice." Reuters, March 29, 2016. www.reuters.com/article/us-usa-election-selectionprocess-factbox/how-selecting-u-s-presidential-candidates-became-the-peoples-choice-idUSKCN0WW001.

Huckman, Robert S., and Gary P. Pisano. "The Firm Specificity of Individual Performance: Evidence from Cardiac Surgery." *Management Science* 52, no. 4 (April 2006): 473–88.

Huntington, Samuel P. *The Common Defense: Strategic Programs in National Politics*. New York: Columbia University Press, 1961.

Irwin, Neil. "Presidents Have Less Power over the Economy Than You Might Think." The Upshot, *New York Times*, January 16, 2017. www.nytimes.com /2017/01/17/upshot/presidents-have-less-power-over-the-economy-than-you-might-think.html.

Jeansonne, Glen. *Herbert Hoover: A Life*. New York: New American Library, 2016.

Jeffers, H. Paul. *Commissioner Roosevelt: The Story of Theodore Roosevelt and the New York City Police, 1895–1897*. New York: J. Wiley & Sons, 1994.

Johnson, Haynes, and David S. Broder. *The System: The American Way of Politics at the Breaking Point*. Boston: Little, Brown, 1996.

Johnson, Jenna. "Donald Trump: They Say I Could 'Shoot Somebody' and Still Have Support." *The Washington Post* (Washington, DC), January 23 2016. www.washingtonpost.com/news/post-politics/wp/2016/01/23/donald-trump-i-could-shoot-somebody-and-still-have-support/?utm_term=. fb8f88dbb739.

Jones, Benjamin F., and Benjamin A. Olken. "Do Leaders Matter? National Leadership and Growth since World War II." *Quarterly Journal of Economics* 120, no. 3 (August 2005): 835–64.

———. "Hit or Miss? The Effect of Assassinations on Institutions and War." *American Economic Journal: Macroeconomics* 1, no. 2 (July 2009): 55–87.

Jones, Charles O. "The Legitimacy of Inexperience: Leadership from Outside." *The Forum: A Journal of Applied Research in Contemporary Politics* 7, no. 1 (2009).

Jones, Sam. "Wednesday Catastrophe: Breaking the Buck." *Alphaville* (blog of *Financial Times*), September 17, 2008. http://ftalphaville.ft.com/blog/2008 /09/17/15992/wednesday-catastrophe-breaking-the-buck/.

———. "Why Letting Lehman Go Did Crush the Financial Markets." *Alphaville* (blog of *Financial Times*), March 12, 2009. http://ftalphaville.ft.com/blog /2009/03/12/53515/why-letting-lehman-go-did-crush-the-financial-markets/.

Judge, Timothy A., Remus Ilies, and Amy E. Colbert. "Intelligence and Leadership: A Quantitative Review and Test of Theoretical Propositions." *Journal of Applied Psychology* 89, no. 3 (2004): 542–52.

Judge, Timothy A., Ronald F. Piccolo, and Tomek Kosalka. "The Bright and Dark Sides of Leader Traits: A Review and Theoretical Extension of the Leader Trait Paradigm." *The Leadership Quarterly* 20, no. 6 (2009): 855–75.

"Just 37% of Americans Can Name Their Representative." Haven Insights, 2017, accessed March 27, 2018. www.haveninsights.com/just-37-percent-name-representative/.

Kahneman, Daniel. *Thinking, Fast and Slow.* New York: Farrar, Straus and Giroux, 2011.

Kalter, Lindsay. "A Closer Look at Joe Biden's Health." WebMD, October 28, 2020. www.webmd.com/a-to-z-guides/news/20201028/a-closer-look-at-joe-bidens-health.

Kamarck, Elaine Ciulla. *Primary Politics: Everything You Need to Know about How America Nominates Its Presidential Candidates.* 2nd ed. Washington, DC: Brookings Institution Press, 2015.

———. *Why Presidents Fail: And How They Can Succeed Again.* Washington, DC: Brookings Institution Press, 2016.

Karabell, Zachary. *Chester Alan Arthur.* New York: Times Books, 2004.

Keefe, Patrick Radden. "How Mark Burnett Resurrected Donald Trump as an Icon of American Success." *The New Yorker,* January 7, 2019. www.newyorker.com/magazine/2019/01/07/how-mark-burnett-resurrected-donald-trump-as-an-icon-of-american-success.

Keltner, Dacher. "Don't Let Power Corrupt You." *Harvard Business Review* 94, no. 10 (October 2016): 112–15.

Keltner, Dacher, Deborah H Gruenfeld, and Cameron Anderson. "Power, Approach, and Inhibition." *Psychological Review* 110, no. 2 (2003): 265–84.

Kessler, Glenn. "How Liberal Was Joe Biden?" Fact Checker Analysis, *Washington Post,* May 17, 2019. www.washingtonpost.com/politics/2019/05/17/how-liberal-was-joe-biden/.

Khurana, Rakesh. *Searching for a Corporate Savior: The Irrational Quest for Charismatic CEOs.* Princeton, NJ: Princeton University Press, 2002.

Klein, Philip Shriver. *President James Buchanan, a Biography.* University Park: Pennsylvania State University Press, 1962.

Kliegman, Julie. "Obamacare 'Has Never Been Favored by a Majority of Americans,' Gingrich Says." Politifact, September 26, 2013. www.politifact.com/truth-o-meter/statements/2013/sep/26/newt-gingrich/obamacare-has-never-been-favored-majority-american/.

Korematsu v. United States. 323 US 214 (1944). Oyez. www.oyez.org/cases/1940–1955/323us214.

Kranish, Michael. "A Fierce Will to Win Pushed Donald Trump to the Top." *Washington Post,* January 19, 2017. www.washingtonpost.com/politics/a-fierce-will-to-win-pushed-donald-trump-to-the-top/2017/01/17/6b36c2ce-c628-11e6-8bee-54e800ef2a63_story.html?utm_term=.4793df10607e.

Krippner, Greta R. "The Financialization of the American Economy." *Socio-Economic Review* 3, no. 2 (2005): 173–208.

Kruger, Justin, and David Dunning. "Unskilled and Unaware of It: How Difficulties in Recognizing One's Own Incompetence Lead to Inflated Self-Assessments." *Journal of Personality and Social Psychology* 77, no. 6 (1999): 1121–34.

Kruse, Michael. "The 199 Most Donald Trump Things Donald Trump Has Ever Said." *Politico*, August 14, 2015. www.politico.com/magazine/story/2015/08/the-absolute-trumpest-121328.

Labash, Matt. "Nine Tales of Trump at His Trumpiest." *The Weekly Standard*, January 22, 2016. www.weeklystandard.com/matt-labash/nine-tales-of-trump-at-his-trumpiest.

Laing, Matthew, and Brendan McCaffrie. "The Impossible Leadership Situation? Analyzing Success for Disjunctive Presidents." *Presidential Studies Quarterly* 47, no. 2 (June 2017): 255–76.

Landau, Daniel. "One Man's Wickedness: Malignant Narcissism and Major Blunders in International Relations." MS thesis, Massachusetts Institute of Technology, 2004.

Lange, Jeva. "Donald Trump Flies Back to New York Every Night to Sleep in His Own Bed."*The Week*, January 8, 2016. https://theweek.com/speedreads/598324/donald-trump-flies-back-new-york-every-night-sleep-bed.

Lee, Michelle. "Fact Check: Has Trump Declared Bankruptcy Four or Six Times?" *Washington Post*, September 26, 2016. www.washingtonpost.com/politics/2016/live-updates/general-election/real-time-fact-checking-and-analysis-of-the-first-presidential-debate/fact-check-has-trump-declared-bankruptcy-four-or-six-times/.

Leuchtenburg, William Edward. *Herbert Hoover.* New York: Times Books, 2009.

Levy, Adam. "DNC Changes Superdelegate Rules in Presidential Nomination Process." *CNN Politics*, August 25, 2018. www.cnn.com/2018/08/25/politics/democrats-superdelegates-voting-changes/index.html.

Lieberson, Stanley, and James F. O'Connor. "Leadership and Organizational Performance: A Study of Large Corporations." *American Sociological Review* 37, no. 2 (1972): 117–30.

Lilienfeld, Scott O., Irwin D. Waldman, Kristin Landfield, Ashley L. Watts, Steven Rubenzer, and Thomas R. Faschingbauer. "Fearless Dominance and the US Presidency: Implications of Psychopathic Personality Traits for Successful and Unsuccessful Political Leadership." *Journal of Personality and Social Psychology* 103, no. 3 (2012): 489–505.

Linz, Juan. "The Perils of Presidentialism." *Journal of Democracy* 1, no. 1 (Winter 1990): 51–69.

Long, Heather. "Trump Organization Is Now America's 48th Largest Private Company." CNN, December 15, 2016. https://money.cnn.com/2016/12/15/investing/trump-organization-48th-largest-private-company/.

Lopez, German. "Donald Trump's Long History of Racism, from the 1970s to 2019." *Vox*, February 14, 2019. www.vox.com/2016/7/25/12270880/donald-trump-racist-racism-history.

Lozada, Carlos. "I Just Binge-Read Eight Books by Donald Trump. Here's What I Learned." *Washington Post*, July 30, 2015. www.washingtonpost.com

/news/book-party/wp/2015/07/30/i-just-binge-read-eight-books-by-donald-trump-heres-what-i-learned/.

Ludwig, Arnold M. *King of the Mountain.* Lexington: University Press of Kentucky, 2002.

Maccoby, Michael. *The Productive Narcissist: The Promise and Peril of Visionary Leadership.* New York: Broadway Books, 2003.

Madison, James. "Federalist No. 10." In *The Federalist Papers,* 63–72. Seattle: AmazonClassics, 2017.

———. "Federalist No. 14." In *The Federalist Papers,* 93–98. Seattle: Amazon-Classics, 2017.

———. "Federalist No. 57." In *The Federalist Papers,* 419–26. Seattle: Amazon-Classics, 2017.

Maranell, Gary M. "The Evaluation of Presidents: An Extension of the Schlesinger Polls." *Journal of American History* 57, no. 1 (June 1970): 104–13.

Maraniss, David. *Barack Obama: The Story.* New York: Simon & Schuster, 2012.

———. *First in His Class: A Biography of Bill Clinton.* New York: Simon & Schuster, 1995.

March, James G. "How We Talk and How We Act: Administrative Theory and Administrative Life." In *Leadership and Organizational Culture,* edited by Thomas J. Sergiovanni and John E. Corbally, 18–35. Urbana: University of Illinois Press, 1984.

March, James G., and Herbert A. Simon. *Organizations.* New York: John Wiley and Sons, 1959.

Marchant-Shapiro, Theresa. *Professional Pathways to the Presidency.* New York: Palgrave Macmillan, 2015.

Masket, Seth. "How to Improve the Primary Process? Make It Less Democratic." *Pacific Standard,* August 11, 2017. https://psmag.com/magazine/how-to-improve-the-primary-process.

Mason, J. W. *What Recovery? The Case for Continued Expansionary Policy at the Fed.* (New York: Roosevelt Institute, July 25, 2017). https://rooseveltinstitute.org/wp-content/uploads/2020/07/RI-What-Recovery-report-201707.pdf.

Mauboussin, Michael J. *The Success Equation: Untangling Skill and Luck in Business, Sports, and Investing.* Boston: Harvard Business Review Press, 2012.

Mayer, Jane. "Donald Trump's Ghostwriter Tells All." *The New Yorker,* July 25, 2016.www.newyorker.com/magazine/2016/07/25/donald-trumps-ghostwriter-tells-all.

McCartney, Laton. *The Teapot Dome Scandal: How Big Oil Bought the Harding White House and Tried to Steal the Country.* New York: Random House, 2008.

McCaskill, Nolan D. "Trump Accuses Cruz's Father of Helping JFK's Assassin." *Politico,* May 3, 2016. www.politico.com/blogs/2016-gop-primary-live-updates-and-results/2016/05/trump-ted-cruz-father-222730.

McCullough, David. *Mornings on Horseback: The Story of an Extraordinary Family, a Vanished Way of Life and the Unique Child Who Became Theodore Roosevelt.* New York: Simon & Schuster, 1982.

McCullough, David G. *Truman.* New York: Simon & Schuster, 1992.

McDermott, Rose. *Presidential Leadership, Illness, and Decision Making.* New York: Cambridge University Press, 2008.

McMillan, Priscilla Johnson. "Cold Warmonger." *New York Times,* May 25, 1997. www.nytimes.com/1997/05/25/books/cold-warmonger.html.

McNichol, Tom. "The Art of the Upsell: How Donald Trump Profits from 'Free' Seminars." *The Atlantic,* March 17, 2014. www.theatlantic.com/business /archive/2014/03/the-art-of-the-upsell-how-donald-trump-profits-from-free-seminars/284450/.

Mcnulty, Colin, and Jennifer White. *Making Obama.* Podcast audio, 2018. www.wbez.org/shows/making-obama-podcast/.

Meacham, Jon. *Destiny and Power: The American Odyssey of George Herbert Walker Bush.* New York: Random House, 2015.

Mead, Walter Russell. *Special Providence: American Foreign Policy and How It Changed the World.* New York: Alfred A. Knopf, 2001.

Mencken, H. L. Wikiquote, accessed April 24, 2018. https://en.wikiquote.org /wiki/H._L._Mencken.

Mendell, David. *Obama: From Promise to Power.* New York: Amistad/Harper-Collins, 2007.

Merry, Robert W. *President McKinley: Architect of the American Century.* New York: Simon & Schuster, 2017.

———. *Where They Stand: The American Presidents in the Eyes of Voters and Historians.* New York: Simon & Schuster, 2012.

Mervin, David. "Political Science and the Study of the Presidency." *Presidential Studies Quarterly* 25, no. 4 (Fall 1995): 669–76.

Messer, Robert L. *The End of an Alliance: James F. Byrnes, Roosevelt, Truman, and the Origins of the Cold War.* Chapel Hill: University of North Carolina Press, 1982.

Minsky, Hyman P. "The Modeling of Financial Instability: An Introduction." *Modeling and Simulation* 5, no. 1, Proceedings of the Fifth Annual Pittsburgh Conference, April 24–26, 1974, 267–72.

Moe, Terry M. "The Revolution in Presidential Studies." *Presidential Studies Quarterly* 39, no. 4 (2009): 701–24.

Morgan, Iwan. "UK Survey of US Presidents: Results and Analysis." Institute for the Study of the Americas: United States Presidency Centre, accessed June 18, 2019. www.community-languages.org.uk/US-presidency-survey /pdf/analysis.pdf.

Morris, Edmund. *The Rise of Theodore Roosevelt.* New York: Ballantine Books, 1980.

———. *Theodore Rex.* New York: Random House, 2001.

"The Most Infamous Brawl in the History of the U.S. House of Representatives." Historical Highlights, History, Art, & Archives of the United States House of Representatives, accessed August 11, 2018. https://history.house.gov/Historical-Highlights/1851–1900/The-most-infamous-floor-brawl-in-the-history-of-the-U-S--House-of-Representatives/.

Mudde, Cas, and Cristóbal Rovira Kaltwasser. *Populism: A Very Short Introduction.* New York: Oxford University Press, 2017.

Mukunda, Gautam. "Don't Trust Anyone over 70." *Foreign Policy,* February 27, 2013. https://foreignpolicy.com/2013/02/27/dont-trust-anyone-over-70/.

———. *Indispensable: When Leaders Really Matter.* Boston: Harvard Business Review Press, 2012.

———. "The Price of Wall Street's Power." *Harvard Business Review* 92, no. 6 (June 2014): 70–78.

———. "Why Donald Trump Might Be the Most Dangerous Presidential Candidate in History," *HuffPost,* January 22, 2016. www.huffingtonpost.com/entry/why-donald-trump-might-be_b_9368144.

Mukunda, Gautam, and William J. Troy. "Caught in the Net: Lessons from the Financial Crisis for a Networked Future." *Parameters* 39, no. 2 (Summer 2009): 63–76.

Murray, Robert K. *The Harding Era: Warren G. Harding and His Administration.* Minneapolis: University of Minnesota Press, 1969.

———. *The Politics of Normalcy: Governmental Theory and Practice in the Harding-Coolidge Era.* New York: Norton, 1973.

Murray, Robert K., and Tim H. Blessing. *Greatness in the White House: Rating the Presidents, Washington through Carter, Final Report, the Presidential Performance Study.* University Park: Pennsylvania State University Press, 1988.

Mutz, Diana C. "Status Threat, Not Economic Hardship, Explains the 2016 Presidential Vote." *Proceedings of the National Academy of Sciences* 115, no. 19 (2018): E4330–E39. www.pnas.org/content/pnas/115/19/E4330.full.pdf.

Naftali, Timothy J. *George H. W. Bush.* New York: Times Books, 2007.

Nakamura, David. "'Maybe I Have a Natural Ability': Trump Plays Medical Expert on Coronavirus by Second-Guessing the Professionals." *Washington Post,* March 6 2020. www.washingtonpost.com/politics/maybe-i-have-a-natural-ability-trump-plays-medical-expert-on-coronavirus-by-second-guessing-the-professionals/2020/03/06/3ee0574c-5ffb-11ea-9055-5fa12981bbbf_story.html.

Neuman, Scott. "Doctor: Trump Dictated Letter Attesting to His 'Extraordinary' Health." *The Two-Way,* NPR, May 2, 2018. www.npr.org/sections/thetwo-way/2018/05/02/607638733/doctor-trump-dictated-letter-attesting-to-his-extraordinary-health.

Newman, Brian, and Adrian Davis. "Polls and Elections: Character and Political Time as Sources of Presidential Greatness." *Presidential Studies Quarterly* 46, no. 2 (2016): 411–33.

Nice, David. "The Influence of War and Party System Aging on the Ranking of Presidents." *Western Political Quarterly* 37, no. 3 (September 1984): 443–55.

Nichols, Curt. "The Presidential Ranking Game: Critical Review and Some New Discoveries." *Presidential Studies Quarterly* 42, no. 2 (2012): 275–99.

Nichols, David A. *Ike and McCarthy: Dwight Eisenhower's Secret Campaign against Joseph McCarthy*. New York: Simon and Schuster, 2017.

———. *A Matter of Justice: Eisenhower and the Beginning of the Civil Rights Revolution*. New York: Simon and Schuster, 2008.

Nocera, Joe. "Donald Trump's Less-Than-Artful Failure in Pro Football." *New York Times,* February 19, 2016. www.nytimes.com/2016/02/20/sports /football/donald-trumps-less-than-artful-failure-in-pro-football.html.

Norrander, Barbara. "Presidential Politics in the Post-Reform Era." Field essay. *Political Research Quarterly* 49, no. 4 (December 1996): 875–915.

NSC 68 (1950). In *Foreign Relations of the United States, 1950, National Security Affairs; Foreign Economic Policy*, v. 1. https://history.state.gov /historicaldocuments/frus1950v01/d85.

Nussbaum, Emily. "The TV That Created Donald Trump." *The New Yorker,* July 31, 2017. www.newyorker.com/magazine/2017/07/31/the-tv-that-created-donald-trump.

Nye, Joseph S. *Presidential Leadership and the Creation of the American Era*. Princeton, NJ: Princeton University Press, 2013.

Oates, Stephen B. *To Purge This Land with Blood: A Biography of John Brown*. Amherst: University of Massachusetts Press, 1984.

Obama, Barack. *Dreams from My Father: A Story of Race and Inheritance*. New York: Times Books, 1995.

O'Boyle, Ernest H., Jr., Donelson R. Forsyth, George C. Banks, and Michael A. McDaniel. "A Meta-Analysis of the Dark Triad and Work Behavior: A Social Exchange Perspective." *Journal of Applied Psychology* 97, no. 3 (2012): 557–79.

O'Brien, Timothy L. *TrumpNation: The Art of Being the Donald*. New York: Warner Business Books, 2005.

Ocasio, William. "Towards an Attention-Based View of the Firm." *Strategic Management Journal* 18 (1997): 187–206.

Ohler, Norman. *Blitzed: Drugs in Nazi Germany*. Translated by Shaun Whiteside. London: Allen Lane, 2016.

Olenski, Andrew R., Matthew V. Abola, and Anupam B. Jena. "Do Heads of Government Age More Quickly? Observational Study Comparing Mortality between Elected Leaders and Runners-up in National Elections of 17 Countries." *BMJ* 351 (2015).

Orhangazi, Özgür. *Financialization and the US Economy*. Cheltenham: Edward Elgar, 2008.

Pace, Julie, and Jill Colvin. "Life in the White House Bubble? Trump's Had Practice." AP News, November 16, 2016. www.apnews.com/f4cb3dc 8949a447695edd65f7aba2108.

Packer, George. *The Assassins' Gate: America in Iraq*. New York: Farrar, Strauss, and Giroux, 2005.

Pager, Devah. "The Mark of a Criminal Record." *American Journal of Sociology* 108, no. 5 (2003): 937–75.

Paige, Glenn D. *The Korean Decision, June 24–30, 1950*. New York: Free Press, 1968.

———. *The Scientific Study of Political Leadership*. New York: The Free Press, 1977.

Palley, Thomas. "Financialization: What It Is and Why It Matters." Working Paper no. 525. Annendale-on-Hudson, NY: Levy Economics Institute of Bard College, 2007.

Panda, Ankit. "Backgrounder: 'No First Use' and Nuclear Weapons." Council on Foreign Relations, July 17, 2018. www.cfr.org/backgrounder/no-first-use-and-nuclear-weapons.

Park, Bert E. "Presidential Disability: Past Experiences and Future Implications." *Politics and the Life Sciences* 7, no. 1 (August 1988): 50–66.

Park, Bert Edward. *The Impact of Illness on World Leaders*. Philadelphia: University of Pennsylvania Press, 1986.

Pasteur, Louis. Wikiquote, accessed June 27, 2019. https://en.wikiquote.org/wiki/Louis_Pasteur.

Paulhus, Delroy L. "Interpersonal and Intrapsychic Adaptiveness of Trait Self-Enhancement: A Mixed Blessing?" *Journal of Personality and Social Psychology* 74, no. 5 (1998): 1197–208.

Paulhus, Delroy L., and Kevin M. Williams. "The Dark Triad of Personality: Narcissism, Machiavellianism, and Psychopathy." *Journal of Research in Personality* 36, no. 6 (2002): 556–63.

Paunonen, Sampo V., Jan-Erik Lönnqvist, Markku Verkasalo, Sointu Leikas, and Vesa Nissinen. "Narcissism and Emergent Leadership in Military Cadets." *The Leadership Quarterly* 17, no. 5 (2006): 475–86.

Peltier, Michelle. "Why Black Women Prefer Clinton to Obama." CBS News, December 3, 2007. www.cbsnews.com/news/why-black-women-prefer-clinton-to-obama/.

Peterson, Merrill D. *Lincoln in American Memory*. New York: Oxford University Press, 1994.

Pfeffer, Jeffrey. "The Ambiguity of Leadership." *Academy of Management Review* 2, no. 1 (January 1977): 104–12.

Pfeffer, Jeffrey, and Gerald R. Salancik. *The External Control of Organizations: A Resource Dependence Perspective*. Stanford, CA: Stanford Business Classics, 2003.

Phillips, Tasha R., Martin Sellbom, Yossef S. Ben-Porath, and Christopher J. Patrick. "Further Development and Construct Validation of MMPI-2-RF Indices of Global Psychopathy, Fearless-Dominance, and Impulsive-Antisociality in a Sample of Incarcerated Women." *Law and Human Behavior* 38, no. 1 (February 2014): 34–46.

Piroth, Scott. "Selecting Presidential Nominees." *Social Education* 64, no. 5 (2000): 278–85.

Polsby, Nelson W. *Consequences of Party Reform*. Oxford: Oxford University Press, 1983.

Popkin, Samuel. *The Candidate: What It Takes to Win—and Hold—the White House*. New York: Oxford University Press, 2012.

———. *The Reasoning Voter: Communication and Persuasion in Presidential Campaigns*. 2nd ed. Chicago: University of Chicago Press, 1994.

Post, Jerrold M. "Current Concepts of the Narcissistic Personality: Implications for Political Psychology." *Political Psychology* 14, no. 1 (March 1993): 99–121.

———. *Leaders and Their Followers in a Dangerous World*. Ithaca, NY: Cornell University Press, 2004.

Post, Jerrold M., and Robert S. Robins. "The Captive King and His Captive Court: The Psychopolitical Dynamics of the Disabled Leader and His Inner Circle." *Political Psychology* 11, no. 2 (June 1990): 331–51.

———. *When Illness Strikes the Leader: The Dilemma of the Captive King*. New Haven, CT: Yale University Press, 1993.

Potter, David M. *The Impending Crisis: 1848–1861*. Edited by Don E. Fehrenbacher. New York: HarperCollins, 1976.

Potts, John. *A History of Charisma*. London: Palgrave Macmillan, 2009.

"Presidential Historians Survey 2017." C-SPAN, 2017, accessed April 2, 2018. www.c-span.org/presidentsurvey2017/?page=overall.

Pressman, Jeffrey L., and Aaron Wildavsky. *Implementation: How Great Expectations in Washington Are Dashed in Oakland: Or, Why It's Amazing That Federal Programs Work at All, This Being the Saga of the Economic Development Administration as Told by Two Sympathetic Observers Who Seek to Build Morals on a Foundation of Ruined Hopes*. Berkeley: University of California Press, 1973.

Quist, John W., and Michael J. Birkner. "Introduction: Bum Rap or Bad Leadership?" In *James Buchanan and the Coming of the Civil War*, edited by John W. Quist and Michael J. Birkner, 1–19. Gainesville: University of Florida Press, 2013.

Rabe, Stephen G. "Eisenhower Revisionism: A Decade of Scholarship." *Diplomatic History* 17, no. 1 (1993): 97–116.

Rablen, Matthew D., and Arnold J. Oswald. "Mortality and Immortality: The Nobel Prize as an Experiment into the Effect of Status upon Longevity." *Journal of Health Economics* 27, no. 6 (December 2008): 1462–71.

Rachael, Reveszm. "9/11: Donald Trump's Bizarre Quotes about September 11 Attacks Prior to Becoming President." *The Independent,* September 11, 2018. www.independent.co.uk/news/world/americas/donald-trump-bizarre-quotes-911-attacks-tallest-building-higher-ratings-muslims-cheering-george-w-a8530571.html.

Ragin, Charles C. *Fuzzy-Set Social Science.* Chicago: University of Chicago Press, 2000.

Ranney, Austin. *Curing the Mischiefs of Faction: Party Reform in America.* Berkeley: University of California Press, 1976.

Rappleye, Charles. *Herbert Hoover in the White House: The Ordeal of the Presidency.* New York: Simon & Schuster, 2016.

Raskin, Jamie. "Raskin Reintroduces 25th Amendment Legislation Establishing Independent Commission on Presidential Capacity." news release, October 9, 2020. https://raskin.house.gov/2020/10/raskin-reintroduces-25th-amendment-legislation-establishing-independent.

Reilly, Steve. "USA Today Exclusive: Hundreds Allege Donald Trump Doesn't Pay His Bills." *USA Today,* June 9, 2016. www.usatoday.com/story/news/politics/elections/2016/06/09/donald-trump-unpaid-bills-republican-president-laswuits/85297274/.

Relman, Eliza. "The 22 Women Who Have Accused Trump of Sexual Misconduct." *Business Insider,* updated September 26, 2018, accessed February 8, 2019. www.businessinsider.com/women-accused-trump-sexual-misconduct-list-2017-12.

Remnick, David. *The Bridge: The Life and Rise of Barack Obama.* New York: Alfred A. Knopf, 2010.

———. "The Wanderer." *The New Yorker,* September 18, 2006. www.newyorker.com/magazine/2006/09/18/the-wanderer-3.

Reny, Tyler T., Loren Collingwood, and Ali Valenzuela. "Vote Switching in the 2016 Election: How Racial and Immigration Attitudes, Not Economics, Explain Shifts in White Voting." *Public Opinion Quarterly* 8, no. 1 (Spring 2019): 91–113.

Richard, Carl J. *The Founders and the Classics: Greece, Rome, and the American Enlightenment.* Cambridge, MA: Harvard University Press, 1994.

Rickey, Branch. Wikiquote, accessed June 27, 2019. https://en.wikiquote.org/wiki/Branch_Rickey.

Ricks, Thomas E. *Fiasco: The American Military Adventure in Iraq*. New York: Penguin Press, 2006.

Ridings, William J., Jr., and Stuart B. McIver. *Rating the Presidents: A Ranking of U.S. Leaders, from the Great and Honorable to the Dishonest and Incompetent*. New York: Carol Publishing Group, 1997.

Risen, Clay. *The Bill of the Century: The Epic Battle for the Civil Rights Act*. New York: Bloomsbury Press, 2014.

Robertson, Ian H. "How Power Affects the Brain." *The Psychologist* 26, no. 3 (March 2013): 186–89.

Robins, Richard W., and Jennifer S. Beer. "Positive Illusions about the Self: Short-Term Benefits and Long-Term Costs." *Journal of Personality and Social Psychology* 80, no. 2 (2001): 340–52.

Rockman, Bert A. "Does the Revolution in Presidential Studies Mean 'Off with the President's Head'?" *Presidential Studies Quarterly* 39, no. 4 (2009): 786–94.

Ronson, Jon. *The Psychopath Test: A Journey through the Madness Industry*. New York: Riverhead Books, 2012.

Roosevelt, Theodore. *The Naval War of 1812, or, the History of the United States Navy during the Last War with Great Britain, to Which Is Appended an Account of the Battle of New Orleans*. Philadelphia: Gebbie and Co., 1902.

———. *The Rough Riders: An Autobiography*. Edited by Louis Auchincloss. New York: Library of America, 2004.

———. *The Winning of the West: An Account of the Exploration and Settlement of Our Country from the Alleghanies to the Pacific*. Philadelphia: Gebbie and Co., 1903.

Rose, Frank A., "As Russia and China Improve Their Conventional Military Capabilities, Should the US Rethink Its Assumptions on Extended Nuclear Deterrence?" *Order from Chaos*. Brookings Institution, October 23, 2018. www.brookings.edu/blog/order-from-chaos/2018/10/23/as-russia-and-china-improve-their-conventional-military-capabilities-should-the-us-rethink-its-assumptions-on-extended-nuclear-deterrence/.

Rosenzweig, Phil. *The Halo Effect . . . and the Eight Other Business Delusions That Deceive Managers*. New York: Free Press, 2007.

Ross, Lee. "The Intuitive Psychologist and His Shortcomings: Distortions in the Attribution Process." In *Advances in Experimental Social Psychology*, edited by L. Berkowitz, 173–220. New York: Academic Press, 1977.

Rossoll, Nick. "More Than 40 Percent of Americans Cannot Name VP Candidates." ABC News, October 2, 2016. http://abcnews.go.com/Politics/40-percent-americans-vp-candidates/story?id=42497013.

Rottinghaus, Brandon, and Justin S. Vaughn. "How Does Trump Stack Up against the Best—and Worst—Presidents?" *New York Times*, February 19, 2018. www.nytimes.com/interactive/2018/02/19/opinion/how-does-trump-stack-up-against-the-best-and-worst-presidents.html.

———. "Measuring Obama against the Great Presidents." The Brookings Institution, updated April 2, 2015. www.brookings.edu/blog/fixgov/2015/02 /13/measuring-obama-against-the-great-presidents/.

———. "Official Results of the 2018 Presidents & Executive Politics Presidential Greatness Survey." Online paper at Boise State University, 2018. www .boisestate.edu/sps-politicalscience/files/2018/02/Greatness.pdf.

"Roundtable Discussion of Richard J. Samuels's *Machiavelli's Children: Leaders and Their Legacies in Italy and Japan.*" *Journal of East Asian Studies* 6, no. 1 (January–April 2006): 1–29.

Rowland, Thomas J. *Franklin B. Pierce: The Twilight of Jacksonian Democracy.* Hauppauge, NY: Nova Science Publishers, 2011.

Rozansky, Michael. "Americans Know Surprisingly Little about Their Government, Survey Finds." News release, Annenberg Public Policy Center, September 17, 2014. www.annenbergpublicpolicycenter.org/wp-content/uploads /Civics-survey-press-release-09-17-2014-for-PR-Newswire.pdf.

Russell, Francis. *The Shadow of Blooming Grove: Warren G. Harding in His Times.* New York: McGraw-Hill, 1968.

Salmore, Barbara G., and Stephen A. Salmore. *Candidates, Parties, and Campaigns: Electoral Politics in America.* 2nd ed. Washington, DC: CQ Press, 1989.

Samuels, Richard J. *Machiavelli's Children: Leaders and Their Legacies in Italy and Japan.* Ithaca, NY: Cornell University Press, 2003.

Saunders, Elizabeth N. "Leaders, Advisers, and the Political Origins of Elite Support for War." *Journal of Conflict Resolution* 62, no. 10 (November 2018): 2118–49.

———. *Leaders at War—How Presidents Shape Military Interventions.* Ithaca, NY: Cornell University Press, 2011.

———. "Transformative Choices." *International Security* 34, no. 2 (Fall 2009): 119–61.

Saunders, Elizabeth Nathan. "Wars of Choice: Leadership, Threat Perception, and Military Interventions." PhD diss., Yale University, 2007.

Scheidel, Walter. "Demography." In *The Cambridge Economic History of the Greco-Roman World,* edited by Walter Scheidel, Ian Morris, and Richard P. Saller, 38–86. Cambridge: Cambridge University Press, 2007.

Schelling, Thomas C. *The Strategy of Conflict.* Cambridge, MA: Harvard University Press, 1960.

Schlesinger, Arthur M. "Our Presidents: A Rating by 75 Historians." *New York Times Magazine,* July 29, 1962, 12–13, 40–41, 43.

Schlesinger, Arthur M., Jr. "Rating the Presidents: Washington to Clinton." *Political Science Quarterly* 112, no. 2 (1997): 179–90.

Schmidt, Frank L., and John E. Hunter. "The Validity and Utility of Selection Methods in Personnel Psychology: Practical and Theoretical Implications of

85 Years of Research Findings." *Psychological Bulletin* 124, no. 2 (1998): 262–74.

Schneider, Benjamin. "The People Make the Place." *Personnel Psychology* 40, no. 3 (September 1987): 437–53.

Schneider, Benjamin, Harold W Goldstein, and D. Brent Smith. "The Asa Framework: An Update." *Personnel Psychology* 48, no. 4 (1995): 747–73.

Schneider, Karen S. "The Donald Ducks Out." *People,* May 19, 1997. https://people.com/archive/cover-story-the-donald-ducks-out-vol-47-no-19/.

Schweller, Randall L. "Bandwagoning for Profit: Bringing the Revisionist State Back In." *International Security* 19, no. 1 (1994): 72–107.

Scott, James C. *Seeing like a State: How Certain Schemes to Improve the Human Condition Have Failed.* New Haven, CT: Yale University Press, 1998.

Scott, Jamil, and Nadia Brown. "Reconsidering Gender Stereotypes with an Intersectional Lens." Online paper, November 26, 2018, presented at 2019 National Conference of Black Political Scientists Annual Meeting. https://papers.ssrn.com/sol3/papers.cfm?abstract_id=3290902.

Segal, David. "What Donald Trump's Plaza Hotel Deal Reveals about His White House Bid." *New York Times,* January 16 2016. www.nytimes.com/2016/01/17/business/what-donald-trumps-plaza-deal-reveals-about-his-white-house-bid.html.

Sellbom, Martin, Yossef S. Ben-Porath, Christopher J. Patrick, Dustin B. Wygant, Diane M. Gartland, and Kathleen P. Stafford. "Development and Construct Validation of MMPI-2-RF Indices of Global Psychopathy, Fearless-Dominance, and Impulsive-Antisociality." *Personality Disorders* 3, no. 1 (January 2012): 17–38.

Shafer, Byron E. *Bifurcated Politics: Evolution and Reform in the National Party Convention.* A Russell Sage Foundation Study. Cambridge, MA: Harvard University Press, 1988.

Shakespeare, William. *The Norton Shakespeare.* Edited by Stephen Greenblatt, Walter Cohen, Jean E. Howard, Katharine Eisaman Maus, and Andrew Gurr. New York: W. W. Norton, 1997.

Shaw, Daron R. "A Study of Presidential Campaign Event Effects from 1952 to 1992." *Journal of Politics* 61, no. 2 (1999): 387–422.

Shehata, Adam, and Jesper Strömbäck. "Not (Yet) a New Era of Minimal Effects: A Study of Agenda Setting at the Aggregate and Individual Levels." *International Journal of Press/Politics* 18, no. 2 (2013): 234–55.

Shenk, Joshua Wolf. *Lincoln's Melancholy: How Depression Challenged a President and Fueled His Greatness.* Boston: Houghton Mifflin, 2005.

Shephard, Alex. "Donald Trump Doesn't Read Books." *New Republic,* May 17, 2016. https://newrepublic.com/minutes/133566/donald-trump-doesnt-read-books.

Sherman, Matthew. *A Short History of Financial Deregulation in the United States*. Washington, DC: Center for Economic and Policy Research, July 2009. http://cepr.net/documents/publications/dereg-timeline-2009-07.pdf.

Sides, John, Michael Tesler, and Lynn Vavreck. *Identity Crisis: The 2016 Presidential Campaign and the Battle for the Meaning of America*. Princeton, NJ: Princeton University Press, 2018.

"Siena's 6th Presidential Expert Poll, 1982–2018." Siena College Research Institute, February 13, 2019. https://scri.siena.edu/2019/02/13/sienas-6th-presidential-expert-poll-1982-2018/.

Simon, Arthur M., and Joseph E. Uscinski. "Prior Experience Predicts Presidential Performance." *Presidential Studies Quarterly* 42, no. 3 (2012): 514–48.

Simon, Herbert A. *Administrative Behavior*. New York: The Free Press, 1968.

Simonton, Dean Keith. "Intellectual Brilliance and Presidential Performance: Why Pure Intelligence (or Openness) Doesn't Suffice." *Journal of Intelligence* 6, no. 2 (2018).

———. "Intergenerational Transfer of Individual Differences in Hereditary Monarchs: Genetic, Role-Modeling, Cohort, or Sociocultural Effects?" *Journal of Personality and Social Psychology* 44, no. 2 (1983): 354–64.

———. "Land Battles, Generals, and Armies: Individual and Situational Determinants of Victory and Casualties." *Journal of Personality and Social Psychology* 38, no. 1 (1980): 110–19.

———. "Leaders as Eponyms: Individual and Situational Determinants of Ruler Eminence." *Journal of Personality* 52, no. 1 (1984): 1–21.

———. "Mad King George: The Impact of Personal and Political Stress on Mental and Physical Health." *Journal of Personality* 66, no. 3 (June 1998): 443–66.

———. "Personality and Intellectual Predictors of Leadership." In *International Handbook of Personality and Intelligence*, edited by D. H. Saklofske and M. Zeidner, 739–57. New York: Plenum, 1995.

———. "Personality and Politics." In *Handbook of Personality Theory and Research*, edited by L. A. Pervin. New York: Guilford, 1990.

———. "Predicting Presidential Performance in the United States: Equation Replication on Recent Survey Results." *Journal of Social Psychology* 141, no. 3 (2001): 293–307.

———. "Presidential Greatness and Performance: Can We Predict Leadership in the White House?" *Journal of Personality* 49, no. 3 (September 1981): 306–23.

———. "Presidential Greatness: The Historical Consensus and Its Psychological Significance." *Political Psychology* 7, no. 2 (June 1986): 259–83.

———. "Presidential IQ, Openness, Intellectual Brilliance, and Leadership: Estimates and Correlations for 42 U.S. Chief Executives." *Political Psychology* 27, no. 4 (2006): 511–26.

———. "Presidential Personality: Biographical Use of the Gough Adjective Check List." *Journal of Personality and Social Psychology* 51, no. 1 (1986): 149–60.

———. "Presidential Style: Personality, Biography, and Performance." *Journal of Personality and Social Psychology* 55, no. 6 (1988): 928–36.

———. "Putting the Best Leaders in the White House: Personality, Policy, and Performance." *Political Psychology* 14, no. 3 (1993): 537–48.

———. *Why Presidents Succeed: A Political Psychology of Leadership.* New Haven, CT: Yale University Press, 1987.

Skowronek, Stephen. *The Politics Presidents Make: Leadership from John Adams to Bill Clinton.* Cambridge, MA: The Belknap Press of Harvard University Press, 1997.

———. "Theory and History, Structure and Agency." *Presidential Studies Quarterly* 29, no. 3 (1999): 672–81.

Smith, Adam. *Inquiry into the Nature and Causes of the Wealth of Nations.* Penguin Classics. New York: Penguin, 1999.

Smith, Jean Edward. *Bush.* New York: Simon & Schuster, 2016.

———. *Eisenhower: In War and Peace.* New York: Random House, 2012.

Somin, Ilya. *Democracy and Political Ignorance: Why Smaller Government Is Smarter.* 2nd ed. Stanford, CA: Stanford University Press, 2016.

Sonmez, Felicia. "Donald Trump on John McCain in 1999: 'Does Being Captured Make You a Hero?'" *Washington Post,* August 7, 2018. www.washingtonpost .com/politics/donald-trump-on-john-mccain-in-1999-does-being-captured-make-you-a-hero/2018/08/07/a2849b1c-9a56–11e8–8d5e-c6c594024954_ story.html.

Spinelli, Dan. "Why Penn Won't Talk about Donald Trump." *Politico,* November 6, 2016. www.politico.com/magazine/story/2016/11/ donald-trump-2016-wharton-pennsylvania-214425.

Stampp, Kenneth M. *America in 1857: A Nation on the Brink.* New York: Oxford University Press, 1992.

Stauffer, John. *Giants: The Parallel Lives of Frederick Douglass and Abraham Lincoln.* New York: Twelve, 2009.

Steinbruner, John D. *The Cybernetic Theory of Decision.* Princeton, NJ: Princeton University Press, 1974.

Steinhauser, Paul. "Poll: Obama Makes Big Gains among Black Voters." *CNN Politics,* January 19, 2008. www.cnn.com/2008/POLITICS/01/18/poll.2008 /index.html.

Stepan, Alfred, and Cindy Skach. "Constitutional Frameworks and Democratic Consolidation: Parliamentarianism versus Presidentialism." *World Politics* 46, no. 1 (2011): 1–22.

Stewart, David O. *Impeached: The Trial of President Andrew Johnson and the Fight for Lincoln's Legacy.* New York: Simon & Schuster, 2009.

Stockman, David A. "Yes We Can: How Eisenhower Wrestled Down the U.S. Warfare State." *The Globalist,* April 29, 2014. www.theglobalist.com/yes-we-can-how-eisenhower-wrestled-down-the-u-s-warfare-state/.

Strauss, Robert. *Worst. President. Ever.: James Buchanan, the POTUS Rating Game, and the Legacy of the Least of the Lesser Presidents.* Guilford, CT: Lyons Press, an imprint of Rowman & Littlefield, 2016.

Strouse, Jean. *Morgan: American Financier.* New York: HarperPerennial, 2000.

Stueck, William Whitney. *Rethinking the Korean War: A New Diplomatic and Strategic History.* Princeton, NJ: Princeton University Press, 2002.

Surowiecki, James. *The Wisdom of Crowds.* New York: Random House, 2005.

Swenson, Kyle. "Harold Bornstein: Exiled from Trumpland, Doctor Now 'Frightened and Sad.'" *Washington Post,* May 2, 2018. www.washingtonpost.com/news/morning-mix/wp/2018/05/02/harold-bornstein-exiled-from-trumpland-former-doctor-now-frightened-and-sad/.

Taleb, Nassim Nicholas. *Antifragile: Things That Gain from Disorder.* New York: Random House, 2012.

———. *The Black Swan: The Impact of the Highly Improbable.* New York: Random House, 2007.

———. *Fooled by Randomness: The Hidden Role of Chance in Life and in the Markets.* New York: Random House, 2005.

———. Various tweets. Twitter, 2016. https://twitter.com/nntaleb.

Taranto, James. "The Rankings." *Wall Street Journal,* September 12, 2005.

Taylor, Mark Zachary. "An Economic Ranking of the US Presidents, 1789–2009: A Data-Based Approach." *PS: Political Science & Politics* 45, no. 4 (2012): 596–604.

Teodoro, Manuel P., and Jon R. Bond. "Presidents, Baseball, and Wins above Expectations: What Can Sabermetrics Tell Us about Presidential Success?" *PS: Political Science & Politics* 50, no. 2 (April 2017): 339–46.

Tesler, Michael, and John Sides. "How Political Science Helps Explain the Rise of Trump: The Role of White Identity and Grievances." *Washington Post,* March 3, 2016. www.washingtonpost.com/news/monkey-cage/wp/2016/03/03/how-political-science-helps-explain-the-rise-of-trump-the-role-of-white-identity-and-grievances/.

Tetlock, Philip E. "Agreeing to Disagree: A Respectful Reply to a Senior Statesman of Political Psychology." *Political Psychology* 16, no. 3 (1995): 671–75.

———. *Expert Political Judgment: How Good Is It? How Can We Know?* Princeton, NJ: Princeton University Press, 2006.

———. "Good Judgment in International Politics: Three Psychological Perspectives." *Political Psychology* 13, no. 3 (September 1992): 517–39.

———. "How Politicized Is Political Psychology and Is There Anything We Should Do about It?" *Political Psychology* 15, no. 3 (1994): 567–77.

———. "Political Psychology or Politicized Psychology: Is the Road to Scientific Hell Paved with Good Moral Intentions?" *Political Psychology* 15, no. 3 (1994): 509–29.

Tetlock, Philip E., and Aaron Belkin, eds. *Counterfactual Thought Experiments in World Politics: Logical, Methodological, and Psychological Perspectives.* Princeton, NJ: Princeton University Press, 1996.

Tetlock, Philip E., and Dan Gardner. *Superforecasting: The Art and Science of Prediction.* New York: Crown, 2015.

Tetzeli, Rick. "Could This Radical New Approach to Alzheimer's Lead to a Breakthrough?" *Forbes*, January 18, 2019. http://fortune.com/longform/alzheimers-disease-cure-breakthrough/.

Thomas, Evan. *Ike's Bluff: President Eisenhower's Secret Battle to Save the World.* New York: Little, Brown.

Thompson, James D. *Organizations in Action.* New York: McGraw-Hill, 1967.

Tilley, James, and Sara B. Hobolt. "Is the Government to Blame? An Experimental Test of How Partisanship Shapes Perceptions of Performance and Responsibility." *Journal of Politics* 73, no. 2 (April 2011): 1–15.

Todd, Chuck, and Sheldon R. Gawiser, with Ana Maria Arumi and G. Evans Witt. *How Barack Obama Won: A State-by-State Guide to the Historic 2008 Presidential Election.* New York: Vintage Books, 2009.

Tolbert, Caroline, and Peverill Squire. "Reforming the Presidential Nomination Process." *PS: Political Science and Politics* 42, no. 1 (January 2009): 29–58.

Tomaskovic-Devey, Donald, and Ken-Hou Lin. "Financialization: Causes, Inequality Consequences, and Policy Implications." *North Carolina Banking Institute* 18, no. 1 (2013). http://scholarship.law.unc.edu/cgi/viewcontent.cgi?article=1365&context=ncbi.

———. "Income Dynamics, Economic Rents, and the Financialization of the U.S. Economy." *American Sociological Review* 76, no. 4 (2011): 538–59.

Trani, Eugene P., and David L. Wilson. *The Presidency of Warren G. Harding.* Lawrence: Regents Press of Kansas, 1977.

Trefousse, Hans Louis. *Andrew Johnson: A Biography.* New York: Norton, 1989.

Troy, Tevi. "The Evolution of Party Conventions." *National Affairs*, Summer 2016.

Truman, Harry S. *Memoirs*, vol. 2, *Years of Trial and Hope.* Garden City, NY: Doubleday, 1956.

———. "The President's Farewell Address to the American People." January 15, 1953. The American Presidency Project, University of California, Santa Barbara. www.presidency.ucsb.edu/ws/index.php?pid=14392.

"Trump Again Calls Himself 'a Very Stable Genius.'" *Axios*, July 12, 2018. www.axios.com/donald-trump-very-stable-genius-nato-summit-twitter-30f4da11-9857-4fe4-b33f-ae1061cbfb46.html.

Trump, Donald J. *Crippled America: How to Make America Great Again*. New York: Threshold Editions, 2015.

———. *Time to Get Tough: Making America #1 Again*. Washington, DC: Regnery, 2011.

———. Tweet. @realdonaldtrump (suspended account), 2013, accessed January 24, 2019. https://twitter.com/realDonaldTrump/status/329390667438624768.

———. Tweet. @realdonaldtrump (suspended account), 2018, accessed January 24, 2019. https://twitter.com/realDonaldTrump/status/949619270631256064.

———. *The Way to the Top: The Best Business Advice I Ever Received*. New York: Crown, 2004.

Trump, Donald J., with Charles Leerhsen. *Trump: Surviving at the Top*. New York: Random House, 1990.

Trump, Donald J., with Meredith McIver. *Trump: Think like a Billionaire: Everything You Need to Know about Success, Real Estate, and Life*. New York: Random House, 2004.

Trump, Donald J., with Tony Schwartz. *Trump: The Art of the Deal*. New York: Random House, 1987.

Trump, Donald J., with Dave Shiflett. *The America We Deserve*. Los Angeles: Renaissance Books, 2000.

Turnham, Steve. "Donald Trump to Father of Fallen Soldier: 'I've Made a Lot of Sacrifices.'" ABC News, July 30, 2016. https://abcnews.go.com/Politics/donald-trump-father-fallen-soldier-ive-made-lot/story?id=41015051.

Twohey, Megan, and Michael Barbaro. "Two Women Say Donald Trump Touched Them Inappropriately." *New York Times*, October 12, 2016. www.nytimes.com /2016/10/13/us/politics/donald-trump-women.html.

Uscinski, Joseph E., and Arthur Simon. "Partisanship as a Source of Presidential Rankings." *White House Studies* 11, no. 1 (2010): 1–14.

Useem, Jerry. "Power Causes Brain Damage." *The Atlantic*, July/August 2017. www.theatlantic.com/magazine/archive/2017/07/power-causes-brain-damage /528711/.

van der Zwan, Natascha. "Making Sense of Financialization." *Socio-Economic Review* 12, no. 1 (2014): 99–129.

Van Evera, Stephen. *Guide to Methods for Students of Political Science*. Ithaca, NY: Cornell University Press, 1997.

Vedder, Richard, and Lowell Gallaway. "Rating Presidential Performance." In *Reassessing the Presidency: The Rise of the Executive State and the Decline of Freedom*, edited by John V. Denson. Auburn, AL: Ludwig von Mises Institute, 2001.

Viser, Matt. "Donald Trump's Airline Went from Opulence in the Air to Crash Landing." *Boston Globe*, May 27, 2016. www.bostonglobe.com/news /politics/2016/05/27/donald-trump-airline-went-from-opulence-air-crash-landing/zEf1Er2Hok2dPTVVmZT6NP/story.html.

Visser, Beth A., Angela S. Book, and Anthony A. Volk. "Is Hillary Dishonest and Donald Narcissistic? A Hexaco Analysis of the Presidential Candidates' Public Personas." *Personality and Individual Differences* 106 (2017): 281–86.

Wadhera, Vivek K. "Losing Touch." *Kellogg Insight,* November 1, 2009. https:// insight.kellogg.northwestern.edu/article/losing_touch.

Wallner, Peter A. *Franklin Pierce: Martyr for the Union.* Concord, NH: Plaidswede Publishing, 2007.

———. *Franklin Pierce: New Hampshire's Favorite Son.* Concord, NH: Plaidswede Publishing, 2004.

Walt, Stephen M. *Revolution and War.* Ithaca, NY: Cornell University Press, 1996.

Waltz, Kenneth N. *Foreign Policy and Democratic Politics: The American and British Experience.* Boston: Little, Brown, 1967.

———. *Man, the State, and War.* Revised ed. New York: Columbia University Press, 2001.

———. "Neorealism—Confusions and Criticisms." Guest Essay. *Journal of Politics and Society* XV (2004): 2–6. www.helvidius.org/files/2004/2004_Waltz.pdf.

———. *Theory of International Politics.* First ed. Boston: McGraw Hill, 1979.

Wasniewski, Matthew. "I've Scalped Him?" *History, Art & Archives of the United States House of Representatives,* February 6, 2014. http://history.house.gov/Blog/2014/February/2-06-I-ve-Scalped-Him/.

Wasserman, Noam, Bharat Anand, and Nitin Nohria. "When Does Leadership Matter? A Contingent Opportunities View of CEO Leadership." In *Handbook of Leadership Theory and Practice,* edited by Nitin Nohria and Rakesh Khurana, 27–64. Boston: Harvard Business Press, 2010.

Wattenberg, Martin P. "The Declining Relevance of Candidate Personal Attributes in Presidential Elections." *Presidential Studies Quarterly* 46, no. 1 (2016): 125–39.

———. "Elections: Reliability Trumps Competence: Personal Attributes in the 2004 Presidential Election." *Presidential Studies Quarterly* 36, no. 4 (2006): 705–13.

Watts, Ashley L., Scott O. Lilienfeld, Sarah Francis Smith, Joshua D. Miller, W. Keith Campbell, Irwin D. Waldman, Steven J. Rubenzer, and Thomas J. Faschingbauer. "The Double-Edged Sword of Grandiose Narcissism: Implications for Successful and Unsuccessful Leadership among U.S. Presidents." *Psychological Science* 24, no. 12 (2013): 2379–89.

Waugh, John C. *One Man Great Enough: Abraham Lincoln's Road to Civil War.* Orlando, FL: Harcourt, 2007.

———. *Reelecting Lincoln: The Battle for the 1864 Presidency.* New York: Crown Publishers, 1997.

Wayne, Stephen J. "Presidential Character and Judgment: Obama's Afghanistan and Health Care Decisions." *Presidential Studies Quarterly* 41, no. 2
(2011): 291–306.

Weiland, Noah, Maggie Haberman, Mark Mazzetti, and Annie Karni. "Trump
Was Sicker Than Acknowledged with Covid-19." *New York Times,* February
11, 2021. www.nytimes.com/2021/02/11/us/politics/trump-coronavirus.html.

Weinberg, Neil. "Schapiro's Promontory Move Latest Sign of Too Much Coziness." American Banker, April 2, 2013. www.americanbanker.com/opinion
/schapiros-promontory-move-latest-sign-of-too-much-coziness.

Weiner, Tim. *Enemies: A History of the FBI.* New York: Random House, 2012.

Weiss, Philip. "The Lives They Lived: Fred C. Trump, b. 1905; the Fred." *New
York Times,* January 2, 2000. www.nytimes.com/2000/01/02/magazine/the-
lives-they-lived-fred-c-trump-b-1905-the-fred.html.

Wells, Samuel F., Jr. "Sounding the Tocsin: NSC 68 and the Soviet Threat."
International Security 4, no. 2 (Autumn 1979): 116–58.

White, Theodore H. *The Making of the President, 1960.* New York: Pocket
Books, 1962.

———. *The Making of the President, 1964.* New York: Atheneum, 1965.

———. *The Making of the President, 1968.* New York: Atheneum, 1969.

———. *The Making of the President, 1972.* New York: Atheneum, 1973.

Whitesides, John. "Black Voters Still Unsure about Obama." Reuters, February
8, 2007. www.reuters.com/article/us-usa-politics-obama/
black-voters-still-unsure-about-obama-idUSN0829251720070208.

Whyte, Kenneth. *Hoover: An Extraordinary Life in Extraordinary Times.* New
York: Alfred A. Knopf, 2017.

Wicker, Tom. *Dwight D. Eisenhower.* New York: Times Books, 2002.

Witt, Edward A., M. Brent Donnellan, Daniel M. Blonigen, Robert F. Krueger, and
Rand D. Conger. "Assessment of Fearless Dominance and Impulsive Antisociality via Normal Personality Measures: Convergent Validity, Criterion Validity,
and Developmental Change." *Journal of Personality Assessment* 91, no. 3 (May
2009): 265–76.

Wohlforth, William C. "The Stability of a Unipolar World." *International
Security* 24, no. 1 (1999): 5–41.

Yglesias, Matthew. "American Democracy Is Doomed." *Vox,* October 8, 2015.
www.vox.com/2015/3/2/8120063/american-democracy-doomed.

Yong, Ed. "How the Pandemic Defeated America." *The Atlantic,* September
2020. www.theatlantic.com/magazine/archive/2020/09/coronavirus-
american-failure/614191/.

Zelizer, Julian E. *Jimmy Carter.* New York: Times Books, 2010.

Index